BODY
AND
SOUL

BODY AND SOUL

The Story of John Garfield

by Larry Swindell

WILLIAM MORROW AND COMPANY, INC.
NEW YORK   1975

Picture Acknowledgments

The Museum of Modern Art, Film Collection: Photographs of the Garfields at home in 1942; of Garfield in group shot at CBS; with troop entertainers; sparring and softball charity activity. Also, stills from *Saturday's Children, The Postman Always Rings Twice, Nobody Lives Forever, We Were Strangers,* and *Under My Skin.*

Picture Collection of the Library for the Performing Arts, Lincoln Center: Photographs from *Counsellor-at-Law, Awake and Sing, Heavenly Express* and *Golden Boy;* film stills from *The Fallen Sparrow* and *Gentleman's Agreement.*

Stills from *They Made Me a Criminal, Flowing Gold, The Sea Wolf,* and *Pride of the Marines* are from *The Philadelphia Inquirer,* as is the portrait on the front of the jacket. Other photographs are from private collections.

Printed in the United States of America.

1 2 3 4 5   79 78 77 76 75

Library of Congress Cataloging in Publication Data

Swindell, Larry.
 Body and soul, the story of John Garfield.

 Includes index.
 1. Garfield, John. I. Title.
PN2287.G377S9   791'.092'4 [B]   74-31470
ISBN 0-688-02907-8

Book design by Helen Roberts

Again, for ELLIE
. . . whose book this also is

Author's Note

The subtitle is not frivolous. "The Story of John Garfield" is less biography than history, embracing both the American stage and screen during what now appears to have been a vibrant period for each. Garfield was a most interesting actor of that period, and significantly was a product of his times. His life and career provide a narrative framework. For historical perspective on the movies' "studio system," I have sought to define Warner Brothers in the way that my earlier book on Spencer Tracy charted the methods of Fox and M-G-M, and as the forthcoming life story of Carole Lombard also portrays Paramount.

Consistent third-person reference to "Julie" must not imply the author's familiarity with Garfield. I never knew him. But he was a most informal person, always Julie to casual or intimate friends. While Mrs. Sidney Elliott Cohn (Garfield's widow) did not choose to participate or advise, the contributions of many Garfield friends and associates will be evident in the text. I am grateful to them all, and forego individual acknowledgment only because many persons have requested anonymity. After two decades, the specter of McCarthyism still shrouds the performing arts.

But I am indebted to many whose assistance would not be apparent: to Monty Arnold and Rod Bladel of the Lincoln Center Library for the Performing Arts; Mary Corliss of the Museum of Modern Art; helpful friends Florence Collis, Joe Gradel, Pat McHugh, and Helen Sutcliffe; Jonathan Dolger of Simon & Schuster; and my editor for William Morrow, the graciously firm Howard Cady. And Eleanor Eby Swindell again has outdone herself as wife, collaborator, and critic—not necessarily in that order.

Richboro, Pennsylvania
December 8, 1974

Contents

I

Wild in the Streets

Projected on the screens of the world, he was the Eternal Outsider, obliged to glimpse paradise but not to dwell there. John Garfield was the vagabond hood, the urban ne'er-do-well, the diamond-in-the-rough prodigy, the nervously embattled G.I. In every guise he conveyed an inner turbulence. As a primitive but idealistic sinner, he was as formidable as steel but vulnerably naive, volatile but plaintive. He was a game competitor but a born loser—urgently forceful and forcefully attractive, but never the master of his fate. Because the cards were stacked against him in the script, he was finally pathetic.

Often he joked that he was playing out his own life on film. He didn't believe that. In almost every movie assignment he would enact a fictional person whose culture and background reflected his own, but he supposed the parallel ended there. He was somehow unable to see himself as others saw him, and he never comprehended the certainties of his own personality that formulated his popular image on film.

Exercising the benefit of hindsight, a later generation would recognize the collective body of John Garfield's movies as a bittersweet American saga for which his own life was the master script. To have known that he would be a cult figure fully twenty years after his death surely would have given him satisfaction, but he would not have fathomed the secret of his surviving fascination. Above all he wanted to be a great actor, but his instinct as well as his most intimate critics told him this was not possible. Yet he was a great symbol and he barely appreciated that.

Neither accepting nor understanding his own significance, he died unaware that he had been the prophet of the new actor in America, on stage and in pictures. Prototype and archetype, he was the first of the rebels: John Garfield, the antihero in revolt against a world he never made.

It was a world vibrant with promise when he entered it, during the first hours of the Woodrow Wilson administration. On March 4, 1913, peace becalmed every continent. Involvement in foreign wars still lay beyond the American imagination. Of only mild concern was the likelihood of a thing called the income tax, whose intended victims saw it as nothing more than a token penalty for being rich. The newly inaugurated President extolled an American life "incomparably great in its body of wealth, in the diversity and sweep of its energy . . . our life contains every great thing in rich abundance."

John Garfield's birth rubbed against the grain of unprecedented optimism as America inhaled its new greatness. Yes, wealth obsessed those times. But poverty was stubborn and it recycled, generation after generation, in the capillaries of New York City, and nowhere so persistently as in Manhattan's raffishly old-world Lower East Side. Among its struggling poor were David and Hannah Garfinkle, whose life held no great things or rich abundance, but who said their first child brought with him the hopeful omen of an early spring.

They named him Jacob. No middle name was indicated at the time of his birth, but Julius was added during the boy's early infancy, possibly to reduce confusion among a quorum of Jacob Garfinkles. Soon he was not called Jakie, but Julie; and Julie it would always be. Professionally his name would undergo an incremental metamorphosis that would culminate in John Garfield, movie star. But the people who knew him would always call him Julie, nothing else. Nor would he ever lose the rumpled charm that made Julie seem so appropriate.

He was born in a bleak three-room flat on Rivington Street, at the gamy core of the Lower East Side that was still the primary repository for Europe's transplanted huddled masses, as it had been for four decades. The apartment building of Julie's birth and early childhood was a congestion of Russian and Polish Jews. David Garfinkle's forebears had been peasants in the Crimea. Hannah was of Ukrainian stock. Both of Julie's parents were first-generation American Jews with a common heritage of poverty.

Rivington Street was a vivid anachronism—a lively ghetto refusing to yield to the automobile that had vanquished most of New York. It was a busy vein of people and pushcarts, of horses and their residue; and always it swarmed with children. On any day it was a scene that might suggest the obligatory prologue to one of those pseudo-sociological melodramas that would be a staple of the movie houses a generation later: usually manufactured by Warner Brothers and featuring, often as not, John Garfield.

To its inhabitants, the Lower East Side was not the vast slum others considered it. It was a collection of many distinctive neighborhoods, each knitted together by ethnic traditions, language, and religion. The ghettos were impoverished, but the dwellers saw themselves in a favorable light, living with more comfort than European respectability had afforded them. The glorious opportunity of America was theirs, and their community throbbed with optimism. There was much singing.

John Garfield's mother seemed attuned to the positive thinking. He would have only dim and tender memories of her, but recalled that she sang funny songs to him, and that her robust laugh almost belied her chronic sickliness. Hannah Garfinkle, gay and radiant, would not be intimidated by travail. She was a neighborhood favorite and a forceful presence in the street where the little Julius sweltered through his first summers. Hannah fretted that her son was always smaller than other boys his own age, and she took his part in the daily scuffles with other children. Julie was an agreeable child, but he learned early to use his fists. He said his mother taught him to fight.

The good humor that sustained his mother was nowhere apparent in Julie's father. David Garfinkle was permanently inoculated with the culture of the old country. He accepted his low estate as God's will. He was pleasant enough and gently handsome, but his vagueness and his slightly stooped carriage conveyed a false suggestion of agedness. In word and deed, he was reliably slow. Lacking the vocational skill of an honest tailor, he accepted the bony wages of a clothes presser for years on end. The making of a living obsessed him, but he had neither talent nor ingenuity for getting ahead.

For many an enterprising young man, the ghetto was a stimulus, a springboard to wealth and power. One of David's early, brief employers was Marcus Loew, a Rivington Street alumnus who graduated into furs, then into the fledgling movie business, where he rode a trajectory to considerable fame and enormous fortune. But for David Garfinkle and his family the ghetto was a treadmill. There was never enough money for even marginal comfort.

But they were not without a cultural outlet. There was the Educational Alliance—a large brick structure on lower Broadway—conceived by Isadore Straus and Jacob Henry Schiff to enrich the Jewish occupants of lower Manhattan and to Americanize the immigrant stream. Eventually it would become the world's largest community center, and during the years of the First World War it imbued the East Side citizenry with a new patriotism and American pride. The Alliance offered glee clubs, dramatics, arts and crafts, and a busy social calendar for adults, and beginning education for the young children. The Garfinkles attended some of the Alliance entertainments, and it was there that Julie saw his first play. He attended kindergarten at the Alliance, and if he had a penny he could choose between an outsized pretzel or a freshly baked yam, hawked on the street by the Alliance building.

The family's finances improved temporarily with the country's involvement in the European war. There was an abundance of work, and David could juggle more than one job. He worked as a steam presser in a factory that made Army uniforms. But Hannah was often in need of medical attention, and then she had a difficult second pregnancy. Afterward she was never well again, and neither were the Garfinkle finances. Expenses went up after the war, so David started taking in extra money as a cantor on weekends and holidays, and for bar mitzvahs and other special occasions.

Max, the promised brother, arrived when Julie was five. He was a quiescent child in contrast to Julie, whose boundless energy had been a foremost characteristic even before he walked. The boys had small opportunity to develop a close, brotherly relationship. Their mother began to waste away, and when Julie was seven and Max only two, she died. Julie would always retain a clear memory of the ambulance coming to their place and collecting not a sick person, but a corpse. The ambulance doctor wrote "death due to physical illness" on the certificate, but Julie would later reflect that it may have been a fatigue as mental as it was physical. He also reasoned that Hannah Garfinkle's death was a blow from which his father never recovered. David took his sons out of the East Side, and soon the family broke up.

In 1940 John Garfield made a pilgrimage to Rivington Street to film some scenes for *East of the River*. He did not recognize his first neighborhood, although the storefronts and apartments had changed only slightly. Yet the first ghetto had cast his image and incited his personality. When Julie started school at the Educational Alliance he was the smallest boy in his class—sturdy and compact—but even then the stubby legs seemed out of proportion to an ample torso. His vagrant black hair, unusually thick, was never without curl. Rivington neighbors remembered a jolly boy whose large smile made his eyes dance. An immodest dimple gave him an early endowment of roguish charm, and they said that even as a moppet, he was an instinctive performer.

After his mother's death, Julie caromed from one family to another in Brooklyn, Queens, and the Bronx. People in all the boroughs were somehow his relatives and had jurisdiction over him. All of his relatives were poor, and Julie was an "extra mouth" to cause distress wherever he went. Yet he enjoyed the odyssey, and lapped up the outpourings of sympathy over his orphaned status. With grownups and with other children, he made friends easily and quickly. He was not a shy child, nor wary of strangers.

For a time David Garfinkle contributed little to Julie's care. He paid occasional duty visits, but his relationship with his son was more of tolerance than affection. They were not pals; and after Hannah's death, David seemed to settle into permanent gloom. Julie was irrepressibly merry, too much so. By his own recollection, he was awakened at night by a family argument, and the object of dispute turned out to be himself.

A day or so later, David arrived to gather up his son and his few belongings and take him to a new home.

Several families of relatives were clustered in the battered section of East Brooklyn tenements known as Brownsville. Under a new arrangement, Julie took meals in one house and slept in another. His only chore was to tend his little brother, with whom he was now reunited. David Garfinkle shared quarters with his sons, but sometimes he would be away from the house for days and weeks at a time.

Julie's scholastic performance in Brownsville was not encouraging. He was adept at drawing, but was a backward reader and a poor speller. His attendance also was suspiciously fitful, but none of his guardians placed a premium on formal education. They accepted the easy judgment that Julie was "slow." If he lacked drive, it was also true that no one pushed him. His father expressed only the regret that Julie was not receiving Hebrew training.

But he was absorbing the training of the street. Later he would recall that it was in Brownsville that he learned "all the meanness, all the toughness it's possible for kids to acquire." At school and around the neighborhood, he fought a lot. Fighting was a daily ritual and a boy wore a black eye as a badge. No grievance was required. Julie recalled that he and a good friend might enter into a bare-knuckles brawl just to settle a controversy over who might be tougher. He learned to take care of himself with his fists. For three years the turbulence of the Brownsville slums was to his liking; and when he moved away, he was unhappy about it.

Again his father had courted and won a woman more forceful than himself. Shortly after David Garfinkle married a stout, rather plain widow named Dinah Cohen, Julie joined them in a small apartment in the West Bronx. They may not have planned it that way, but none of the Brooklyn relatives would accept Julie as a permanent responsibility. On the other hand Max—now called Mike—had been assimilated by his new family, and he remained in Brownsville because everyone thought that would be to his best interest.

Dinah Cohen Garfinkle had no particular fondness for Julie, but she did not shirk the challenge of an often unruly ten-year-old stepson. She reasoned that a mother's attention was his foremost need. So she would see that his clothes were mended and that he would attend school regularly and do his homework. She did not expect an easy time, but she intended to have the day. But she conveyed no tenderness, and Julie recognized Dinah as his natural enemy. If she struck him, he would hit back.

In Julie's conflict with Dinah or with others, David Garfinkle seldom took his son's part. Living together again, father and son did not develop a bond. If Julie reached out, David only withdrew. "I don't understand that boy!" was his regular lament, and it carried truth. There was no ground for understanding. David's fatherly wisdom was a lean fund of religious platitudes. Julie answered them with ridicule. Nor could David muster interest in the new things that captivated his son—racing cars and zeppelins, boxing gloves and Jack Dempsey, the Yankees and Babe Ruth, or the picture shows with Charlie Chaplin and Tom Mix.

They all adjusted to their hostility, but Dinah regarded Julie as the deterrent to the serenity she had sought through David. In time there would be general agreement that the Garfinkles had made a good marriage, but it was on a more solid footing at those times when Julie was not around. As time passed, that became quite often. Julie found his natural habitat, and it was the street.

John Garfield was never able to disguise the affection he felt toward his shabby boyhood environment, even when he made it sound woeful. Triumph over adversity, against the customary formidable odds, was his fulfillment. It was the thing that made him "different" among the movie heroes. He thrived on underprivilege, and professionally he would make it work to his benefit. Curious social workers concluded that the boy was grievously deprived—of love, of attention, of every advantage—and this allowance was made when he was officially classified a "problem" by juvenile authorities, before *delinquent* was a fashionable word. But Julie was not unhappy in the Bronx.

He was his own best biographer for the coming-of-age on

the streets of New York in the twenties. Interviewers usually found he wanted to talk of nothing so much as his errant youth.

"If I hadn't become an actor, I might have become Public Enemy Number One," he once said; and, liking the sound of that, he would say it again and again.

That he could have been anybody's sworn enemy was unlikely. Julie was too congenial. No chip rested on his shoulder, although he had a reasonable claim to one. Still intent on impressing his chroniclers as a "tough guy," in later years he tended to exaggerate his youthful rowdiness. But delinquent he was.

In his first Bronx neighborhood he was quickly taken in by a kid gang, and when the Garfinkles moved to a more turbulent street that was proving ground for a bigger and faster gang, Julie wanted in.

"Every street had its own gang," John Garfield would explain. "That's the way it always was in poor sections. We didn't fight with other gangs unless someone really had a grudge. Mostly we stayed to ourselves, the old safety in numbers thing. But we caused trouble. We *tried* to make trouble. Why? For recognition, I suppose."

Often there were contradictions in his many summaries of misspent childhood and youth, but always the craving for attention was acknowledged. Surely this was partly caused, as he said it was, by his failure to receive attention at home; but around his comrades Julie behaved in an extroverted style that had a theatrical essence. He was center stage, doing zany impersonations or carrying on conversation in unnatural voices and exaggerated accents: "making crazy," his friends called it. Everything he attempted was accomplished better, Julie said, if there was some kind of audience. This was the case when he won admittance into his first gang.

The leader was a haggard, tubercular youth named Simon, who dictated the boys' activities and was receiver of their spoils. When Julie sought entry, Simon decreed that he would have to pass an initiation test that included stealing a cantaloupe from a neighborhood fruit stand.

Boys regularly snatched apples and other modest-sized produce, but a cantaloupe was a large order. Still, the code said you were a yellow punk until you proved otherwise. A show of real courage gave a boy status in the gang regardless of his age or size.

About half a dozen boys gathered across the street from the fruit stand to observe Julie's performance under pressure. Their presence gave him ample determination, and also distracted the vendor. Doubtless remembering past maraudings, the vendor began shouting at the boys, and they answered with obscenities. Julie pilfered the melon, still unnoticed by the vendor. Moments later he was received into the gang, and Simon ate the cantaloupe. No matter, Julie would acquire a connoisseur's taste for stolen fruit. He had the quickest pair of hands, and could run like hell.

Another tale, involving a different neighborhood gang, found Julie proving his daredevil credentials by hanging head downward, by his knees, from a fourth-floor roof. The gang had dared him.

"Not just a dare," John Garfield recounted. "I was a dumb kid, but I wasn't a sucker. I was *paid* for that stunt . . . ten cents. I wanted to go to the movies and didn't have the dime. Another kid had a dime but wouldn't part with it unless I made it worth his while. I remember the picture was *The Iron Horse*. I liked it."

His adventures spanned several neighborhoods. Sometimes his father had trouble making the rent, so the Garfinkles would be on the move. In Julie's mind, each apartment was somehow crummier than the previous one. He changed school often and lost touch with former pals. He did hear that Simon, his first leader, had died. Another street kingpin—a homeless tough named Benny—was picked up by the police for an unspecified offense, and never heard from again.

"But the cops weren't our enemies. They were the best friends we had, though we may not have realized that. They were more understanding than our parents. You see, most of the cops had run in street gangs when *they* were kids. If you were a poor boy you didn't have much choice. You might not finish school, and anyway you didn't figure to get the good jobs. But maybe you could be a cop. Yeah, a hood or a cop, that was the choice. Still playing the same game, only on different sides."

Many boys were even poorer than Julie. They were improperly nourished and always hungry, or not sufficiently clothed for the mean winters. Some were fatherless or motherless or both, but often parents rated as liabilities. Even the term *orphan* could certify a boy's independence. Julie did not usually acknowledge a stepmother. Dinah was "the woman my old man is living with." But meals were regular at the Garfinkles' and Dinah was a good cook. Sometimes Julie was absent at mealtime, but he would steal food from Dinah's pantry and share it with his friends.

Even years later, he discounted Dinah. "Not having a mother, I could stay out late, I didn't have to eat regularly, or drink my milk at four o'clock. I could sleep out and run away, which I did a lot of."

Sometimes he bunked at another boy's house or would say he had. In the steamy summer when school was out, he often slept outdoors with other boys, on the flat rooftops of the apartment buildings. He daydreamed of owning a penthouse and being able to spit on the street from his own observatory.

Some boys moved away to "better" streets and others simply outgrew the milieu, perhaps moving on from simple mischief to professional thievery. There were always new boys to fill the gaps, and gang members were coached regularly to obey the only law of the street: *don't rat on nobody.*

Personable, inventive, and the best athlete on the block, Julie inevitably became the leader of his own gang. He fancied himself more idealistic than rival leaders, and for a time his gang was called the Arrows, out of admiration for Robin Hood. He instructed his chums to steal only from the rich, to benefit the poor. "And that was us."

The most common crime was stealing milk bottles from doorsteps. Julie drank a lot of milk in the predawn hours. They also stole the empties, worth one or two pennies, and with the added revenue from scavenged pop bottles, the boys managed to attend the movies regularly. The silent photoplays inspired the kid gangs. If a movie was particularly exciting, the boys would "play" it later, sometimes even charging admission for their dramatizations. That was Julie's idea. Dinah Garfinkle, who could not recall a time when Julie did not think himself some kind of actor, remembered that she often paid a penny or two to see improvised plays in which Julie always took the leading role. She said he always won applause for his ability to mimic well-known performers, both bodily and facially.

Julie staged the plays in the cool basement of an abandoned carpet mill that also served his gang as headquarters until police boarded the entrance. That forced the boys to find other sanctuaries for smoking and talking rough and otherwise commemorating their puberty. "People thought we were holy terrors, but mostly we just talked. But the talk was strictly gutter," John Garfield said. "We were all pretty wise to sex before we were able to do anything about it, but maybe not so wise as we thought."

In all things, gang talk was stronger than gang action. "We thought we were tough, but we didn't carry guns, like some gangs did. We all had knives, but they were for whittling and playing mumbly-peg and making things, not for fights. We never robbed at the point of a gun, or a knife either. Just potatoes we'd steal from a grocery store, or crackers. But that's a poor boy, not a bad boy."

Poverty was a thing he learned to exploit. "When I think back, the neighbors were always saying 'Oh that poor Julie, that poor orphan,' and I loved it. Once, when I was living in a mostly Italian neighborhood, the Italians would invite me in for big dinners, they felt so sorry. I knew what being hungry was like, but I was never hungry very long."

He recounted the pleasures of poverty, and there were pastimes lighter than stealing. Julie excelled at marbles and sometimes hustled other players for pennies. In summer, when stickball ruled the street, he was an accomplished swatter with a broom handle; and in winter he was a quick, decisive shinny artist, chasing a tin-can puck on his own greased sneakers or in someone's borrowed roller skates.

Every winter there would be snowball fighting, not always a playful sport. Sometimes a snowball war underscored ethnic conflicts, with fierce name calling accompanying the heaved missiles. John Garfield said he disliked "getting hit on the noggin with a snowball made of coal and ashes. That hurt. I also knew what it was to be called names, but that didn't hurt as much."

He sustained a permanent sledding scar when a large girl (who grew to giant dimensions in his later imagination) crashed into him with her sled and sliced open his leg. His recovery was complete except that the spot remained sensitive; and it was the only visible reminder of his well-advertised roughhouse childhood.

Even without funds, resourceful boys could find a good time. A gang could get into the Polo Grounds or Yankee Stadium after the fourth inning and see a lot of baseball without paying admission. Except for the camaraderie, watching sports contests left Julie unsatisfied, restless to be not an observer but a participant. So he had an early fascination for boxing, and a gymnasium on Jerome Avenue was a favorite haunt for the boys who could lay claim to worn-out gloves and get in their own sparring licks.

A pitfall was the certainty of encounters with small-time hoodlums who canvassed the slums, always on the prowl for smart kids who could be exploited. As a gang leader, Julie was regularly confronted by minor thugs and their propositions.

"Being the boss of a gang was important. It compensated for the attention I wanted at home, and missed. I resented my father thinking of me only as a disgrace to his name, so I fought him in childish ways. But maybe I wasn't really so tough. We played friendly with some of the underworld types because they always gave us cigarettes. On the other hand, we were pretty innocent about most of their dealings."

Confrontation with juvenile authorities was a continuing ordeal for the Garfinkles, but the trouble was seldom over stealing or destroying property. More often it was over Julie's ditching school. He was expelled from public schools three times, and he was usually on some kind of probation.

As a young boy he had been seriously ill with scarlet fever, causing permanent heart damage that would not be detected until after he was grown. But more important to a child, it caused him to miss much school, and getting behind made Julie resent the classroom even more.

David Garfinkle shrugged his declining interest by saying, "If Julie wants to be a bum, he's a bum." But Dinah often met with teachers, principals, and truant officers; she wanted Julie to have an education.

"They were finally calling me every time he was absent, sick or not sick," she would recall many years later. "Sometimes they were ready to expel him and I talked them out of it. It seemed then I was going to the school about as often as Julie was."

Some effort to keep up with his studies came through on Julie's part, but younger pupils began to pass him by. When he was twelve, his sixth-grade teacher decided he could not continue at that level, but Julie wanted to quit school rather than return to fifth grade. The Garfinkles, fearing that a demotion might push Julie to make good his frequent threat of running away from home, met once again with school officials. And then someone suggested a transfer to the Angelo Patri school as a possible solution.

The Garfinkles hadn't heard of Angelo Patri or his school with its "special cases" from all over the city. David reckoned that reform school would do Julie more harm than good; and besides, the school, located at Lorillard Place off 189th Street in the East Bronx, was too far away. School officials insisted that Patri's school was not a detention center, but specialized in the rehabilitation of problem youngsters and had a good record for that. And they suggested that something might be worked out for boarding Julie near the school.

Something was, and this was to Julie's liking. An uncle with whom he had a good rapport lived at Hoffman Avenue at 189th Street, at easy walking distance from the Patri school, and he agreed to take Julie in for the period of the school term. So in September, 1926, Julie was enrolled in P.S. 45. And, in later years, his every reference to Angelo Patri had a ceremonial tone.

"For a lost boy to be found, someone has to do the finding. Dr. Patri found me, and for reaching into the garbage pail and pulling me out, I owe him everything. The good things that came my way would not have been possible but for that sweet, funny man."

II

The King or the Beggar

It was not a reformatory and the principal was dismayed that many people held that opinion. But neither was P.S. 45 like any other school in the New York of its day. It revolved around personal expression and abounded with it.

Angelo Patri, riding in on America's largest immigrant wave of 1889, was twelve years old and unable to speak or write in English when he arrived with his family at Ellis Island. But he graduated with honors from City College of New York before he was twenty, and already was committed to teaching other immigrant children to understand America and seize its promise. In 1913—the year of John Garfield's birth—he became principal of hapless P.S. 45, a school of predominately poor children in a Bronx quarter rather resembling Manhattan's Little Italy, where he was raised. Patri quickly turned the school inside out.

He incorporated some of the teaching methods of Maria Montessori, his more famous Italian contemporary and personal friend; and Patri followed John Dewey's *Ethical Principles,* especially the tenet that "conduct is the real test of learning." Patri believed a teacher should "ask the child" and "know the child"; and that rather than doing *for* pupils, the teachers should get the pupils *to do for themselves.* He deemphasized book learning and devised a tailor-made curriculum for each pupil. The whole idea was to encourage *talent.*

P.S. 45 had shops in painting, drawing, writing, metal and wood crafts, sewing, weaving and gardening; but Patri's own interests inclined toward the finer arts. P.S. 45 got an enviable reputation in a hurry, partly because the experimentation yielded favorable results, and also because Patri himself had a flamboyant love of the limelight. He charmed the audience with his own impassioned performance of the grateful immigrant, and soon "the Angelo Patri school" had a terrific press. By accepting out-of-district delinquency cases, Patri obtained extraordinary financial assistance from the city; and Patri, always in demand as a speaker, got a newspaper column of his own ("Our Children") with evergrowing syndication, a vehicle to advance his theory that every child had a God-given vocation, a *gift* that had to be discovered.

The teachers Patri hired shared his enthusiasm for the artistic; they were not likely to uncover a student's remarkable potential for tax accounting or automotive repair or home economics. Patri himself was a concertgoer, a devotee of opera and ballet, a Sunday painter, and a lover of theatre and films. To Patri, classical artistry was the pinnacle of the "personal expression" encouraged in his school, so he would boast of grooming "another Caruso" or "the next Pavlova." He was tuned to musicians, painters, sculptors; but he was often heard to say that actors were his favorite people, and an autographed portrait of Eleanora Duse adorned a wall in his office.

In that office, on a fall day in 1926, Angelo Patri made his first acquaintance with a fairly new student who had been ordered to see the principal as a disciplinary measure. Playing in the outfield during a recess softball game, the boy had scaled a chain fence to retrieve a ball that had been socked into the street, and in his leap he had trampled some Patri-planted dahlias.

The boy Patri regarded had a Jewish name but a fair-skinned, dark-haired handsomeness that could as easily have been Italian. He was short but substantial—a sturdy body carried on short legs. Patri sensed the boy's uncertainty and embarrassed guilt, but also detected a tendency to pose. Julius Garfinkle, Patri reasoned, had a compulsion to show off; and he could find nothing wrong with such a tendency.

And Julie was confronted by a striking picture of a man,

with comical overtones. At fifty, stocky Angelo Patri had a large, square head with a thick wavy mane gone white in the best Italian tradition. And he wore a bright green suit, an individual trademark since having first bought one to impress some of his Irish students on St. Patrick's Day.

Julie expected to be booted from his new school, but Patri dismissed the flowerbed incident by pointedly rhapsodizing on the beauty flowers bring to a world that needs it. Patri suggested that Julie could also become a flower, a thing of beauty, if he could be left untrampled. When the principal asked what he wanted to do with his life, Julie mumbled an ambition for prizefighting.

"He seemed full of antagonism, as if he believed everybody —all grown people—were against him," Patri recalled. "But there was really nothing wrong with Julie, and I liked him. He had a nice embarrassed smile, and because he lacked confidence, he had that bad stammer. . . ."

Julie was hardly aware of a tendency to stammer until Angelo Patri made a big thing of it. In assigning him to a corrective speech class, Patri delivered Julie to his inevitable discoverer.

She was Margaret O'Ryan—a stout, agreeable young woman who had an easy way with boys. She was confident Julie and she would get along, and they did. She was the first teacher he ever *liked,* and it amounted to a schoolboy crush. Mrs. O'Ryan thought she could build Julie's confidence by getting him to recite in front of the class, and she assigned Thomas Paine's words about the summer soldier and the sunshine patriot, "These are the times that try men's souls . . ."

He memorized the text flawlessly, and Mrs. O'Ryan noted that Julie didn't stammer when he knew what he wanted to say. But his recitation was also monotonous. She told Julie to think of himself as addressing the people of the colonies with an important message that would arouse their devotion to country. He gave the speech again, this time with patriotic fervor. Mrs. O'Ryan was gratified by his quick response; and because she was also the dramatics instructor at P.S. 45, she began casting Julie in the one-act plays that were performed at student assemblies.

The one-act plays were an extracurricular activity for the after-classes hours, and they took Julie away from the school gym where he had been working into the boxing program. Some of his pals demeaned play-acting as a sissy pastime. But when Julie absorbed a hard punch thrown by another boxer and it hurt more than he would let on, he decided that his attention to dramatics would conveniently deliver him from having to face up to the truth that he was really no great shakes as a boxer. He was flashy enough; and the boxing instructor, a Mr. Hoblitzel, was so taken by Julie's footwork that he made the boy an unofficial teaching assistant. But Julie found that his gloved fists packed little power potential, and that he could wilt under another fighter's steady attack. But by backing away from the ring sport, he could still claim excellence at it.

Prizefighting was at its professional pinnacle during those Dempsey-Tunney years, and for poor boys it spelled economic opportunity. The champion boxers had large houses and fast cars and fancy women, so the ring was an honorable ambition for wishful thinkers. But making a living as an actor didn't occur to many boys in the Bronx.

About that time, it certainly occurred to Julie. From his earliest acting exercises in Margaret O'Ryan's classroom, he extracted an earnest and clear-cut will to become an actor. And at least one of his fellow boxing students didn't deride Julie's newfound theatrical interest. A wiry Italian youth named Joe LaSpina had some promise as an artist and helped out on the school plays by designing and painting scenery. Joe had heard of people acting in movies for thousands of dollars a week; and besides, his idea was that haunting the backstage scene was a sure way to meet the pretty girls. Sure enough, the school's loveliest numbers were its would-be actresses, for whom getting into the movies was the fantasy equivalent to contending for a boxing title. Julie was aroused by girls now, and Joe seemed to know them all. Soon the two boys were producing their own plays away from the schoolgrounds and casting girls of their choice.

According to Angelo Patri, "Julie found himself the moment he began acting for Mrs. O'Ryan. He could be convincing in any part, the king or the beggar." Patri recalled a time when Julie was playing a blind man and Mrs. O'Ryan told him to "go stand in the corner and don't come out until you've convinced yourself you're blind." And John Garfield said, "Mrs. O'Ryan may not have heard of Stanislavsky, but she was sure up on his system." He believed she had professional merit as a director.

Most students were overblown and declamatory, nervous about being on stage. But Julie was relaxed and his delivery was conversational, with just a hint of tension. Mrs. O'Ryan said Julie had natural talent, and of course Patri was delighted. Obviously, they both told Julie, he should concentrate on becoming an actor.

Julie tried the thought out on the Garfinkles, but his parents and other relatives and most of his friends thought the idea of Julie trying to become an actor was nonsense. Not that Julie needed their encouragement: Angelo Patri provided more than enough of that. Patri, who regularly became involved in the daily lives of his most diversely promising students, got to know David Garfinkle and they became friends, although the principal's ideas made no sense to Julie's father. But the Garfinkles had to admit that Patri was keeping Julie out of trouble, and they accepted Patri's assurance that Julie was improving in all his subjects at school, although it was only half-true. Math courses still baffled him and Julie had something less than mastery of the social studies; but he won an award for penmanship and continued to excel in art, now with watercolors. Patri said these developments validated Julie's artistic temperament. He said Julie had a need to express himself, but David Garfinkle felt his son had always expressed himself too much and too well.

Once Patri paid an impromptu visit to the apartment where Julie still boarded with his uncle. After the polite introductions, he asked to see Julie's room or the place where he slept. Not only did Julie lack a room of his own, he also had no bed. He slept in a hallway, on a mattress of old coats. The next day Patri had sheets, blankets, mattress and a spring bed delivered for Julie, whom he came to regard as an investment.

In the fall of 1927, Julie played the young soldier in Barrie's

The Old Lady Shows Her Medals at P.S. 45; the Garfinkles accepted Patri's invitation to the play and admitted their surprise over how believably Julie became an entirely different sort of person on stage. Soon afterward the New York *Times* sponsored the city schools' annual debating competition, and Patri coaxed a scarcely reluctant Julius Garfinkle to enter the P.S. 45 contest. The American Revolution was the governing theme, and one of Julie's girl friends had written a term paper on Benjamin Franklin. They turned it into a speech for Julie to deliver, called "Franklin, the Peace Maker of the Constitution." However spurious his facts, Julie won the school championship. Patri was one of the judges, but when Julie represented P.S. 45 in the Bronx borough competition, the judging was impartial. No matter, there were nine contenders and again Julie won. Angelo Patri was to say, "I don't know where Julie got the idea that Franklin was the great mind behind the Revolution, but I remember how beautifully he handled it."

The Garfinkles were astonished and proud. Dinah scraped together enough money to take Julie to a clothing store where he selected his first long-pants suit, to wear in the city-wide debate. Then a large collection of Julie's relatives journeyed to Manhattan, where the debating finals were held in a cavernous municipal auditorium. The crowd seemed enormous, and it was the first time Julie had the sensation of real fright before an audience; but he had "found the limelight . . . found an acceptable way of showing off. . . . I didn't want it to end."

Stimulated by the throng and by the exacting competition, he gave what he knew was his most forceful presentation. But he didn't win. Instead he received a runner-up medal for having advanced to the tournament final. It didn't subdue his disappointment, however, and afterward he was humiliated by the snickers of his peers when all the contestants were guests at an elegant dinner. Julie had never seen a finger bowl before. He didn't want anyone to suspect he didn't know what to do with one, so he drank the water from his.

After receiving his intermediate diploma from P.S. 45, Julie was back home in the summer of 1928 for a new round of quarreling. His voice had changed abruptly and a sudden growth spurt carried him very near to what would be his full height. He decided he should be treated with the respect due a man, and his father said if Julie was a man, he should be learning a trade and paying for his keep.

He got a job selling the Bronx *Home News* on a street corner he had won with his fists for his own territory. Dutifully he turned over the newspaper revenue to Dinah, but he kept the dollars he collected irregularly at the local gym for sparring with the novice professionals. Such income was no longer an encouragement. The gym was a snake pit of watchful promoters who used folding money for greeting cards and kept their eyes on any boy who looked like a possible comer. But they no longer showed real interest in Julie. He reasoned that if there was no future in it, getting battered around was hardly worth it.

Holdovers from his old gang still coaxed Julie to "make crazy," and he passed the hot hours acting out some scenes and improvising his own tall tales—still good for a laugh, but no longer satisfying to one who had decided on acting as a livelihood. His ambition was fortified that summer by encounters with two persons who already called themselves professional actors. One was Eddie Kogan, a boy of about Julie's age but slightly better economic circumstances. Eddie had more flair than training for the theatre, but was beginning to pick up small stage roles in minor Bronx and Westchester stock companies, and he advised Julie to forget about staying in school and just plunge into the job hunt. One day Julie was shooting baskets with Eddie Kogan, and the boys were joined by a young man who lived in the vicinity, near Beck and Longwood Avenues. He had good spring but poor shooting skill, and he introduced himself as an actor: Clifford Odet, who would add an *"s"* to his surname that year when he started appearing in small parts in plays staged by the Theatre Guild.

It was the first Julie had heard of the Guild and the first time he soaked up the kind of talk that kept Clifford Odets alive— talk of plays, theatres, actors, playwrights. Unlike Eddie Kogan, Odets felt that Julie should learn the general mythology of the theatre before making a first professional assault. He also told Julie that if he wanted to become a popular actor, he would do well to get a name other than Julius Garfinkle, which was not calculated to please the ladies who attended the matinees.

Julie did not want to invest three or four more years in a high school diploma. He sought his father's permission to drop public school if he took up a trade in earnest—provided he could keep some of his income to support acting lessons in one of the dramatic schools he had heard about through Eddie Kogan. David might have consented, but now the tenacious Angelo Patri arranged for Julie's enrollment at Roosevelt High School, in Patri's own territory. More importantly, Patri had pulled strings to obtain a dramatic scholarship for Julie with the Heckscher Foundation. Linked physically but not administratively to the Roosevelt school, the Heckscher Foundation was a stimulant for underprivileged but *gifted* children. Julie became a member of Heckscher's dramatic workshop.

Julie got off to a rocky start in high school and never regained his footing. Acting had become his consuming interest and he just couldn't summon attention to the general curriculum. But he thrived on the sessions at the Heckscher workshop, which gave him his first acquaintance with the dramatic classics. He did scenes from Molière and Jonson—even Aristophanes—and enjoyed himself even when he failed to understand the lines he spoke. Of course there was a lot of Shakespeare, whose poetry often demanded more than Julie's knack for simplicity; but he had no difficulty grasping the low humor of the rustic clowns who fancied themselves actors in the play-within-the-play of *A Midsummer Night's Dream*.

It was the Heckscher Foundation's major offering in the fall of 1928. Two complete casts were selected, and Julie was assigned to both Bottom and Quince, playing the two roles on alternate nights. Julie reveled in the general acknowledgment that he was the play's comic delight in either part; but while David and Dinah had honest applause for the performance they attended, there was no dissuading them from their opinion that Julie's increasingly apparent ambition was foolish. The

Heckscher scholarship would terminate in the spring, and Julie was secretly resolved to leave DeWitt Clinton High School at that time, having bounded there from Roosevelt.

On a night when Julie was overplaying Nick Bottom, Mr. and Mrs. Angelo Patri attended the Heckscher performance accompanied by the eminent actor, Jacob Ben-Ami. Julie had not heard of Jacob Ben-Ami, but during the backstage congratulations after the performance, he recognized the authority of a star actor. Ben-Ami had been in the forefront of the Yiddish drama's New York renaissance, most notably with the Jewish Art Theatre; then Arthur Hopkins tapped him to appear in English versions of *Samson and Delilah* and other plays he had done in Yiddish. Now that he was a successful Broadway star, his old friend Angelo Patri had sought him out to assess the ability of a nice Jewish boy who was in danger of getting in with the wrong crowd. Jacob Ben-Ami asked Julie how badly did he *need* the theatre?

Affecting nonchalance, Julie grinned and said he supposed acting beat working. Ben-Ami's scowl indicated that even if Julie's answer was given jokingly, it was not satisfactory. Ben-Ami issued some lofty statements about "the theatre" that made Julie wonder if they were talking about the same thing; but he said yes, he wanted to work hard to become a good actor.

Jacob Ben-Ami knew of a very good place for Julie to begin training if he was interested in acting as his life's work. It was called the American Laboratory Theatre and there would be a tuition fee, but Ben-Ami said he would be most pleased to recommend Julie's acceptance as a pupil there, on the basis of the performance he had just witnessed.

Other persons came forth with congratulations and exaggerated praise, and Julie savored all of it, though straining to overhear the conversation that continued between the Patris and their distinguished guest. He was sure he heard Jacob Ben-Ami say that the boy was rather handsome after all, which should certainly prove no hindrance to a dramatic career.

III

Vagabond Promise

At sixteen, Julie knew almost nothing about the world of professional theatre. The names of the powerful and influential on Broadway were strange to him, and he was entirely ignorant of the international movement. Had he a fair appreciation of the credentials borne by Richard Boleslavsky and Maria Ouspenskaya, he might have been awed and fearful about offering himself for their appraisal. But it would become his pattern to comprehend the fame or skill of a mentor or colleague only after having first attained his friendship.

Julie dropped out of DeWitt Clinton High School in his sophomore term. At home he was scolded routinely for his action, but his father was rigid in refusing to participate in raising four dollars every week for lessons at a place called the American Laboratory Theatre. Angelo Patri made a personal appeal to Julie to remain in school; but once Julie had convinced his old principal that the regular high school program could not help him develop into a fine actor, he started working on Patri for financial assistance. Patri finally agreed to give Julie a regular weekly "loan" of five dollars—sufficient to underwrite the expenses of theatrical training and subway fare as well.

So there was Julie, in the office on West Fifty-second Street, telling the secretary that he was supposed to see a man named Boleslavsky. It was a name easily interchangeable with Constantin Stanislavsky, of whom Julie also had heard nothing.

But now and for years to come, Julie would hear much about Stanislavsky and his method.

A Russian of privileged birth and an actor from childhood, Constantin Stanislavsky despaired of the artificial and exaggerated acting that was the world standard throughout the nineteenth century. Ibsen and then Strindberg had spawned a new drama of psychological insight that florid technique could only discredit, and Stanislavsky sought an artistic truth that would embody a completely new approach to directing and acting. He formulated his "system" by synthesizing the traits of the great actors, past and present, and by applying his own new theories, particularly the actor's reliance on what he called "sense-memory." Stanislavsky established the Moscow Art Theatre in 1898, producing Chekhov's *The Sea Gull* that same year and embracing the theory of *ensemble* playing. Maria Ouspenskaya became the Moscow Art Theatre's leading character actress; and Richard Boleslavsky, first a juvenile in Stanislavsky's troupe, soon won regard as Russia's finest young leading actor.

Boleslavsky forsook the new Soviet Union in favor of America in 1920. Being adept at English as well as vividly handsome, he might have become a matinee idol on Broadway; but his consuming interest lay in preaching Stanislavsky's gospel through stage direction. When the Moscow Art Theatre made its historic tour of the United States in 1923, Boleslavsky was a sort of liaison between Stanislavsky and the Broadway scene. Ouspenskaya, still with Stanislavsky's company, wanted to retire into teaching; and because she also spoke English, she stayed on in America to give acting lessons in the "system." Ouspenskaya's classes attracted only a minor cult following until the Theatre Guild—the dominant producing organization of the day, with money and culture consciousness —decided to develop the American Laboratory Theatre as a "collective education" workshop in all aspects of dramatic production. The Guild enlisted Boleslavsky to coordinate activities of "the Lab" and stage its experimental productions; and he, in turn, brought in Ouspenskaya to supervise the classes in acting.

In the spring of 1929, Julie met them both at the same time: Boleslavsky, fortyish but looking much younger, a tall man and rather spectacular; and Ouspenskaya, just past sixty but frail and seemingly ancient, a tiny woman whose glinty stare withered Julie.

He lied about his age a year's worth, but even at a presumed seventeen, Julie was the youngest student as well as the newest one. Yes, he said in his interview, he was "experienced," but Madame—as everyone called Ouspenskaya—thought otherwise. Julie had expected to get right down to the business of acting, but Ouspenskaya told him that first he must *prepare.* What did he know about *motivation?* It was a word he didn't believe he had heard before. There were a lot of questions Julie couldn't answer, but he was put at ease when he sensed that Madame was merely amused.

She said, "Good, we do not have to worry about the wrong things you have learned, for it is apparent you have learned nothing." When she asked why he thought he wanted to act, Julie said, "I don't know. Why did *you* want to?" Ouspenskaya said she didn't know why she had wanted to act, and that his answer was acceptable because it was honest. He was no longer afraid of her.

He wasn't frightened by people so much as by their knowledge and his own ignorance. Other students at the Lab had a literary foundation for the theatre and at least a smattering of popular sophistication. Hearing chatter about the Lunts, the Shuberts, and others whom he knew nothing about, Julie felt suddenly inadequate. Once he overheard gushing praise of the Lunts in their current Theatre Guild vehicle, *Caprice,* and to engage a new friend, George Tobias, in small talk, Julie pretended to have seen it.

"They know every trick of acting, those Shuberts. The play's not much, but it's worth the money just to see them."

"The *Shuberts?"* Tobias glowered.

"Yeah. Mr. and Mrs. Shubert. They're man and wife, although she uses another stage name. Christ, I thought everybody knew *that."*

White lies would be his defense, a way of staking false claim to a cultural education he lacked. Although he was easy to see through, lying would become a habit and then an obsession. Even being unmasked was a thing Julie could take good-naturedly, and it did not discourage him from hatching new falsehoods. He would always envy the ability of others to discuss plays and players, critics and playhouses, and theatrical philosophy.

Julie enrolled in morning and afternoon classes at the Lab, but dropped the later session to take a job in the garment district. It was a way to keep peace with his father and also have a meager amount of spending money; and he figured to have a prolonged life at the Lab if he swallowed it in easy doses. He pushed clothes carts for long hours and turned over part of his earnings to his father. He was paying his own board, although he was acquiring a new relationship with the Garfinkles, to whom he would soon become more accurately a now-and-then visitor than a living-in son.

Most of his evenings were given voluntarily to the Lab. Julie would get off work and head back toward Fifty-second Street, alternately walking briskly or sprinting in excitement, and would haunt Boleslavsky's rehearsals of new and untried plays. He helped build and paint scenery, he pitched in with crew work, and decided there was no aspect of the theatrical life he couldn't enjoy. He took up easily with most of the students who were slightly older than himself, and all living in Manhattan in a self-consciously bohemian way. Julie, eager to adopt their style, let his hair grow long. He became a chain smoker on "borrowed" cigarettes and enjoyed quantities of his friends' cheap wine, but retained his preference for beer among the bootleg alternatives. Although his enlistment at the Lab would occupy only one hard-paced year, it was his formative experience for both mind and body—a time of political awakening and sexual initiation. Life was adventure. Julie's sleeping habits now were largely improvised, and he was a welcome and agreeable guest in cold-water flats maintained by other male students, or the girls, or sometimes by both.

They liked his congeniality but no one detected the kind of talent in Julie that would guarantee his social acceptance. Nor did Julie's conduct in Lab classwork arouse a suspicion of professional aptitude. He played only one role in a Lab production: a walk-on, without lines, in *Big Lake,* by a novice dramatist named Lynn Riggs. Riggs soon afterward created a mild hit with *Green Grow the Lilacs* for the Theatre Guild, and it would be the genesis for the milestone musical, *Oklahoma!*

Not all of the talk at the Lab was about the theatre. Talking pictures were a reality passing beyond the novelty phase, and they seemed to augur some kind of peril for a legitimate theatre that had enjoyed its greatest boom throughout the twenties. Hollywood, with its bottomless reservoir of money, reached across the country to pirate the cream of the performing craft from Broadway. Jolson and the entertainers went first, but then the studios corralled the premium actors—Jeanne Eagels, Ruth Chatterton, and Ann Harding; Walter Huston, Paul Muni, and the venerable George Arliss. Nor was the quest merely for *names:* the picture companies signed scores of young featured players who were the hoped-for new generation of the theatre. Some would have gaudier destinies, setting new standards of fame as film stars. In the vanguard were Barbara Stanwyck and Claudette Colbert, Fredric March and Robert Montgomery. To the kids at the Lab, these young stage hopefuls were all traitors; and while Julie had always enjoyed the movies and fancied Hollywood as some kind of great place, he quickly accepted the idea of the picture companies as villains in a grand conspiracy against the theatre.

During one of Julie's early classroom sessions at the Lab, a clamor erupted over Edward G. Robinson's defection. First the Guild's fine young character actor had agreed to make a single picture at Paramount's eastern studio on Long Island, saying he was not forsaking the stage. Then a contract materialized and he was off to Hollywood. Some of the actors and other Guild personnel called for sanctions against Robinson who, while not under contract to the Guild, was under "moral agreement." That's what Herbert Biberman contended, anyway.

The volatile Herb Biberman, whose manner of talking in a

pant suggested a fellow about to catch a train, was a principal stage manager and sometime director for the Guild, but spent a good part of his time at the Lab, occasionally exchanging ideas with Richard Boleslavsky but more often ingratiating himself with the novitiate, going on eloquently about "the movement." Biberman had a way of taking the students under his wing, and for no reason that was easily foreseen or understood, he singled out the young Julius Garfinkle for special attention. Biberman explained that the theatre could afford to lose plenty of actors to the movies—there would always be good actors—but an Eddie Robinson was something special. The *movement* needed him because he had true intellect and that was rare. Robinson was shaping up as a leader in the *movement,* but his gifts would have no outlet in Hollywood, which was politically barbaric. Herb Biberman said there was no great loss in Robert Milton going to Hollywood—Milton was one of the Guild's esteemed directors—because he was not Left-oriented. It was Julie's first inkling of a political division in the theatre. Let the George Abbotts and John Cromwells and George Cukors go to Hollywood, Biberman declared, it was good riddance because they were "Broadway people" after all. Julie sensed that when Biberman spoke of the movement, he didn't mean Broadway.

Certainly idealism in its various forms flourished more in the atmosphere of the Lab than in the hardened arteries of Broadway itself. And in Richard Boleslavsky's opinion, to succumb to any movie offer was nothing short of high treason.

Then the stock market crashed. Wall Street, said *Variety,* had laid an egg. This amused the young folk at the Lab who could not foresee or even imagine the economic consequences; and besides, there was President Hoover in December, telling the American people that conditions were fundamentally sound. But one immediate effect of the crash was to jeopardize the financial sovereignty of the Guild, and with it, the Guild's subsidy of the Lab. Certainly Boleslavsky was not amused, for he had been thoroughly assimilated by capitalism. He had invested heavily in the bull market and now he was wiped out, with no alternative but to commit high treason and go to Hollywood.

Months earlier Boleslavsky had rejected a lucrative offer to direct talking pictures for Paramount. Now he was reduced to accepting an offer from the then-minor Columbia company on Hollywood's "poverty row"—a cluster of independent studios along Gower Street. Boleslavsky was granted a leave of absence from the Lab to direct one picture, but he would stay in Hollywood to the end of his days and be counted a success there. (When Ethel Barrymore consented to appear with her brothers in *Rasputin and the Empress,* she stipulated that only Boleslavsky should direct; he also guided a couple of Garbo vehicles and at least one certified classic, the March-Laughton *Les Miserables.*)

With Boleslavsky's departure, the Lab ceased to be an important experimental force in the New York theatre, although the darkening economic picture seemed to ordain its demise in any event. Julie may not have sensed that circumstance was bringing the Guild into more active administration of Lab activities, which in turn brought him more directly under the spell and influence of Herbert Biberman.

The Guild had one of 1929's popular Broadway successes with *The Camel Through the Needle's Eye* and Biberman, as stage manager, began to employ Julie as an unofficial assistant on that production. It also marked Julie's debut as an actor on Broadway, again without acknowledgment, and for only one performance.

Biberman's first assistant was George Freedley, poor of health but with a rich, encyclopedic command of theatrical facts and statistics that later would earn him eminence as a scholar-historian. In *The Camel Through the Needle's Eye,* Freedley also acted the small role of a young medical student. While they worked the backstage chores during performance, Freedley dazzled Julie by enumerating things he knew about the drama, and by mouthing all the actors' dialogue and exaggerating their gestures: he had memorized the entire play.

Freedley's part was only a few lines, and Julie begged

nightly to "let me go on in your place." Not given to frivolity, Freedley would not indulge Julie's whim, but one night when he wasn't feeling well he finally agreed to let Julie go on for him. Julie got into makeup and costume and made a bouncy entrance that startled the other actors, doubtless projecting too much youth for anybody's medical student.

Claude Rains confronted Julie with a near-smile that spoke amusement, and it threw Julie: he forgot his lines and stood there sputtering. Rains calmly ad-libbed a little speech incorporating all the medical student was supposed to say, then calmly waved Julie off stage.

Director Philip Moeller heard what happened and wanted to fire Julie, but since Julie had not been properly hired he could hardly be fired. George Freedley persuaded Moeller that Julie was really a boy of some promise, and Moeller became friendly. Julie stayed with *Camel* through the rest of its run and then assisted Biberman and Freedley in another Guild production, *Karl and Anna*. Again the director was Moeller, who didn't object to Julie (still uncredited) sometimes going on stage in a crowd scene.

Julie was awed by the polished Guild actors he observed nightly. Aside from Claude Rains, who later would be of capital importance to Julie's early film career, the *Camel* company boasted such Guild mainstays as Henry Travers and Helen Westley. The radiant young Miriam Hopkins—on the eve of her first Hollywood fling—played the lead. Alice Brady and Otto Kruger were in *Karl and Anna;* so were Frank Conroy, Claude Rains again, Biberman himself, and Biberman's wife, the serpentine Gale Sondergaard.

The actor who most fascinated Julie was Morris Carnovsky, who was still being billed as "Edgar Kent" when he appeared in the first Broadway play Julie saw—Eugene O'Neill's *Dynamo,* produced by the Guild. Carnovsky, bald and unbeautiful, was barely thirty, but already playing character roles. He was one of the Guild actors often attracted to the Lab by his earnest interest in the Stanislavsky technique—already referred to merely as "the system" or "the method." Julie was intrigued that Carnovsky, so unaffected offstage, was no more histrionic

when playing a role. Instead, his quality of *being* was opposed
to thespian showiness, and Carnovsky, Julie thought, exempli-
fied what Ouspenskaya wanted her pupils to become. As an
actor of understatement Carnovsky was not unique; but Julie
decided he was the finest actor in town, and in years to come
he would not abandon that opinion.

Julie was also impressed that so many actors, able and well
past their apprenticeship, still felt they had so much to *learn*
and came to the Lab with an exuberance often not matched
by the younger pupils. There was Stella Adler, an experienced
actress, already a champion of Stanislavsky; the furtive Lee
Strasberg, then only a minor actor; and the patrician Franchot
Tone, another Guild actor hopefully exploring the Stanislavsky
system. Also frequenting the Lab were Cheryl Crawford and
Harold Clurman, Guild employees who were not actors. Herb
Biberman explained to Julie that a dissident faction within the
Guild was beginning to grow, and starting talk of a revolution.

These people had begun to get together socially, spurred
mainly by the adventure of eventually organizing a company
of their own. Julie would hear afterward of a meeting held in
this or that person's apartment. Aching to be invited, he attempted to chum-up to Lee Strasberg, who, with Harold Clurman, seemed the likely cofounder of the company-to-be. But
when Julie asked Strasberg outright if he might attend one of
the "group meetings," Strasberg only glared at him and said
no, offering no further explanation.

About that time, the Guild put Romain Rolland's *The Game
of Love and Death* into rehearsal, to immediately follow *Karl
and Anna* and employ the same leading players—Alice Brady,
Otto Kruger, Claude Rains, and Frank Conroy. Biberman got
Julie into the company to do a soldier bit in a crowd scene,
and in the backstage environs he heard the entrenched Guild
actors disparage the *radical* element. Any offshoot company,
they believed, could only be short-lived and not likely to get
anything on the boards. But Julie's fellow supernumeraries in
the Rolland play were sympathetic to the upstarts, thinking
wishfully of joining the new company, devouring every rumor
of the group meetings. One of the soldiers in the mob was a

pleasant chap named Henry Fonda, who also hoped to be asked.

The Guild regulars viewed most of the young people affiliated with the Lab as radical spirits; and Julie sensed that the people studying at the Lab or haunting it really were his kind of actors. Mostly they were starvation cases, despite the acknowledged professional stature of some; and being neither effeminate nor egomaniacal, they were hardly the fashion or the pride of the acting profession. But with patriotic zeal they called themselves prophets of a theatre yet to come, and Julie believed them.

The Guild, having fitfully entertained notions of an experimental wing of its own, chose to silence the criticism that was percolating from within by staging a Soviet play called *Red Rust* that had intrigued Harold Clurman, who read plays for the Guild. So the "Theatre Guild Studio" was launched, with a production committee consisting of Clurman, Cheryl Crawford (the Guild casting director), and Herb Biberman who, it was agreed, would stage *Red Rust*. Biberman was relieved of his stage managing position on *The Game of Love and Death* before its opening, and on his invitation Julie quit the ensemble of the Rolland play to appear in *Red Rust,* which also required an enormous cast.

Getting into *Red Rust* provided Julie with a passport to the informal gatherings of the expanding clique that polarized around Clurman and Strasberg. He rubbed elbows with Franchot Tone and Luther Adler and Morris Carnovsky and they seemed friendly enough but kept their distance: obviously they regarded him as a harmless kid—one of Biberman's hangers-on—and not as a prospective member of an independent company that Biberman chose not to join himself. Both Clurman and Strasberg seemed indifferent politically, and when they lectured their young flock on the art of the theatre, they were not obsessed by the propaganda aspect. Biberman, on the other hand, was an exuberant Marxist who believed that the theatre existed as an agent for social revolution. He evangelized his convictions and found, in Julie, a willing and pliable listener. At this point Julie felt indebted mainly to Biberman for his *start*. For the crowd chores in *Red Rust* as a student and laborer, plus opportunity to display his physique as a boxer in one of the play's more effective scenes, Julie earned twenty dollars a week—astronomical by his standard, and hardly less so by his father's. He also understudied one of Biberman's prize chattels, Lionel Stander.

Not all of the actors clustered around Clurman, Strasberg, and Cheryl Crawford—and already talking about "our group" —were directly involved with *Red Rust*. Carnovsky was only an observer, as was the talkative young man Julie remembered from their brief acquaintance in the Bronx—Clifford Odets— who had begun taking small roles for the Guild and had a nice rapport with Clurman.

Odets sought to be helpful toward Julie, whose name was about to appear on a playbill for the first time. Odets had written a radio script that had been recently aired on station WIP in Philadelphia, and the name of its principal character was Garfield Grimes. He proposed it as a likely stage name for Julie, who liked the Garfield part. A compromise was reached, and the *Red Rust* program identified him as Julian Garfield.

Red Rust opened at the Martin Beck Theatre a few days before Christmas, 1929. It ran through February, creating something of a stir as the first play from the Soviet Union to have a substantial engagement in the United States. David and Dinah Garfinkle came to see the play, but were not comfortable. David grumbled about the money he had spent to see and hear something he couldn't understand or be interested in, and his reaction provoked a shouting argument during one of Julie's now-and-then forays into the Bronx. Julie ridiculed his father's ignorance: "You're too stupid ever to know anything about *expressionistic* theatre!" And noting that Julie's uninhibited speech was peppered with profanities he wasn't accustomed to hearing only reaffirmed David's conviction that "actors are a bunch of *bums*." He was also plainly hurt that his son was denying even his family name.

Mr. and Mrs. Angelo Patri, however, were impressed by the *Red Rust* performance they attended, and Julie accepted their congratulations. Now that Julie was a professional actor drawing a weekly salary, Patri reasoned that it would no longer be necessary for him to *loan* Julie money for his tuition, and even suggested that Julie might wish to work out a repayment plan. But the backstage meeting proved to be Julie's last encounter with Angelo Patri for many years.

So in the spring of 1930, just seventeen, Julie left the Lab —to face the ordeal of the unestablished actor. After *Red Rust* closed there was a Theatre Guild retrenchment program that prevented Herbert Biberman from tossing even the crumbs of crew work out to Julie.

The Guild was not dissatisfied with the *Red Rust* experiment, but neither was it encouraged to a point of perpetuating the activities of its "studio." Knowing that *Red Rust* was a one-shot oddity for the Guild crystallized Harold Clurman's goal of an independent repertory company; soon his group became The Group indeed. Organized under that name, it proceeded slowly in acquiring actors for a permanent company and in mapping a production plan. There was a feverish little status game concerning who would and who would not be invited into the company. Ruth Nelson and Eunice Stoddard, students with Julie at the Lab, had played fair-sized roles in *Red Rust* and accepted invitations to join the Group. Those in the *Red Rust* cast not included in the Group were Julie's chum George Tobias and Herb Biberman's wife, Gale Sondergaard; both would be in the movies some years later, at Warner Brothers with John Garfield. Both Clifford Odets and Luther Adler recommended Julie to Clurman, Strasberg, and Cheryl Crawford—who became the Group's triumvirate of directors— but he was given no serious consideration. Not unexpectedly, there were some grievances about the makeup of the company, and Luther Adler decided not to commit himself. But Clifford Odets, a character member, advised Julie to stay busy in the theatre, and eventually he'd get him into the Group. From the beginning, Group members indicated they expected their ensemble to endure perhaps forever.

Julie "made rounds," but found the Broadway offices gloomy. The showmen had taken a beating in the stock market and their activities seemed less glamorous because they were less secure. But Julie's ragamuffin presentation of himself could hardly have produced results. He had no photographs or résumé; he lacked poise and assurance; he was in that fatally in-between stage for a young actor, unable to play either a child or an adult; and he was hardly a conventional stage juvenile. The best he could do was extract a promise from Philip Moeller that the Guild would summon him should it need a juvenile of his "certain type." Julie's only recommendation was that he had worked at the Lab.

Many years later, returning to New York after a decade of film stardom, John Garfield reflected on his early training, saying he had been a washout at the Lab. He doubted he had revealed promise, and remembered that when Ouspenskaya asked him to "become a cup of steaming tea" he was only baffled. Madame's lectures on emotional truth were beyond his grasp, and he didn't think she had been complimentary toward his work in the prepared scenes. Later when they were both working at Warners, he visited Ouspenskaya. She politely said she remembered him, but he doubted it.

She remembered. Maria Ouspenskaya, still a working actress as an octogenarian, said, "Indeed I remember John Garfield quite well. He was Julius, I believe, a charming boy with a most expressive body. I was not aware of a dramatic talent, but then one is never surprised, especially when there is a vivid personality. He was . . . I think charming is the right word. And he was so eager to be of some kind of help."

Yes, it was charm, of a certain kind. That its basis was distinctly sexual was a thing Julie did not fully understand, but it gave him an anchor of confidence nevertheless. He found the girls at the Lab as covetous of his favors as the gum-chewing Bronx girls had been, and was taken to bed by more than a few of them, including some older and diversely experienced women bent on instruction. He found the bedroom exercises generally more fascinating than Ouspenskaya's classroom rituals. Because sex was easily obtainable for him, he was not confronted by romance until it flowered at home, in the Bronx.

One Sunday afternoon he had taken a subway to the Bronx for a family visit, and after dinner he dropped in on one of his casual girlfriends. His hair was actor-long and he was over-dressed, Barrymore collar and all. It was near the beginning of his year at the Lab, and the girls around the old home base were aflutter just to know someone who was *almost* a real actor. At the girl's house Julie took his first notice of another visitor: a pretty girl of fifteen, with straight black hair worn in a bob, and whose figure was undecided. Her name was Roberta Seidman and she regarded the swaggering Julie as one of her friend's rough-talking "bohemian" swains. But she was impressed that he went to something called the American Laboratory Theatre, and she would not easily forget how good-looking he was. They would not meet for another year; and when that occurred, Roberta Seidman would be a shapely eye-catcher with new reason to be impressed. By then, Julie could exaggerate his importance to the Civic Repertory Theatre.

Julie paid a call to Eva LeGallienne's Civic Repertory Theatre down on Fourteenth Street and had the good fortune to encounter—quite by accident—Jacob Ben-Ami, whose memory, it seemed, was excellent. Of course he recalled Angelo Patri's talented boy, and yes, he'd be happy to introduce him to Miss LeGallienne, and with a healthy recommendation besides.

The lady explained that no parts were available, since they would soon be laying off for the summer. But he could help out with the backstage chores, and because Ben-Ami's report was so enthusiastic, he could join the Civic in the fall as a regular apprentice if he was still interested. Julie should expect no pay, and little chance of acting roles of any size; but it could certify him with Equity, the actors' union. When the summer layoff came, Julie was broke. But he said he'd be back.

He went home, and the Depression was burrowing in. Julie's father did not have regular work; he and Dinah were sorely pressed. There was no backstage work to be had, and Julie also was unable to reclaim his job in the garment district. Even the modest part-time jobs that usually went to teen-aged boys in the summer, now were being taken by grown men coming off the breadline.

To combat his frustration, Julie went back to the gym to work into a boxing trim, sights set on the Golden Gloves. If you won in the Gloves, it was a sure bet you could win as a pro, and Julie thought he could smell the money.

He had abandoned the Garfinkle name for good, but this Julian business was no good for a fighter. So he was Julie Garfield, 126 pounds stripped, whose first match—in the prelims —would be his last. From the opening bell he took a pounding from a brawny Irish youth. Julie pranced around, landing some fast, soft shots that left his opponent unimpressed. Then Julie left himself open and caught a left hook that dazed him, before a right uppercut sent him to the canvas. He heard the referee begin the count, and he knew he was able to get back to his feet; but staying down for the full count and deciding once and for all to become an actor seemed a sensible thing to do at the time. It was scored a knockout.

Staying home got on the retired prizefighter's nerves, but the ordeal was more trying for David and Dinah. They regarded Julie's friends as mostly of questionable character, and the Garfinkles were wary of rumors involving some of the girls in the neighborhood. Dinah was always one to intercept a lot of talk. Julie had taken up with Joe LaSpina, his pal from P.S. 45 days, and Joe had sexual expertise and knew a lot of girls. Yet Joe did not know Roberta Seidman, who teased Julie's imagination as he caught fleeting glimpses of her now and then, wondering if she remembered him.

In that summer of 1930, Julie attained his full height—five feet seven if he pulled in his stomach and remembered to think tall. In later years, movie studio biographers would add on extra inches, but Julie was always ashamed of his lack of real height. But the girls never complained, and from the beginning they were too easy a mark for him. He was the beau ideal of the Bronx, dark but fair, with deep brown eyes already fixed in a characteristic squint. His mouth was sensual, and the curls that fell loosely over a low hairline could only be appealing. But the girls were most impressed that Julie had been on Broadway—that someday he might be a rich movie star.

David Garfinkle remained rigidly skeptical. When Julie heard of a Shakespeare company playing the Bronx, he found Fritz Leiber doing *Macbeth* and needy of spear-carriers. Julie and Joe LaSpina filled the order at fifty cents a performance, prompting David to ask, "Is this the big money you talk about?" Julie had always enjoyed summer but this one passed too slowly. He was miserable until he rejoined the Civic Repertory for its fall season.

The idea of a public repertory theatre had flickered in America—all talk and no action—until Eva LeGallienne went to work, renovating a theatre on Fourteenth Street and opening the Civic Repertory in 1926. Her productions played to a dollar-and-a-half top, and a seat near the back sold for twenty-five cents. The caliber of Civic productions varied, but usually it was the best theatrical buy in town. Critics were too often condescending, but in retrospect the Civic Repertory was an unquestioned success and an exciting footnote to the twenties, the most interesting years of American theatre. Great artists, Nazimova among them, sacrificed their customary fees to appear in Miss LeGallienne's programs.

Although not operated as a school, the Civic was a workshop for total stagecraft, with the best apprentice program of its day. The new apprentice decided his name was Jules Garfield; Julian, he reasoned, seemed to place him in a drawing room, where he surely did not belong. He was instructed in his new tasks by a graduate apprentice only a few years older than himself—Burgess Meredith, commonly called Buzz. Another of the younger actors with whom Julie immediately formed a strong friendship was Howard DaSilva, just out of Carnegie Tech. The atmosphere was not unlike the Lab.

Julie was the chore boy, the *gofer:* he would go for the coffee. He swept the theatre, washed windows, and cleaned toilets. He also built furniture, sewed costumes, gathered props, painted flats, took tickets, learned about lighting, and talked acting, acting, acting.

Actors at the Civic, like those around the Lab, had no time for prissy airs, and they employed the vivid expletives that were staples of Julie's vocabulary. Earthy talk had been a problem for him at school and at home, and in a few instances had made it hard for him to hold a job. But blue was the color of common shop talk at the Civic, and Eva LeGallienne could cuss with telling effect.

A pool hall not far from the theatre was headquarters for the boy apprentices. Julie bummed cigarettes and hustled other players for lunch money. The boys were always broke but needed only a nickel apiece for subway fare, and if they could win it at the pool table, they rode uptown to Times Square and then walked to the Union Church on Forty-eighth Street where free lunches were served to actors—an innovation of the Depression credited to actress Selena Royle. Sometimes the boys would wash dishes, a way of rubbing elbows with other actors and hearing about plays and opportunities for casting. They weren't so dedicated to Civic Repertory that they wouldn't have angled for a paying part elsewhere.

But hard times were hurting the theatre and Julie began to feel fortunate in his apprentice assignment. He took some grudging satisfaction in hearing that plans for the Group Theatre apparently had snagged, and that some of the Group "company" were applying at the Civic. Yet he felt stifled not being more of an *actor* at the Civic, where again he was limited to the crowd scenes. But he supposed his time would come, and he was encouraged that Buzz Meredith was going to have a good role in a revival of *Liliom*—the play that had brought Eva LeGallienne into prominence some years before.

Along with standards from the classical repertoire, the Civic season included some new American plays, including *Alison's House,* in which Miss LeGallienne took a leading role. After it had played its engagement and was well on its way to being forgotten, the surprise announcement was that it had won the Pulitzer Prize. In that drama about Emily Dickinson's poetic legacy, Julie understudied the role Howard DaSilva played. Otherwise Julie did a walk-on as a soldier in a revival of *Journey's End*. He had an opportunity to become a cast replacement in one of the featured parts, but speech betrayed him. While false English accents were not encouraged for that very British war drama, Julie's rubbery Bronxese was a problem that would plague him throughout his career.

Leona Roberts, a veteran Civic actress who had taken a liking to Julie, tried to help him with the accent. She thought his trouble was in slurring over the vowel sounds, and she gave him a volume of Poe's verse and told him to practice reading aloud the narrative poems emphasizing the open vowels—*The Raven, The Madman,* and especially *The Bells.* He memorized the poems, and in doing so acquired his literary hero; but he would never' have a good ear for the subtleties of speech, and the accent held on stubbornly.

Although he made new friends easily, the Civic scene was less to Julie's liking than the Lab had been. There was a constant backstage bickering and he thought its origins were often petty. Never one to hide his feelings, he said things that probably were leaked to Miss LeGallienne, whose displeasure with him seemed apparent—to Julie if not to others.

If something was missing he was automatically suspected, and once he was accused outright of stealing Alma Kruger's shoes. Julie felt he had been convicted without a hearing until the shoes were located in a pawn shop and the broker identified another apprentice as the thief. Even then, neither Miss LeGallienne nor anyone else apologized to him. Such injustice apparently weighed heavily on Julie, who remembered the incident of the shoes vividly, all of twenty years later.

Away from the environment of the Lab and the adjacent Theatre Guild, Julie missed the everyday dialogue of social protest. The people around the Civic Repertory seemed dedicated only to their craft, and only Howard DaSilva among the younger actors advertised a political conscience. Julie had fallen out of touch with Herbert Biberman and he had no opportunity to observe a Morris Carnovsky or a Luther Adler with silent admiration for their art which, he reasoned, was enhanced by their politics. He was not so much able to define "leftist" as to know he wanted to be one.

But his discomfort at the Civic was mainly a matter of economics. He resented always being broke. He was spending more time in the Bronx now, taking meals at home and sleeping there to keep expenses down. But his father was after him to get a steady job and help pay the bills, and Julie didn't want to work, he wanted to *act*. He thought about quitting the Civic Repertory, but didn't want to give his father the satisfaction.

Julie failed in brief stints as busboy and then elevator operator. The jobs weren't beyond his capacity, but his temper was easily ignited and he would insult his way back into the ranks of the unemployed. Once again he was selling the *Home News*.

Joe LaSpina got Julie a job at a garage, passing him off as a skilled mechanic. Joe was himself an automotive wizard, but in P.S. 45 he had been one of Angelo Patri's diamonds in the rough—a boy with a wretched home life, always in trouble with the police, but showing a definite talent as an artist. Since art didn't pay, Joe worked fairly steadily as a garageman; and by devious means, he usually had a car to drive.

Joe's favorite scheme was to complete his repair work on a fancy car in the late afternoon, but telephone the owner with sincere apologies that the work was going to take longer than had been figured. Joe promised to deliver the car, personally, to the owner's home later that night.

In the interim, Joe and Julie would take the car for an evening spin, picking up girls who could be impressed by the slicked-up boys, or the sleek car, or by all three. Joe was coughing a lot and probably was tubercular, but fought the temptation of heading westward to some nice, dry climate in one of his "borrowed" cars. Julie's concurrence would have been all the encouragement he needed, but Julie would draw the line at stealing a car. Still, they talked often about seeing the country together, and Joe taught Julie how to drive.

Once when Julie and several other boys were out for a jaunt in one of the cars Joe had appropriated, they invaded a block party during its peak of merriment, and Julie saw her: Roberta Seidman, now even prettier than he remembered, and nicely filled out. He asked her for a dance and she accepted. Years later she would still remember that they talked about the proper way for a gentleman to hold a lady while performing whatever dance they were doing.

"He wanted to take me home, but my girlfriend gave me

the 'no' signal because he was known around the neighborhood as a *wolf*. But I said yes anyway . . . and he didn't even try to kiss me good night."

This girl, Julie knew, was different. Perhaps he had been seeing her at various growth stages over the years, and once when he was living on Livonia Street she might have thrown a stone at him because of some vulgarism on his part; he couldn't be sure. Here now was a rosebud whose stature and firm jaw indicated a strong pride. Her dark brown hair was carefully curled and she had bright, expressive eyes. He thought she was the most beautiful girl he'd ever seen.

She wasn't the typical Bronx product. That she had a mind of her own was spectacularly evident. Her real name was Rose, but she loathed it, and chose Roberta by and for herself. She thought Julie had too high an opinion of himself, one that he did not yet deserve, and she told him so. That, of course, was the clincher: he decided she was *the girl*.

Then it wasn't Roberta at all, but Robbie, sometimes spelled Robby or later on, in Hollywood, Robbe. She was saucy, positive, extremely bright; and if looks were the come-on, Robbie's vivaciousness and wit excited Julie's real interest. She shared his sense of a world that existed beyond the choking boundaries of the Bronx; and while she doubted that Julie really knew what he wanted to do with his life, his designs on an artistic career intrigued her and gave their relationship an early intensity.

Robbie lived with her parents and sister in an apartment a cut above the ones Julie was accustomed to, but the stigma of poverty was definite. Still, it was a *home,* with a genial air. The Max Seidmans were an affable couple, proud of their daughters, and their parlor conversation ranged over a wide territory and stimulated Julie. In their presence he was comfortable and spontaneous—more the young friend of the family than the patronizing suitor. The Seidmans shared David Garfinkle's skepticism toward Julie's ambition to act, but they were sympathetic. Max Seidman and David Garfinkle became casual friends, and Robbie's father told David not to worry, Julie probably just had to get some things out of his system.

If the Seidmans were fond of Julie, the Garfinkles adored Robbie. When Julie, still only seventeen, announced that sooner or later he was going to marry Robbie, his father said, "Julie, that girl is too *good* for you." He meant it, and said it regularly. But his relationship with Robbie helped to improve relations between Julie and his own family.

She did not fall easy victim to his charm, and she gave him a hard time. He talked of the fame and fortune he would win, and she said, "Don't say it, *do* it." Robbie accepted it as her mission to be Julie's driving force, to prod him toward the level of accomplishment that would take both of them out of the Bronx, forever. Yet she doubted that she was in love with him and told him so, and this spurred him. She wasn't intimidated by his wolfish tendencies. She had other boyfriends and knew what most of them were after. If Julie got fresh, she could handle him; she called the shots.

So they went biking together, they took in the movies, and they romanced on Robbie's tenement rooftop while a popular song of the day assured them that the very best things in life were free. But they both wanted more than the moon and the stars.

With the end of his Civic Repertory apprenticeship in sight and the summer of 1931 approaching, Julie made vain attempts to catch on with stock companies. Prosperity hadn't turned that corner, and fewer companies were "going out," so competition was exacting. He signed on with Fritz Leiber's tattered Shakespeare troupe once again, this time for a dollar a performance and a go at Malcolm in *Macbeth,* and Roderigo in *Othello.* As one of the forest exiles in *As You Like It,* he came on with a song. The Leiber players performed in open parks and public school auditoriums in New York, mostly in the Bronx, and the receipts were so bleak that the company folded even before the hot weather set in.

Then there was a new quarrel at home. David Garfinkle had persuaded a friend to put in a good word for his son at a local factory, and it resulted in a job offer for Julie—ostensibly for the summer only, but David said it might be permanent if Julie could get the theatrical foolishness out of his head and put his mind and body toward earning a living. Julie said he wouldn't take the job. After the shouting contest, during which David had invited him to leave the house for good, Julie relented and said he would go to the factory, but only until he'd lined up an acting job for sure.

Then Julie received a postcard from Joe LaSpina in Indiana. Joe had lost his job at the garage—they found out about his defrauding customers in various ways—and had hitchhiked westward. He would be working a wheat harvest in Nebraska later in the summer, and wanted Julie to thumb his way out to join him there.

Acting on impulse, Julie pawned a few belongings in hope of scraping together five dollars before heading west to link up with Joe. He did not disclose his intention to his father, but decided to tell Robbie: it would give her an excellent opportunity to talk him out of going. She didn't care enough for him, but the possibility of his taking a long powder might change things between them. He didn't expect to really *go*.

John Garfield remembered: "It was a warm day and we were up on the roof of Robbie's house. I said I was going away because I felt it was my need, and all she said was, 'Everybody knows his need.' There I was, shoving off, and she wouldn't give me a tumble."

The spurned lover was stuffing cans of food into a knapsack when his father crept in. He told Julie to put everything back, he wasn't going anywhere. Dinah came in with groceries, and over a noon meal they argued about Julie tramping off like a bum. Where would he sleep? What would he do for money? Julie said since all actors are bums, if he could succeed as a bum it might mean success as an actor next. The Garfinkles, both having temporary employment, returned to their jobs that afternoon after Julie promised anew to report to the factory. But later he repacked the knapsack and went outside, and kept on walking.

"I think I broke my father's heart, leaving like that . . . but kids are selfish and don't know their cruelty. Out on the road with my thumb waving, suddenly I felt happier than I'd ever been before. What I really wanted was to be on my own, and I saw the turning point."

Hitching short rides, he made Newark by nightfall but walked the road until dawn, unable to thumb a westbound ride. At a roadside diner he met a salesman who was driving to Cincinnati and didn't mind company. The salesman paid for Julie's meals all the way. After that the thumbing was easier and food wasn't much of a problem. Julie invested in candy bars which gave him energy and a feeling of being full. When he met Joe LaSpina in Nebraska he still had most of the four dollars he had carried out of New York.

The wheat harvest was still two months away, but Joe knew that out in California they needed fruit pickers. Julie had not been west beyond New Jersey until this junket, but now he would see the whole country.

In the Colorado Rockies the boys ran out of money and the cold mountain roads ran out of traffic. Snow still lay frozen on the highest hills and every cold night was a challenge. They built fires but couldn't get warm, and Joe would cough through the night.

"Only a few cars would go through, and they weren't wasting gas on a couple of hobos," John Garfield recalled. "We were dirty, unshaved, really seedy. Joe was miserable, but it was a new experience for me, and I think I liked even the pain of it."

A forest ranger told them of an abandoned cabin where they could sleep. Inside it they found shelves of canned food, and while Joe started a fire, Julie reached for a can of soup. It was filled with rocks. Every can contained ore specimens; there wasn't a morsel of food. But the boys had a warm night's sleep before discovering, in the light of morning, that a box very close to the fire they had stoked all night contained dynamite and blasting powder.

Back on the road, they received food at far-scattered homes in exchange for woodchopping and other chores; and at Grand Junction they hopped a freight train they thought would take them to California. Soon Julie knew all the whistle signals: "And I knew by the chuffing of the steam in the cylinders how fast a train was going on the upgrade. We waited until a train was pulling hard and slow near the top, then we'd hop on between the tender and the first mail car."

On every freight they put in with stowaways: career vagrants who often didn't know where the train was headed; likely criminals on the run; and the new flotsam of the Depression—confused men seeking a future that would recapture the past. Most hobos harbored a Micawber-like faith that something would turn up. Whoever these men were, Julie decided it was nice to have friends under a trestle when the rain was coming down.

The enemy was the goon—the railroad policeman who was everywhere then, in his busiest years. Julie and Joe learned from the veteran hobos to hop off the moving train before it pulled into the station, then make fast tracks to reboard beyond the station when the locomotive was again in motion. Sometimes they would hear shots ringing, and their fellow travelers told of many killings.

California turned out to be Seattle—but the Northwest was not yet blighted by the times and there was good pay for a man strong enough for lumberjacking. The boys got work and bought some clothes. They slept at the logging camp and went into town every night for some wild oat-sowing. Julie survived his first drunken stupor but his wallet didn't, and he didn't know which one of the friendly girls snatched his week's wages. He had a good time and would have stayed longer, but the dampness bothered Joe, so they decided to move southward to Los Angeles, again by the freights.

In Sparks, Nevada, not far from Reno, a layover stretched into several days because the area was swarming with goons. Camping among the derelicts gave Julie an experience he would enjoy retelling in years to come; Preston Sturges conceived the film of *Sullivan's Travels* after hearing Julie describe his hobo adventures.

"Every railroad junction had its hobo village, and I learned something of the force that keeps a man going when he has nothing to live for. Not all hobos were misfits. There were doctors and lawyers among them, alcoholics, even an occasional ex-actor. One night we were around the fire putting away some of that delicious hobo stew and Joe said something about me being an actor and couldn't I 'make crazy.' They wanted a sample, so I did some bits of Shakespeare, like the Pyramus and Thisbe thing I still remembered from school. Then I recited *The Raven,* which I'd memorized back at the Civic Repertory. And I got this strange feeling. Every eye and ear was turned on me and I realized that for a moment I was helping those men shut out the rest of the world. You know, there's nothing like a hobo's applause. They don't try to impress anyone with polite custom. If they clap it's the real thing. That was the first time I thought maybe Angelo Patri was right, that I had a *gift.*"

They picked pears and peaches in California's Imperial Valley, and they started mustaches to emulate the *braceros*—their migrant Mexican coworkers. The work was long and hot and tedious, and they slept in filthy, roach-infested shacks. They took their money and rode the rails to Los Angeles, where Julie talked about trying the movies and Joe got temporary work as an auto wrecker. Julie attempted to get in touch with Richard Boleslavsky, but didn't know which studio employed him. Finally he bluffed his way into a truck-driving job without a test, and left for San Francisco in a ten-ton truck loaded with cantaloupes; his chore would be to drive back. But on the route the driver said, "Okay, kid, you take over now." Julie failed to live up to his bluff—he couldn't handle the truck—and the driver reclaimed the wheel. He was fired, but Julie rode to the next town and hitchhiked back to Hollywood.

Then they headed for Nebraska by the least likely route—through Mexico. Joe knew some Italian that could serve as Spanish. They stayed close to the border and rode the trains that skirted it on the U.S. side. They did a brief turn as waiters in Arizona and jumped a fast passenger train that shot them into Austin, Texas, where they were arrested as vagrants. No trial, no hearing: just thirty days, the judge said. When Julie insisted that he was an actor and the jailer sought proof, he produced a worn newspaper clipping relating the New York debate competition. Then Julie polished off *The Raven* and the boys were released, but not until they had a good meal under their belts.

That gave them their formula. Northward through Texas, Oklahoma, and Kansas they entertained for room and board, or at least for food. Joe drew pictures, and Julie gave dramatic readings. It was the part of the country where times were hardest and small banks were failing regularly, but people still craved diversion.

"We weren't as hungry for food as they were for culture. If I could get a bunch of farmers together long enough to give a sampling of good old Poe, we'd eat. Joe would tell them about New York and then sketch Grant's Tomb or the Brooklyn Bridge and they ate it up. They still thought the Woolworth Building was the tallest and Joe would draw it, but then he'd do the Chrysler Building and the plan of the Empire State, which was just being built. They were a great audience."

One experience would haunt them. Riding the rails into Nebraska, the boys struck up conversation with an experienced but inebriated hobo. As they came into a railroad yard and the hobo prepared to get off, he lost his balance and fell between two freights—theirs and another on the next track. The boys looked back to see a smashed body that lay motionless on the ground between the freights racing away from it.

In Nebraska they worked a bumper wheat crop and Julie learned to drive a combine. The farm was prosperous and there was plenty to do, but also time enough to enjoy the local girls who were very attentive to the young vagabonds—especially to Julie, with his fleshed-out summer tan and the now-full, trimmed mustache that made him look like Warner Baxter, so they said. The boys were invited to stay on as hired hands; there would be hog-butchering in the winter. Joe liked the prospect; he was feeling better now, and besides, he did not want to return to New York, where he intimated he might be in trouble with the law.

But Julie was homesick. As his appetite for adventure was satisfied, he did a lot of thinking about Robbie, wondering if she would still bother with him when he got back home. He also felt contrite toward his father and hoped the parable about the prodigal son would hold true in his case. But mainly, his vagrant experience gave him a want of purpose. He felt he could survive forever, trading rhymes for food and shelter, shuffling to no final destination. The odyssey had given him the sense of an audience, but proving himself as an actor could also mean proving himself to his father. Soon a new theatre season would be taking shape and he wanted to push every contact. He decided to go home, and packed for a solo journey.

A rural festival celebrating the end of the harvest became his farewell party. There was dancing and all sorts of playing around, and on his last night Julie got drunk on homemade hooch. He awoke in the middle of the night, throat on fire, and staggered to a well where he drank water by the bucket. After he worked off his hangover they told him the well water was contaminated, but Julie felt fine when he said good-bye to Joe LaSpina, who was destined to die before another wheat harvest came around. Julie was whistling in Iowa when he caught a ride straight to Philadelphia; without Joe as a companion, riding the rails had no appeal for him. He hitchhiked into the Bronx the next day, still six dollars to the good. When he embraced his father, David's tears were real; so was the typhoid fever Julie had contracted from that Nebraska well water.

IV

Forward to the Left

His absence made Roberta Seidman's heart grow fonder. She still scoffed when eighteen-year-old Julie talked of marriage, with little money and fewer prospects. But the fire was still burning, and Julie sensed that Robbie was his girl, whatever else might happen. She was attentive throughout his convalescence. Robbie's own expanding knowledge about the new plays and the people who made them was an indication that she could needle Julie into action on his promise to make good in the theatre. He felt the pressure.

Julie put together a modest résumé, and an uncle who was an amateur photographer made some studies of a surly-handsome juvenile. And Jules Garfield began making the usual casting rounds. He heard that the Group Theatre was about to materialize on stage at last—still subsidized by the Theatre Guild but working independently of it—in a new Paul Green play, *The House of Connelly*. From Art Smith, a member of the company, Julie learned that his name had come up in an early discussion about filling out the large cast, but that nobody knew where he was.

The House of Connelly opened at the Martin Beck Theatre on September 28, 1931, and it took New York by storm: not the regular playgoing audience so much as the people who were, of themselves, the Broadway theatre. The level of acting was uncommonly high according to every report, and the cast enlisted many of Julie's friends, including his foremost professional heroes. When he saw *The House of Connelly* on stage, Julie decided that getting accepted into the Group Theatre must go above every other goal. It was also apparent that many another young actor in New York carried the same thought.

But while *The House of Connelly* was still fresh on the boards, Julie obtained his first role of consequence in a Broadway play, and came very near to playing the lead. Through Herbert Biberman, Julie met the mercurial James Light, known to be looking for a teen-aged boy for the play he was about to direct, called *Lost Boy.*

Light auditioned Julie for the title role—a fifteen-year-old delinquent with a slum background and a grudge against his father. James Light recognized the authentic article when he saw and heard Julie, and he offered plenty of encouragement.

One of the boy wonders of the theatre, James Light had been associated earlier with Eugene O'Neill, Kenneth Macgowan, and Robert Edmond Jones at the Provincetown Playhouse. His future might still have been ahead of him but for a drinking problem that would plague him always and deny recognition of his major talent. Light would remain on the theatrical scene for years, but always on the periphery— brilliant, theatrically creative, a respected adviser—but not personally reliable, and not to be trusted with an obviously first-rate play. But among theatre people, James Light was first to recognize an extraordinary quality in Jules Garfield, even though he didn't give Julie the leading role in *Lost Boy.*

Light contended that Julie's stage projection was too mature to play a fifteen-year-old, and the role finally went to the more experienced Elisha Cook, Jr., who was already in his middle twenties, but who played psychotic teen-agers almost exclusively. Julie and another boy did share the understudy assignment, however, and James Light further compensated Julie with a colorful second-act part, as a companion inmate at a reformatory.

Lost Boy was a shrill melodrama with a tragic ending that pointed an accusing finger at society. Julie thought it was terrific. It rehearsed through the Christmas holidays and opened in the first week of the new year at the Mansfield Theatre, just up the street from the Beck, where *The House of Connelly* was anchored. The critics, who took little note of Jules Garfield's participation other than to lump him with the cast as a whole in generous praise, were only mildly respectful toward the play itself. The notices did not excite a rush to the ticket window. Leonardo Bercovici, one of the producers, led a battle to keep the play running in the hope of an audience building through favorable word-of-mouth. But grim times were changing playgoing habits, fewer people were coming into the theatres, and they came wanting to laugh or to see famous stars: *Lost Boy* offered neither.

The quick failure was a theatrical commonplace—*Lost Boy* ran only two weeks—but that was something Julie could adjust to. He cleared four hundred dollars, including rehearsal pay, and that was solid encouragement. He took Robbie out on their first expensive dinner date. And *Lost Boy* had given him an actor's foremost need beyond talent—a *credit*. Having worked with James Light also enhanced his credentials.

At the Equity office, Julie learned that Elmer Rice was forming a second company of his established Broadway success, *Counsellor-at-Law,* for an engagement in Chicago. Julie answered the audition call but so did most of New York's unemployed actors, for the play had an exceptionally large cast. Julie was in competition for the "youth" parts with his fellow Lab students, Civic Repertory apprentices, and other bygone acquaintances.

Elmer Rice, formerly Reizenstein, directed his own plays and had a major reputation resting mainly on *The Adding Machine* and *Street Scene,* although *Counsellor-at-Law*—with Paul Muni registering a sensational personal success—was his most formidable commercial hit to date. Rice conducted the audition and had Julie read the small part of an errand boy, then the shoeshine boy—an engaging bit role. Julie did not function well in "cold" readings and it was evident that Rice was not impressed. Otto Kruger, who took Muni's title role in the Chicago cast, remembered Julie from his Theatre Guild activity and had also seen him in *Lost Boy.* He urged Elmer Rice to take a chance on the boy, and Rice agreed to give him a second reading. Julie thought he read much better the second time, but when the cast for the Chicago company was posted in the Equity office, his name wasn't on it.

A few days later, Elmer Rice was lunching with a group of theatre folk that included James Light. Rice had a minor problem: the youth cast as the shoeshine boy had become ill and would have to be replaced; did anyone want to suggest an adolescent type who was hopefully not in school and could be pressed into immediate service for Chicago? When James Light suggested Jules Garfield, Rice remembered his audition and admitted that the boy had been better each time he read. But he had vetoed him because of an unusual handicap: he considered the boy too handsome. Light said hire him, the boy's good. Julie joined the company only a few days before it left for Chicago. The boy whose illness had cleared a path for him did not have much of an acting career, but as Meyer Levin he became a prolific and successful novelist.

In his first rehearsal Julie serenaded Elmer Rice with a perfect, and perfectly innocent, Bronx accent—giving Rice the impulse to switch Julie to the plum role of Henry, the office boy. Although it was not a strategic role, Henry was on stage for much of the action. It was a part with colorful opportunity, basically comic but with some good serious moments.

Not only was it a prestige assignment, it guaranteed Julie a salary more than double what his father could earn in the best of times. David Garfinkle, weary at last of ridiculing Julie's aspirations, elected to congratulate him instead.

In his unharnessed excitement Julie dusted off the marriage proposal to Robbie, offering to take her to Chicago. She parried the invitation, but Julie felt she'd accepted a rain check. The Seidmans had mixed feelings about the romance. Robbie's parents had become fond of Julie, but Max Seidman said one good reason for not marrying an actor was that he would always be running off to Chicago or some place even worse. Robbie wanted to finish high school, but on plain emotional terms she was still the pursued object, much less certain of their relationship than Julie. He claimed he had her parents' consent even before Robbie had agreed to the idea of marriage.

Julie had just turned nineteen when he left for Chicago, where he could enjoy bachelorhood under conditions of unprecedented personal affluence. Less than a year before, he had passed through Illinois as a hitchhiker. Now he rode into Chicago on the 20th Century Limited, and would live like a gentleman in a respectable hotel, in the company of actors.

Counsellor-at-Law pleased the finicky Chicago press and all of Julie's first personal notices were favorable. The play captured a large audience that would carry the engagement at the Harris Theatre for twenty weeks. Otto Kruger was politely received as the lawyer up from the ghetto—the role Paul Muni had created—as was the serene Mary Servoss, who played his wife.

Eddie Kogan, whom Julie had known in New York, inherited the part of the shoeshine boy vacated by Julie, and they were roommates and companions all over town. They took in ball games, shot pool, and watched the girls go by. Other lively friendships were established with Sam Bonnell, Ned Glass, and Vincent Sherman.

Julie's pulse would race in a group atmosphere. The Chicago company was not afflicted by the usual backstage bickering, and he formed close ties. Harry Mervis, a veteran with a background in Yiddish theatre, became a father figure to the younger actors, and was a catalyst for the frenetic discussions that inevitably focused on economic and political revolution in America. Mervis was an emotional spellbinder, but Julie profited most from the conversation of Vincent Sherman, with whom he shared a dressing room at the theatre.

Sherman was a sort of older brother to Julie during the run of the play, but he would also become a lifetime friend and eventually one of the Garfield directors at Warner Brothers. In *Counsellor-at-Law* he played the eloquent young Communist who was then a fixture in a good many of the theatre's more serious-minded plays. With his own genuine concern about the prevailing social system, Sherman rather resembled the role he enacted. He found Julie more curious than knowl-

edgeable, anxious to understand the conditions that had everyone so worked up, but ignorant of the ideological factors
determining the conditions. He introduced Julie to *The Nation*
and *The New Republic,* and Julie pursued his own cram course
in back issues at the Chicago Public Library. Books and the
libraries that accommodated them had been anathema to him,
but now they symbolized his need. The Chicago experience
impressed itself upon him in other ways. The city throbbed
with rugged vitality and there was anger there: breadlines were
more in evidence than in New York, and Julie came to recognize a look of hunger more cutting than any pain he'd felt in
his belly. Before he left Chicago, he had the makings of a
political conscience.

Shortly after *Counsellor-at-Law* settled down for its Chicago
run, a sensational film *about* Chicago opened downtown: the
much-publicized *Scarface* that the two Howards—Hughes and
Hawks—had spent so much time and money shooting. It was
a controversial exhibit, but an instant smash hit nationally;
and Paul Muni was its coruscating star. In the parlance of
Hollywood, he was suddenly very hot property; and as a consequence, Otto Kruger was summoned to Broadway to replace
Muni, who was again ticketed to Hollywood.

Harry Mervis took over Kruger's part and gave a colorful
reading, but ticket sales dipped below the break-even point
and curtailed what would have been even a longer run. When
the company was packing for the return to New York, Julie
said he couldn't understand how an actor of Paul Muni's dedication could leave a great part such as George Simon in
Counsellor-at-Law in favor of *any* movie. Regarding the young
player who appeared to be filling out daily into a rugged handsomeness, Harry Mervis said, "Julie, some day they'll offer you
a sackful of money to make movies. You can make your own
decision then, and we'll judge you."

Originally, Paul Muni had not caught on in films, but had
completed the *Scarface* project before essaying *Counsellor-at-
Law* on the stage. Subsequent developments made the actor's
price soar, and the Warner brothers met it. Julie saw *Scarface*
in Chicago and was impressed by the Muni performance. He

was also dazzled by the picture's content, for he had seen Al Capone in the flesh, at a ball game in Chicago's Wrigley Field.

Back in New York, he was again too late to catch on with a stock company. In those days before most theatres were air-conditioned, even the top stage attractions often closed for the summer, leaving New York a ghost town for actors. Fritz Leiber's players were back to strolling the boroughs, but Julie did not want to backtrack from his claim to relative prestige. The only likely alternative was the Borscht Circuit—the Jewish summer resorts—where theatrical entertainments were devised by the "social staff," for which Julie's background now qualified him.

He heard of a camp in Vermont that had an opening as assistant to the social director—in this case a young minor actor and unproduced playwright out of Cornell, Sidney Kingsley.

The Twin-a-Wani Lodge was a seasonal retreat for New York Jews who still had money, and who sometimes had good contacts in show business. If you worked it right, Sidney Kingsley told him, it could be a stepping stone. Julie stressed his identity as Kingsley's assistant social director, but he was also expected to be a dishwasher and busboy and dispenser of other mundane chores. The pay was meager, but since everything was on the house for the employees, it was all profit— and Julie was bent on accumulating a pillow of cash. Even in Chicago he had spent money cautiously, intent on getting a nest egg that would serve as a persuader for Robbie. She hadn't exactly pined while he was away, and had gone to work with an aim to do some saving of her own.

The Twin-a-Wani Lodge, airy and pleasant even at the peak of summer heat, gave Julie pleasures both intellectual and physical in the summer of 1932. Julie helped Sidney Kingsley with the amateur theatricals, both prepared and improvised, and he charmed his way into status as a camp favorite. He acted in skits written mainly by Kingsley, but had his best rapport with an audience around the campfire after supper, reciting the verse of the redoubtable Poe. *The Madman* now was the consensus favorite. He found ways of making everyone aware of his dramatic success in Chicago, and this made him a bright flame around which would flutter the female moths both young and old—but tending to the latter. Twin-a-Wani was an adult camp with a decided shortage of ingenue charmers; but women of maturity were willing, even desperate, to test Julie's virility. He made many friends.

In other moments he thrived on long talks with Sidney Kingsley, who talked a lively game of social protest. Kingsley cursed the absence on Broadway of what he called volatile theatre; he had acted in a sensational play entitled *Subway Express* that was on the order of what he had in mind—the stuff of life itself. No longer driven to performing, he wanted to write because plays and not players were what Broadway needed; and he knew the plays were inside him if he could make that all-important breakthrough. He told of a play he had written and rewritten, called *Crisis* and set in a hospital. The company he most anxiously wanted to perform the play was the Group Theatre which, as a body, was off somewhere at another summer camp providing local entertainment, but also rehearsing the plays they would bring to New York for the 1932-33 season. Julie said he hoped to get into the Group Theatre as an actor. So did everybody else, Kingsley warned him.

On a humid midsummer night, Julie and Sidney Kingsley sprawled on a lawn and talked for hours after the vacationers had retired. Julie recounted his odyssey of the slums—the street gang adventures, his encounters with cheap crooks on the one hand, and his brushes with the law on the other. Kingsley said society is always the villain and Julie liked the sound of that. He told of his travels with Joe LaSpina, and of having recently learned from Joe's parents that his wayward artist friend had died of tuberculosis.

Some interest in New York over his hospital play caused Kingsley to leave the Twin-a-Wani Lodge prematurely. Julie lost touch with him, but barely a year later he saw Kingsley's *Crisis* on stage, only it had become *Men in White* as produced by the Group Theatre, and had won the Pulitzer Prize for drama. Kingsley's next play, even more successful, would be an abrasive, youth's-eye view of New York slum life. Julie liked to tell people that he had planted the seed for *Dead End* in Sidney Kingsley's fertile imagination.

Julie inherited Kingsley's mantle as camp social director, but almost immediately he also abdicated. Elmer Rice reached Twin-a-Wani by telephone from New York.

"Elmer told me to get my ass back home. I was going to do *Counsellor-at-Law* on Broadway with Paul Muni, who was back from Hollywood and itching to be on stage again. I was packed before the next train came through."

Supposition was that *Counsellor-at-Law* had been laid to rest, but the scenery was stored away, and Muni's still-accelerating movie fame made a reopening feasible. So Elmer Rice was putting together a company to include the best available members of both the New York and Chicago companies, and he wanted Julie for the office boy.

The prospect of acting with Paul Muni was an unexpected dividend. The Chicago production, despite Otto Kruger's earnest effort, lacked the spark that Muni's acting gave it, both in its color and its discipline. The brilliance and undeniable star presence were missing on Broadway when Kruger came in from Chicago to replace Muni, and the play lost its box-office punch. It closed, and then it was Otto Kruger's turn to accept a call to films, and he became one of Hollywood's busiest players. Yet *Counsellor-at-Law* would be a stage bonanza all over again, for 1932 was Paul Muni's year.

Scarface was still playing a first-run stand on Broadway; and not long after *Counsellor-at-Law* reopened in September, the other film Muni had gone west to make was also released in Manhattan—the hard-hitting *I Am a Fugitive from a Chain Gang*. Broadway learned afresh that if anything is better commercial insurance than a solid theatrical name, it is a solid movie name—and now Paul Muni was both.

He was a paradox, and other actors were often puzzled by his craft. Austrian-born Muni Weinsenfreund had been a youthful legend of Yiddish theatre in America before gaining fame in English under his new name. Here he was at thirty-

seven, a slight figure, still suggesting a not-quite-grown schoolboy of tentative good looks: the most painfully shy person
Julie had ever met. Obviously insecure in his offstage moments, he was guided by his wife Bella, without whom he
conceivably would become hopelessly lost, on an invisible
dog's leash. Yet something happened when he began acting a
role. He glittered on stage, every component of a complicated
mechanism functioning smoothly. His acting was rich in detail
but the performance never varied. Every action, even the
tiniest gesture, was orchestrated into his total conception of
the role. Other actors Julie observed would add little pieces
of business from time to time, but Paul Muni had a manner
that communicated his displeasure if they tampered with a
fixed performance in a scene that involved *him*. Julie marveled
at Muni's power of concentration but wondered if he ever had
fun.

Julie always had a good time when he and Dorothy Day,
as the lawyer's receptionist, started the dialogue in the opening
scene. They made a game of it, varying the timing, sometimes
starting casually, at other times almost frantically. No one
seemed to mind so long as they knew what they were doing,
but when Muni took stage, Julie and the other actors kept to
their established routine.

In the New York engagement Jules Garfield obtained feature billing, something he had not had in Chicago. He got
the hometown-boy-makes-good treatment in the Bronx *Home
News,* and relatives and long-forgotten friends came to the
Plymouth Theatre to see him. Julie obtained house seats for
David and Dinah Garfinkle, right in the front row; so close
that while he was on stage Julie could hear his father say in a
loud whisper, "You know, Dinah, that boy is really *good.*"
His parents came backstage and praised Julie before some of
the other actors, and Julie introduced them to Paul Muni.

The New York company included many of the Chicago
players but also several of Muni's original coplayers, among
them Martin Wolfson, a friend from Julie's days at the Lab,
and John Qualen, later to act in John Garfield movies. In
their midst Julie was becoming a gregarious funmaker whose

most celebrated accomplishment was his Paul Muni imitation—voice, face, and body—for which he had the benefit of a more than casual physical resemblance.

The return engagement played three months, then the play was taken on an eastern tour. He spent the Christmas holidays in New York with Robbie before going on the road, and their devotion was reconfirmed. That they would eventually marry was something they both accepted, and it would remain for Robbie to decide when. He promised to be a good boy during his travels.

The tour began in Washington, and people in Baltimore, Philadelphia, Pittsburgh, and Cleveland would also line up in imposing numbers to see Paul Muni in the flesh. Snow blanketed the East during the first weeks of 1933, and Washington was bleak and frigid during Julie's first visit there. The very air was turbulent: the wheels of government were in paralysis as the lame-duck Hoover administration waited out its time. Julie and some of the other actors attended veterans' rallies and talked with men who had marched in the ill-fated bonus army. City streets filled up by day with jobless men; hunger and agitation were everywhere. Julie felt guilty about his affluence and tried to put coins into every open hat, but there were too many.

In Philadelphia some of his fellow players gave Julie a surprise twentieth birthday party that also became a festive, hopeful salute to the New Deal. Earlier in the day he had been in a large group gathered around a radio in Elmer Rice's Ritz-Carlton suite to hear the newly inaugurated Franklin Roosevelt tell a nation the only thing it had to fear was fear itself. During the bank holiday that followed, they sensed a tempo of government back on its feet. They were still playing Philadelphia when beer returned on a legal basis, and that provoked Julie to declare himself a Roosevelt Democrat.

On the road he could be faithful to Robbie in his own fashion but pursue a last fling with zeal, and the library became his proving ground. He developed a surefire technique, hustling the prettiest librarian he could find in each city. He would seek their guidance in locating books about the theatre, and during the search would identify himself ever so casually as an actor in the new play that was in town—yes, the one with Paul Muni, who was a good friend of his. One book led to another, and Julie learned that librarians knew their cities well—the places of interest, the good but cheap restaurants, and the likely spots for successful trysting.

His Baltimore conquest was Rebecca Surmeier, who would remember that every girl in the library was jealous for Julie's attentions. When he was visiting her on the job, they would accost her with trivial "business" ("Becky, do you know where the overdue notices are kept?"), and would flutter their eyes and flash let's-get-acquainted smiles at Julie. His chosen librarian in Philadelphia was Florence Abromowitz, who recalled that Julie's winning manner certainly extended to other women; her own mother was in the palm of his hand, and Julie had an open invitation to dinner throughout the local engagement—plus ample family encouragement to pursue romance in earnest. But the evidence of every report was that Julie was remarkably chaste throughout the tour, and the only failing he had in the eyes of his far-flung lady friends was a tendency to talk too much about Robbie.

After the Cleveland booking the company returned to New York for a second return engagement, a thing almost without precedent. Elmer Rice had booked the Forty-sixth Street Theatre and there were early indications that the box-office vitality had not diminished. Julie still expected to be involved with *Counsellor-at-Law* indefinitely—there was talk of yet another eventual tour through the Midwest. Julie felt secure enough now to marry. Any more traveling, and he wanted to have Robbie with him.

He arrived back in New York ahead of schedule and took the subway uptown in hope of surprising Robbie at home. Robbie was out to the movies with friends but expected very soon; and Mr. and Mrs. Seidman welcomed the well-groomed young man in the freshly pressed suit and the squeaky new shoes. They had coffee and many cookies and talked away the hours, awaiting Robbie's return. When she arrived home her surprise was not so much in finding Julie there as in learning that he had obtained official consent for nuptials, and that her parents had no reservations about Robbie marrying an actor. Plans for an early wedding might have been put into motion except that, almost as certainly as it had been established, Julie's economic security vanished and the vagaries of the actor's life were reaffirmed.

Hollywood was again cited as the villain. Warners had alerted Paul Muni for a return to the West Coast where a new vehicle was being readied, but Muni did not like the script and was hoping the project would be canceled. If not, he wanted it delayed long enough to enable him to do the movie version of *Counsellor-at-Law* for the Universal company, which held the screen rights, and for whom Elmer Rice was doing his own movie script.

Right after the play opened to near-capacity business, Universal notified Rice and Muni that Warners had refused absolutely to surrender Muni's services—even briefly—for what promised to be a prestige film. So Universal signed John Barrymore, and Warners ordered Muni to report to his home studio for something called *The World Changes*. Since the survival of *Counsellor-at-Law* on stage was a simple matter of Muni remaining in the cast, the decision was to close the play on his departure.

The company plunged into gloom. It was late May, not a favorable time for lining up new work; and indications were that Universal was not interested in enlisting very many of the able stage actors for the movie edition. Yet the studio approached young Jules Garfield about recreating the role of the office boy, Henry.

Rice had recommended Julie for the part, but when Universal's David Werner met with Julie and said a term contract would have to be part of the arrangement, Julie was confused. Rice advised him against agreeing to any deal that would keep him in Hollywood indefinitely; and Julie, seeing that even a Paul Muni could be wretched about having surrendered his independence, thanked David Werner and said he wasn't interested. He didn't even find out how much money he was rejecting. He merely accepted Elmer Rice's opinion that he was a promising but green talent who would find the best opportunity for development on the stage. Bobby Gordon, a young screen player without stage experience, played the office boy in the movie, in which only John Qualen repeated an original stage role. Under William Wyler's direction, *Counsellor-at-Law* was Universal's 1933 Christmas release and not especially successful.

Before the play had closed, the Warner company had expressed its own interest in Jules Garfield. Lew Stewart, of the Warner home office in New York, wanted to arrange a screen test. Told by some of the other actors that Stewart did a lot of testing but very little signing, Julie gruffly said he wasn't interested, he certainly didn't want to go to Hollywood. But he accepted Stewart's offer of one day's work in a picture being shot in Manhattan. He wound up with fifty dollars and an incomparably obscure motion picture debut—one he never acknowledged later, but in which the prototype John Garfield is clearly visible, if only briefly.

The picture was *Footlight Parade,* an early entry in the Warner cycle of backstage musicals initiated by *42nd Street,* now considered a classic of the genre. A camera unit had taken over one of the vacant Manhattan theatres to shoot portions of the "Shanghai Lil" production number. Busby Berkeley's regiment of lanky chorines adorned the arena, and Berkeley was there to supervise their stepping. James Cagney, a snappy tapper, was the energetic tar looking for his Lil— inevitably, Ruby Keeler. Lloyd Bacon, anchored in a chair adjacent to the camera, was nominally the director.

They had Julie decked out in a sailor suit. He had no lines, only cues for smiling and responding to the ladies and the footworks. The sequence took several hours to shoot, and Julie passed most of the time waiting for the camera settings. When there was action, he never knew when he was on camera.

A few days later, while they were getting ready to go on

stage for the final performance of *Counsellor-at-Law*, Julie
told Sam Bonnell there wasn't enough money in all of Hollywood to make the boredom of moviemaking worth his while.
How much were they *paying* Paul Muni, anyway?

The American theatre had lurched sharply to the Left, and
on the threshold of his twenty-first year, Jules Garfield believed he was part of a movement.

The Group Theatre, his personal holy grail, was gravitating
toward the heart of that movement. And if the Left movement
was not being sustained primarily by the Group, perhaps it
was keeping the Group itself alive. The times may suddenly
have seemed less promising for Jules Garfield, but they were
bleaker for the Group. If the theatre was a fabulous invalid,
the Group was a walking cadaver, an exaggerated death rumor
like Mark Twain's. It did not lessen Julie's craving for membership.

Since its maiden success, the Group had disentangled itself
from the Theatre Guild, only to have failure follow failure in
its subsequent productions. Yet the Group's reputation soared,
or its notoriety did, or both. The nucleus of its charter membership was intact, but strong actors had been added—Luther
Adler officially, J. Edward Bromberg, Russell Collins, and an
exceptionally promising youth out of Yale, Elia Kazan. Julie
had a base of friendship with all of them, and with Art Smith,
Morris Carnovsky, Bill Challee, and others of the original
company. They were the people he counted on to clear a path
for his candidacy, but then the hard-pressed Group submitted
itself to a severe retrenchment.

But if the Group was to become, historically, the most
famous and influential component of the Left movement in
the theatre of the thirties, in its early days it did not lead the
vanguard. The Group was conceived out of artistic rather than
political aspiration, but from the beginning the Theatre Union
was committed to social crusade. Ultimately the Theatre Union
formed a bridge between *Counsellor-at-Law* and the Group
for Julie; but it also illustrated a contrast between the American theatre of the twenties and thirties—the difference be-

tween knowing a problem existed, and coming to grips with it. The twenties had been a bountiful decade for Broadway. A score of new dramatists surfaced with talents blazing, urging their theatre to larger and more imposing themes: O'Neill in his formative years, George Kelly, Sidney Howard, Maxwell Anderson, Elmer Rice, S. N. Behrman, Robert Sherwood, and Philip Barry. There was enlightenment, there were hints of political awareness; yet the brave new world of theatre was predominately glib during the optimism of the Coolidge joyride. The twenties may have yielded a theatre of ideas, but the thirties produced a theatre of protest. Elegant plays of foreign origin were no less fashionable, as the Theatre Guild displayed the Lunts in every variation of continental plumage; but inevitably a reaction mounted against a theatre that stayed resolutely remote from the very real problems of the day.

The Theatre Union did not openly espouse a Marxist stance, but it was a *proletarian* theatre—Sherwood Anderson, one of its founders, gave it that label—and its credo was pacifism. It opposed racial and religious bigotry. It was born during the first Broadway return engagement of *Counsellor-at-Law,* and both Paul Muni and Elmer Rice were among the twenty persons who agreed to finance its charter in equal measure. Some of the other underwriters were playwrights Sidney Howard and John Howard Lawson, and the great Negro actress, Rose McClendon, who had acted in the Group's *House of Connelly* and in an earlier Paul Green play, *In Abraham's Bosom.* There was no official acting company, but Julie was offered a role in the first Theatre Union production—*Peace on Earth,* an antiwar drama. He elected instead to go on tour with the Muni company, but he was a *Peace on Earth* cast replacement later, ending a brief period of unemployment after *Counsellor-at-Law* finally closed. He played a substantial role, but his weekly pay was only twenty-five dollars; and from Broadway elegance he returned to a shabby old haunt. The Theatre Union's headquarters and playhouse was the Civic Repertory on Fourteenth Street, abandoned when Eva LeGallienne decided to call it a day for her bold experiment.

By the fall of 1933, all theatrical companies that rubbed

against the conservative grain had melted into a large radical fraternity, and the Theatre Union was its axis. It was a magnet for active and potential Communists—the militant partisans and the benign idealists who attempted to translate Marxist doctrine into an American solution. Julie played a lot of poker and absorbed a lot of protest talk. Bidding for recognition, he began to read the *Daily Worker*—or started carrying it around, to advertise the political intellect he lacked but coveted.

There was distinct rivalry between the Theater Union and that foremost topic of conversation, the Group Theatre. Julie thought he detected some rank jealousy when the more avowed Communists assailed the Group's dereliction of social responsibility. Getting into the Group seemed to be the objective of everyone Julie knew, including its foremost detractors. An unofficial Group emissary to the Theatre Union was J. Edward (Joe) Bromberg, a splendid character actor who also was both a zealous radical and a companionable fellow. Bromberg defended the Group, its ongoing program, and Harold Clurman and the other leaders against an unflagging barrage of criticism; but he would report that criticism to the Group hierarchy, often in scolding language.

Another Group regular Julie began to see around the Theatre Union was Clifford Odets. After the final performance of *Peace on Earth*, Julie and Robbie went to the inevitable party and were greeted as great old friends by Odets, who was getting nowhere in his effort at hustling a pretty Theatre Union youngster named Ruth Hussey. Leaving the girls to chat, Odets cornered Julie into one of his serious discussions. He had started to teach classes at the Theatre Union, stressing practical applications of the Stanislavsky system. Odets suggested that Julie might benefit from his classes. Julie doubted he could meet the tuition. Odets said, "We'll compromise. When you don't have the money, you can get in free." Robbie, the pragmatist, advised Julie to encourage every prospect of association with Group people. So Julie began attending Odets's weekly classes.

Always intending to discuss some aspect of acting, Odets would more likely detour into another area and get mired there, filibustering on whatever aroused his passion at that moment. But whether Odets entertained only a handful of students or a larger group, he gave pointed and increasing attention to Julie, often more personal than professional.

Odets was captivated by Julie's unbridled charm, but also by his rank ignorance. Odets was a fund of information: names, dates and statistics poured from him; artists, works and movements; Ideas and Theories on the theatre and other aspects of life and art. He was an exhibitionist with knowledge, yet he had a compulsion to share and to teach, and in Julie he found an ideal repository. Julie became a regular visitor to the rancid apartment Odets rented on Horatio Street in Greenwich Village. On an earlier occasion he had dined inelegantly with Odets and some other Group actors when they had been experimentally living together; but the special aspect of Julie's relationship with Clifford Odets was nurtured in the loud privacy of Odets's apartment.

The living room centerpiece was a large wind-up Victrola whose built-in shelves housed a respectable collection of classical records, with one shelf to spare for liquor. Music was mandatory and Odets insisted on maximum volume; so while Beethoven's notes rattled the loose wallpaper, Odets shouted above the music, telling Julie about what the composer was trying to accomplish, or proclaiming the supremacy of Koussevitzky. Thus began the most meaningful friendship Julie would know, and it was an association enriched by high personal regard and mutual envy.

Odets's aptitude for knowledge made Julie aware of his own thirst, yet Odets happily would have traded selves with the handsome boy who was seven years his junior. Odets advocated D. H. Lawrence's concept of natural man. He wanted to possess women physically rather than intellectually. The rugged, naturally virile Julie became his ideal.

Odets explained Stanislavsky in a way that Julie could understand. Without demanding that Julie become a teacup or anything else nonhuman, Odets put the stress on concentration as the mood maker for the "sense-memory" association— the actor finding his own common denominator with the role of his playing. Yet Odets doubted that he was especially beneficial to Julie, believing instead that Julie came naturally by the attributes most of the Group actors merely aspired to. "You really should be in the Group," Odets insisted. Julie's sincere response was, "Let that be arranged."

Yet Odets was also frustrated by the Group. He championed its spirit of brotherhood but was discouraged by his own negligible contribution. That Odets continued to be assigned only bit roles seemed to confirm that he would never achieve fame or any other measure of success as an actor. Yet when the Group had dismissed some of its less promising actors after the initial season, Odets was retained. Perhaps his aggressive sociability persuaded the others that he might accomplish something extraordinary. He hankered to direct, and offered his services to the Theatre Union after getting no encouragement to direct from within the Group. He had always been a sort of clandestine playwright, and in the previous summer the Group had tested a scene from one of his plays before a camp audience.

The play was *I Got the Blues,* and Julie read it about the time a producer named Frank Merlin optioned it for production. Odets suggested Julie to Merlin for the role of the young protagonist, but Merlin failed to deliver a production and the option lapsed. Odets again dangled his script hopefully before his Group brethren and was not intimidated by Lee Strasberg, who said, "You don't understand, Cliff. We don't like your play. We just don't like it." Odets liked what he had written, and the idea of Julie playing the son had taken hold. Odets played advocate to Julie's desire to crack the Group. When Julie asked his new friend what his chances were of getting in, Odets said they were about as good as the Group eventually deciding to do *I Got the Blues* on Broadway. That notion presumed the Group's survival—a thing often taken for granted without justification.

Odets's loyalty to the Group was being severely tested. Only Harold Clurman seemed to have admiration for *I Got the Blues,* and he had reservations. Odets also believed that only Clurman liked him personally, which may have influenced his reaction to the script. But when the Group directorate was under fire for having *commissioned* the writing of a play that it apparently intended to stage, willy-nilly, Odets reminded them that "You can get me cheap."

He put out feelers to both Clurman and Strasberg about adding Jules Garfield to the roster of Group actors. Their response was that the Group was overstocked with players and could stand a trimming. They remembered Garfield vaguely from *Red Rust* and were aware of his later progress; and while Julie found Clurman friendly but detached, Strasberg remained aloof.

Julie's quest of Group membership became an obsession that Robbie shared. She no longer doubted his commitment to acting, and rated the Group as the key to his growth. Robbie had graduated from high school into salesgirl status at the Manhattan Macy's, but resolved to marry Julie only after he had a firm anchor in the theatre. Now she urged him to pitch for a Group apprenticeship. He had hoped to gain entry at a more respectable level, but there was exacting competition even for the apprentice slots, which sometimes delivered an Elia Kazan or an Alan Baxter.

Odets thought the likeliest approach would be through the lady member of the triumvirate—Cheryl Crawford, whom Julie hardly knew. Odets prepared Miss Crawford for Julie's overture, and urged her sympathy. Cheryl Crawford remembered that her first meeting with Jules Garfield spanned several days in the spring of 1934.

The Group once again had come off the ropes with a surprise success early in the season: Sidney Kingsley's *Men in White*. It gave the company some unexpected stability and a renewal of optimism. An ambitious program was in the offing; and yes, the Group needed apprentices. Yet fear of rejection gnawed at Julie and destroyed the cheeky confidence that usually characterized his job-hunting.

Day after day he lingered outside the Broadhurst Theatre on Forty-fourth Street where the Group had its offices, gumption deserting him. Cheryl Crawford became aware of a nicelooking boy waiting on the inside steps each day as she mounted the stairway toward her office. Something formidable about her had stopped him cold; and she sensed that this boy, whom she felt she should know, was too shy or frightened to confront her. So she surprised him with a friendly greeting that implied recognition, and Julie fumbled out a request to join the Group as an apprentice.

She said she'd see what she could do. Impressed by Julie's persistent sincerity and by his good but limited credits, Cheryl Crawford recommended taking Julie as an apprentice and neither Clurman nor Strasberg dissented. Odets delivered the news. Julie and Robbie were delirious.

In later years Julie could get teary-eyed just recalling it. "We stayed up all night, drinking a little and singing old ballads, and seeing who could cry the loudest. It was the best night of all. Weeping can be a wonderful thing, and we were so happy."

V

The Group

The Group Theatre was officially born in 1931 after a long gestation period, with beginnings so remote as to render it impossible to track actual conception. The Stanislavsky concept of total artistic truth brought young people into union. They got together and talked, they read plays, and the idea grew of forming a permanent company of their own. They gave concert readings of new and unorthodox plays, often by poets such as Waldo Frank and Ireland's Padraic Colum. The "Theatre Guild Studio" experiment with *Red Rust* gave the fetus a heartbeat.

The Guild itself was tied umbilically to the Group's maiden production, tossing in a thousand dollars to help produce *The House of Connelly,* the Paul Green play the Guild had released into Harold Clurman's care. The rest of the money came less easily, and recruiting actors was a happier task than the gathering of capital. But the illustrious young company assembled by Clurman had a Guild aura: Franchot Tone, Morris Carnovsky, Sanford Meisner, and some of the lesser lights, Clifford Odets among them.

From beginning to end, the Group would be a man's company, and it may have been unconsciously conceived that way. Although some able and dedicated young women were enlisted, the actresses as a rule didn't meet the measure of the men and never would. But then, some of the more promising women didn't respond enthusiastically to the idea of a team effort.

There was the time Eunice Stoddard, one of the original Group actresses, was in a Guild offering of Turgenev's *A Month in the Country* and recognized a distinctive quality in a young actress playing a very small part. She alerted the Group overseers, who also sensed the younger girl's exceptional personality. They invited her to join the Group, but the twenty-year-old Katharine Hepburn decided against it, preferring to gamble on making it as an *individual*.

Twenty-eight persons answered the first roll call in a vacation camp at Brookfield Center, Connecticut. There was a summer prelude of rehearsal, followed by an initial season of three plays on Broadway. Had *The House of Connelly* failed, the Group might have died in infancy. But its success was one of the season's exciting developments, and it sustained the Group through the two clear failures that followed: a Depression drama called *1931—*, by Claire and Paul Sifton; and *Night over Taos,* a pretentious tragedy by the eminent Maxwell Anderson, one of the Group's first financial supporters. (Later the Group would make a historic misjudgment, rejecting an opportunity to produce Anderson's *Winterset*.) Even the failed productions attained some honor, and Lee Strasberg made a name for himself as director of all the first season's plays.

The 1932-33 season jolted the Group's equilibrium if not its confidence, but misery brought kindred souls together. The Group had evolved from an idea into a reality, capable of riding out the failures of Dawn Powell's *Big Night* and John Howard Lawson's *Success Story*. The failure of the Lawson play prompted Franchot Tone to leave the Group in favor of an M-G-M contract, and also caused Sidney Howard to withdraw *Yellow Jack,* which had been planned as the season's third Group production. Odds were against the Group's longevity, but then the 1933-34 season opened with *Men in White*. It had been held in low esteem by many of the Group regulars, but it saved the day by building a strong box office and then snaring the Pulitzer Prize. Although the Group encore was failure with another John Howard Lawson play, *Gentlewoman,* the permanence of the company was established.

Julius Garfinkle.

Angelo Patri in 1928.

At age 17 in 1930.

Garfield with Florence Abromowitz.

Clifford Odets in 1936.

Maria Ouspenskaya.

Richard Boleslavsky.

Robbie Garfield welcomes her husband on his return from the Caribbean, where he entertained U.S. troops.

After a day of filming, Garfield relaxes at home with his wife in 1942.

Gloria Dickson.

Margot Stevenson.

Anne Shirley.

Hedy Lamarr.

Lana Turner.

Barbara Payton.

Warbling for wartime charities for CBS: Garfield, Douglas Fairbanks, Jr., Maxie Rosenbloom, and a guitar-plucking Groucho Marx.

Warners' East Side Kid and its Irish Peacock: Garfield and Errol Flynn in 1942.

Garfield introduces son David to the press in 1943.

Six-year-old Katherine has a new tie for Daddy in 1945.

Entertaining troops in the Italian war theater in 1944, Garfield is flanked by Jean Darling (left) and Sheila Rogers.

Garfield warms up for *Body and Soul*, sparring with trainer Johnny Indrisano.

Softballing for charity with Joe E. Brown and Peter Lawford, 1949.

On the stand as a technically "friendly" witness for the House Un-American Activities Committee, April 23, 1951.

Iris Whitney in 1946.

As much for its artistic enterprise, the Group captured the attention of theatre people with its members' unorthodox lifestyle. The Group Theatre was not its members' occupation, it was their *life*. It resembled a large marriage: they ate and slept, and worked and relaxed together. Otherwise the company would not have survived hardship. Time and again the Group actors accepted salary reductions to keep their plays running. Sometimes they agreed to work without pay, and the directors often forfeited their salaries. Group artists shared their expenses and accepted responsibility for one another's welfare; and like a family they closed ranks against every external threat.

At the time of the Group's most abject penury, about half the company occupied a large, dilapidated brownstone on West Fifty-seventh Street. Elia Kazan said, "We were the first flower children. Love we had plenty of. You see these kids today living in communes? Well, so did the Group Theatre."

They called their flat "Groupstroy"—"stroy" being a Russian suffix denoting a collection of similar objects. Groupstroy rented for fifty dollars a month. Each tenant had fixed chores, and the cooking duty rotated. Often the house was overcrowded with guests. Franchot Tone, Margaret Barker, and other Group members of relative affluence would arrive to treat the inmates to delicacies not possible within the small grocery budget.

Their extreme togetherness enhanced a notoriety that had been ascendant since early reports of Group boys and girls swimming in the raw during summer rehearsal breaks. The popular idea was that the free thinkers were free lovers as well; they were radicals, anarchists, and other shades of Red; they were intellectual freaks with a preponderance of sexual deviates. The truth was that they were young and united.

No pauper's paradise, Groupstroy was rather a trial. The novelty of the arrangement wore thin for the residents, who tired of Clifford Odets's potato pancakes and other penny-pinching meals. And the big house was cold, with no steam heat. It reeked of gas fumes, and the kitchen oven was always open to distribute warmth. Living in Groupstroy, Morris Carnovsky said, was "not a charming experience." But it was an appropriate setting for palavers on politics and art, and it stimulated Odets. He occupied a closet-sized room off the kitchen, and in that cramped quarter he began the writing of *I Got the Blues*. Art Smith and Elia Kazan were also occupied with the writing of plays, doing their bit for the theatre's Left movement, with which the Group was soon identified.

The Group's communal existence collected people who were properly married and others who were less legally joined. A natural consequence was the romantic pairing-off within the family as a whole. Both permanently and temporarily, the Group eventually bound several members in actual marriage: Lee Strasberg and Paula Miller; Morris Carnovsky and Phoebe Brand; Elia Kazan and Molly Thacher; William Challee and Ruth Nelson; Harold Clurman and Stella Adler.

By the summer of 1934, the Group had experienced comparable shares of agony and ecstasy. To the bewilderment of the apolitical Harold Clurman, the company had taken on a strong ideological bias identity. Some members could not have loved the Group so much, loved they not communism more. Some carried party membership cards, and they often confused the issue of the Group's primary mission. Whatever the mission, perhaps no one suspected that as the Group entered its fifth season, its finest hours lay ahead. The company was on the threshold of its fulfillment when Jules Garfield came into the picture.

The Group had taken over a hotel-sized bungalow in the Catskills, near the village of Ellenville, for the largest camp gathering of its history. Actors, technicians, designers, nonprofessional spouses, and hired help numbered more than fifty, not including animals.

Julie's apprentice chores were not unlike those he had discharged for the Civic Repertory years earlier, but he felt less subservient. Everyone pitched in, veteran and novice together. Apprentices could kibbitz with the ranking actors or beat them on the tennis court. Julie found a favorite sport: he was a tennis natural, able almost immediately to hold his own against the Group's best; and among the Group, tennis was an almost daily passion. The Group roster included many of Julie's oldest friends, and others with whom he would soon experience real kinship. He became aware of his own singular charm without betraying conceit: he had an extraordinary capacity for making friends, and quickly he became a company favorite with the more illustrious artists as well as his fellow apprentices. The latter group included a teen-aged Bernard Zanville who, many years later, was destined for a Warner Brothers grooming under the name of Dane Clark—as a likely successor to the studio's John Garfield.

Since Ellenville was his first exposure to Group behavior, Julie was not aware of inordinate tension. The intramural argument about passive or active communism still simmered. The more militant party-liners scolded the directors for selecting plays that were not sufficiently relevant. The actors nourished grudges against the three directors, individually and collectively; and artistic differences threatened to divide Clurman, Strasberg, and Crawford among themselves. The directors were civil to one another, cautious about the strain they silently acknowledged, and which threatened to become serious. That the company as a whole had a hollow feeling about the play being prepared for the fall opening certainly did not help matters.

Gold Eagle Guy was an oddity—the only original drama written on direct commission from the Group . . . without Clurman's blessing. Now Clurman issued Cassandra-like warnings about flaws in Mel Levy's script, and there was distress among the actors because the play was not topical. It appeared that Strasberg and Crawford had saddled the company with a panoramic period piece about a shipbuilder, and that it was evolving into the Group's most expensive production. With a sprawling cast and complicated multiple settings, *Gold Eagle Guy* represented, in Clifford Odets's sarcastic observation, "the triumph of matter over mind." The demands of the new play upon the Group's resources were such that subsequent productions for the upcoming season could not be put into summer rehearsal. Indeed, no agreement had been reached

about a play to follow *Gold Eagle Guy*. Clurman was warm-
ing to Odets's *I Got the Blues,* but Strasberg remained opposed.
Another possibility was to revive an earlier Group failure,
John Howard Lawson's *Success Story,* which had never been
without adherents.

Departing from earlier practice, they opened *Gold Eagle
Guy* in Boston as the final event of a "Group Theatre season"
underwritten by Boston civic officials. The season began with a
reassembled *Men in White,* previously unseen in The Hub, and
popularly received on the strength of its Pulitzer credential.
Success Story followed and was not accepted, so plans for a
Broadway revival were abandoned. Julie worked the stage
crew for both plays and also for *Gold Eagle Guy,* but in the
new play (Boston advertised a "world premiere"), he also
had a small role. As a shipboard sailor he had few lines, but
he made a spectacular fifteen-foot leap on stage to retrieve a
lady's scarf. He was gratified by opening night applause after
his feat, and it got a mention in a review.

In the turmoil of the Boston season Julie was drawn ever
closer to Clifford Odets, who confided that "Harold has
promised they'll do my play. If he directs it, I know you'll be
in it." His spirits buoyed, Odets had undertaken a new play
called *Paradise Lost,* and had brazenly named the young son
Julie.

On Halloween evening, 1934, Julie and Odets were dining
on five-cent hamburgers in a stand-up Boston café before going
to the Majestic Theatre where *Gold Eagle Guy* had just
opened. Directing Odets's attention to *The New Masses,* a
leading leftist magazine of the day, Julie indicated a notice of
a playwriting contest.

"All those plays you wrote, send 'em in. You may win,
and if you do they'll put on your play and give you fifty
dollars."

Odets read the notice and shrugged. "They want *revolutionary* plays. My things are about families. Individuals, not
the masses. But I could do it . . ."

Odets went into hiding, emerging only at night to act a small
role in *Gold Eagle Guy*. In three days he completed a six-

scene, continuous-action play called *Waiting for Lefty*. He mailed it as a contest entry, then invited Julie to read the play in his room at the Bellevue Hotel. Since Julie was his most appreciative audience and had told him about the contest, Odets wanted him to be *first*. But later Julie heard talk about Clifford's taxi-strike play and concluded that quite a number of Group people, including Harold Clurman, had been set up as the play's "first" reader. Before the company broke camp in Boston, they read *Waiting for Lefty* aloud in the basement of the Majestic Theatre. Even Lee Strasberg liked the play, and Luther Adler suggested that "the Group Theatre has produced the finest revolutionary playwright in America." For Odets, this was the beginning of the respect he craved from the Group. For Clurman, there was now ample justification for producing Odets's full-length *I Got the Blues*.

The Boston reception of *Gold Eagle Guy* had been uncertain, and there was considerable uneasiness among the company as the production was mounted in New York's Belasco Theatre that November. The actors frankly did not believe in the play, but it was all they had. Rumors again hinted at the Group's impending mortality. Julie fretted, but was reassured by Odets, who insisted that, come what may, the Group was going to do his play. Both he and Julie tried to convince Robbie that there was no reason for the marriage to be postponed any longer.

The weeks that followed were tumultuous. Julie and Robbie agreed they wanted only a small wedding, but the parents wanted tradition and trimmings. The nuptials were arranged for a Sunday evening when Julie would not have a performance. Or so they thought: the Group scheduled a benefit performance for their dark Sunday, and Julie would honor every commitment, even on his wedding night.

They were married in the Bronx under a ceremonial canopy. Nothing about the affair was small, and the Seidmans gave their daughter a catered reception. After the ceremony Julie excused himself, hurried downtown to do the benefit, and joined Robbie belatedly for the reception. Most of the Group members were there, many of them meeting David and Dinah

Garfinkle for the first time. Actors mingled with a landslide of relatives, many of whom were virtual strangers to Julie. He did not immediately recognize the good-looking youth named Mike Garfinkle—his brother Max.

The festivities were enhanced by a resurgence of Group optimism. *Gold Eagle Guy* had opened to respectable notices and a healthy run was anticipated. Clifford Odets, one of the most eloquent wedding guests, brandished a fifty-dollar check as proof that he had won that playwriting contest after all; yes, and Odets would himself direct a performance of *Waiting for Lefty* for the New Theatre League. To Julie and Robbie, the Group seemed better at that moment than any alternative honeymoon.

They moved into a small Greenwich Village flat, shared with another couple. Robbie hated the place and dubbed it the "Mud Hole"; she shared Julie's adventuring spirit toward the Group, but not all of his illusions. He had wanted her to quit her job at Macy's, but Robbie held firm. She vowed to work until they could afford a decent and private residence. Her judgment that they still had to contend with much uncertainty was vindicated too soon. Riding the yo-yo of Group Theatre fortunes, the Garfield marriage felt every jerk.

Despite its polite press and a virtuoso account by Joe Bromberg, *Gold Eagle Guy* was not finding an audience. The word of mouth validated the actors' initial reservations about the play, and the specter of failure hovered once more over the Group. They hoped to keep *Gold Eagle Guy* on the boards through January, but there was talk of cutting the season short at that point. This ignited a panic of uncertainty among the actors. Lee Strasberg felt that Group players should be released from their obligation for the balance of the normal season and permitted to earn a living by acting for other producers. But the actors were not so concerned for their own stomachs as for the Group's survival. They wanted to continue.

The dilemma had not been resolved by January 5, 1935, when Julie and Robbie Garfield, subdued by distress, left their apartment for a walk up to Fourteenth Street. It was a frigid Sunday, the lame-duck *Gold Eagle Guy* was dark, and the occasion was the first performance of Odets's *Waiting for Lefty*—at, inevitably, the Civic Repertory Theatre. Odets and the Group's Sanford Meisner were directing an all-Group ensemble. Julie was working backstage and would appear in the crowd scene at the finale; Robbie was in the audience with some other Group wives. The theatre was filled and some people stood; the audience was composed mainly of committed radicals. After a one-act play by Paul Green as a curtain-raiser, the anchor event was "a new award-winning play featuring members of the cast of *Gold Eagle Guy*."

The performance crackled with tension. *Waiting for Lefty* took its audience by surprise, and the actors' awareness of that response spiked the labor drama with an added intensity. Odets's propaganda exercise alluded to a New York taxi strike of almost a year earlier. The climax of the play was an impassioned decision to "Strike, Strike, Strike!" The audience rose to its feet in a unified frenzy and joined the chorus. They had become a part of the play and didn't let it end. They spilled onto the stage and embraced the actors, and soon everyone was cheering an astonished Clifford Odets. Harold Clurman called the "Strike, Strike, Strike!" chorus the birth cry of the thirties. Once again the Group had been saved.

The sensation of *Waiting for Lefty* was well reported in the press, and additional Sunday benefit performances were booked at the Civic Repertory. In a showdown meeting with the directors, the Group actors unanimously affirmed their desire to continue the season. Clifford Odets was an instant celebrity and the timing was right for Clurman to propose *I Got the Blues* as the next regular production. Strasberg capitulated but pleaded for a change of title, and in committee fashion they adopted *Awake and Sing* and everyone was pleased. The new title was positive, and it was Biblical—from Isaiah: "Awake and sing, ye that dwell in dust."

Odets read *Awake and Sing* in its latest revised form to the Group actors and they gave it an exuberant endorsement. Art Smith said that in that moment the Group would have liked anything that was by Odets, even *Abie's Irish Rose*. Harold Clurman actually leaned toward the unfinished *Para-*

dise Lost, but sensed that the Group should proceed while it had momentum. The directors decided to close Gold Eagle Guy on January 23, sooner than planned, and get into the new production immediately, retaining the Belasco Theatre. The company was now flat broke, but Franchot Tone agreed to guarantee production costs from Hollywood. Immediately upon the final curtain of Gold Eagle Guy, Clurman announced that Odets's Awake and Sing would be the next Group production and that he would stage it—Clurman's maiden effort as a director.

The clamor over Waiting for Lefty did not subside. The Sunday performances continued to fill the Civic Repertory, but Clurman withdrew several of the Lefty actors to take roles in Awake and Sing. Odets himself replaced Luther Adler in the important role of Dr. Benjamin, enabling Adler to take the part of Moe Axelrod in Awake and Sing. Clurman put together as strong an ensemble as the Group could provide. Stella Adler was cast as the dominant Bessie Berger, the "Jewish mother" long before she became a commodity figure. Art Smith was her amiable, emasculated husband. Phoebe Brand would play Hennie, the restless daughter. Joe Bromberg was the affluent Uncle Morty; Morris Carnovsky the philosophical, music-loving patriarch; and Sanford Meisner the ineffectual foreigner tricked by Bessie into marrying the pregnant Hennie. With Luther Adler as the lame Moe who loves Hennie, and with Roman Bohnen set to appear briefly as a broken janitor, every role was entrusted to a veteran Group player with the exception of Ralph, the impressionable young son pleading for "a chance to get to first base."

Clurman was now living with Odets in the Horatio Street apartment and it was there that he offered the role to Julie. He said some of the passed-over players would resent seeing a leading role given to an apprentice, but only briefly: Julie's performance could be his proof. Odets later insisted that he held out for Julie over protestations by all the directors and some of the actors, but other reports did not bear that out. Lee Strasberg, who had almost terrified Julie years earlier, had become his close friend from Julie's first days in the

Catskills. And while Clurman remained distant to Julie, he reasoned that the part of Ralph was uncastable from elsewhere within the Group. It was a young company—most of the Group actors were now in their thirties—but while Carnovsky, Bromberg and perhaps others could convincingly impersonate men of twice their age, simulating actual youth on stage was a meaner challenge. Kazan was almost as young as Julie, and Meisner had physical characteristics that could translate into a stage juvenile. But Ralph was uncorrupted, not yet scarred, a romantic: Odets said the actor had to be really handsome as well as authentically young. It narrowed down to the apprentice boy.

Harold Clurman said, "Julie was the logical choice. The part required a certain quality and he had that quality. If anyone doubted that he was an able actor, doubt vanished after rehearsals began."

Julie had his own doubts. During the rehearsal period he was frightened by the caliber of performance all around him. At home he was tense, preoccupied. Robbie tried to snap him out of his moods and they would fight. What others diagnosed as a standard case of stage fright, Morris Carnovsky saw as a genuine loss of confidence, and he took Julie under his wing. At Ellenville, Carnovsky had helped Julie with his speech, and he had the knack for saying just the thing that would restore him. Carnovsky emerged as a father figure and pulled Julie through the ordeal. Julie's main fear was that he would not live up to Odets's abnormally high expectations.

A calculated few days before *Awake and Sing* faced press and public, *Waiting for Lefty* was presented formally for the reviewers and again was a whistling success. This aroused interest in the full-length Odets play that was about to bow; and the presence of a Group apprentice in one of the leading roles provided another angle for good coverage. *Awake and Sing* received extraordinary attention prior to its opening. It seemed important. On February 19, 1935, it brought out the well-dressed first nighters.

In the dressing room before the opening curtain, Julie was frozen in nervousness and Robbie was the one who seemed outwardly to be going all to pieces. An almost arrogantly confident Odets, making the rounds, stopped in to wish Julie good luck. Then it was time to begin.

In a later recollection, John Garfield explained an application of the Stanislavsky system to his going-to-death scene (the electric chair) in the film, *The Castle on the Hudson*. "Naturally I hadn't ever *been* to the electric chair before, so it required a little imagination to go back into my past and find the emotion I needed. But not so much imagination after all. When I got on stage for the first performance of *Awake and Sing* it *felt* like the electric chair . . . and that feeling is what I was remembering when the movie cameras were grinding."

The first moment was almost killing, but after that it was tense pleasure. Julie didn't let down Odets, or Clurman. As Ralph, he combined anarchic strength with a small boy's innocence. He sensed that the audience was responding to him, and did not think him misplaced on a stage with some of the best actors he knew. After the play Odets, choked with emotion, embraced Julie and said he was "merely perfect." The Garfinkles, cautious in a strange environment, greeted Julie backstage with wonderment. The Seidmans also attended the opening and gave joyful congratulations, and Robbie was beaming. All was for the best in the best of all worlds . . . for just this one time.

There was a party to await the reviews, and the Scotch flowed. Joe Bromberg said it was important to get really smashed before the first notices came in, and they all tried. The critics were not ecstatic, but neither were they soberingly uncordial. It was evident that the play had scored. Brooks Atkinson alone was a dissenter (an attitude he would modify sharply in years to come), saying, "The shrill turbulence of the Group Theatre performance is partly the fault of unsifted direction but largely the result of Mr. Odets's fresh response to human life. It leaves a final impression of nebulous thinking." But Atkinson was not nebulous about Jules Garfield, who "plays the part of the boy with a splendid sense of character development." The esteemed critic was in Garfield's corner from the start and would never leave it.

The production was the artistic fulfillment of the Group. Individual performances were not emphasized in the reviews, which generally focused on Odets as the *star;* but as the newer, less familiar face in the company, Julie was the big news of the show. Although not a smash commercial hit, *Awake and Sing* promised to carry the Group through the season, and the box office started to build. Two weeks after the opening, Julie's apprentice status officially ended after less than one year. Alan Baxter quit the cast of *Waiting for Lefty* to accept a movie offer from Paramount, and Julie replaced him on the regular roster, voted full membership by the company as a twenty-second birthday present. Odets had started telling reporters that Jules Garfield was his personal "find," and he had started telling Julie that someday he would write a play just for *him.*

Group actors regularly entertained overtures from Hollywood, and now the movie people were knocking on Jules Garfield's dressing room door. He discouraged a couple of studio feelers, and was surprised that Robbie could so easily agree to his refusal of more money than he could ever earn on the stage. But Robbie considered the Group as Julie's *home,* and a steadying influence as such. Now that Julie was on regular salary they lived less frugally, but Robbie held on to her sales job and they started moving gypsylike from one tinny Manhattan apartment to another, bidding for more respectable quarters, but still usually doubling with other Group folk.

All that remained to make the spring of 1935 the Group's most bountiful chapter was to give *Waiting for Lefty* a regular engagement on Broadway. Since it was not of length sufficient to occupy an evening, Odets got to work on a companion play. *Till the Day I Die* was one of the first anti-Nazi dramas, and a long one-act play that could employ the *Lefty* actors. The double bill had a spring opening on Broadway and satisfied audiences less secular than those that had hailed *Lefty* downtown. The Group was in the unusual position of having two shows and three plays, all by the same author, in healthy simultaneous New York engagements. Odets was the man of the moment, and business was still fair when the Group closed up shop for the muggy summer.

For the first time, the Group did not hire out a summer camp. Everyone felt they had earned a vacation and needed one, although the members continued to cling to one another—houseguesting, weekending together out of the city, or staying home and accepting the humidity, as the Garfields did—but always together. Clifford Odets found himself in demand as a celebrity, and Julie got involved in one of Odets's political causes: the investigation of labor conditions in Cuba under the new Batista dictatorship. An organization was formed to go to Cuba with Odets on a fact-finding mission, but shortly after the investigators arrived, they were arrested and deported. They had misread the scene: Batista had won the confidence of the Communist faction and had cornered the Cuban labor force. The experience humiliated Odets, but Julie was stimulated by the sheer adventure of it.

The Group had experienced an Odets spring and largely anticipated an Odets fall. *Awake and Sing* reopened in September, this time on a double bill with *Waiting for Lefty*. Together the plays accommodated most of the actors in the company, and in turn each would be occupied with one of the two new projects planned for the fall season. The Odets double bill was transferred to Philadelphia for several weeks, and there the new plays were put into rehearsal prior to playing there in tryout. It was an arrangement often identified with stock companies—performing one play by night while rehearsing another by day—in this case, rehearsing two plays.

Of the actors in *Awake and Sing,* Carnovsky and the Adlers went into Odets's long-awaited *Paradise Lost* under Clurman's direction, along with Sandy Meisner, who took the role of the son named Julie. The other project was *Weep for the Virgins,* a gamy drama by Nellise Child, a playwright nurtured by the Group as its hoped-for "female Odets." Julie joined Art Smith, Joe Bromberg, and Phoebe Brand in *Weep for the Virgins* under Cheryl Crawford's direction, and heading the cast as a put-upon mama was Evelyn Varden, an actress new to the Group.

Morale was high. *Awake and Sing* was saluted by Henry Murdock of the Philadelphia *Inquirer* as "an American classic," and *Lefty* was dutifully cheered. Yet most of the company expressed the conviction that *Paradise Lost* would eventually be considered Odets's "best" play. The Philadelphia engagement did not discourage that estimate. Odets's parents were living in Philadelphia and he was patronized as the hometown boy who had made good. Amid the general optimism, and perhaps honoring an intuition, Robbie decided to chuck her Macy's job and keep an eye on her husband in Philadelphia.

Murdock, the helpful columnist who, years earlier, interviewed Julie during the first *Counsellor-at-Law* tour, now found him the same quiet, likable kid—"modest about his work, greatly in love with the theatre and with the Group who were giving him opportunity to play a variety of roles." Julie raved about *Paradise Lost* and confessed his disappointment at not being a member of the cast. But he explained the Group's need of authentic lowlife types for *Weep for the Virgins,* and he reckoned he was one of those. Julie got his Bronx pal Eddie Kogan (the shoeshine boy in *Counsellor-at-Law*) into a small role in *Virgins.* And Vincent Sherman, another acting chum from Chicago days, had a minor part in *Paradise Lost* and a likely future with the Group. Julie's sense of security was rising, and he tried to talk Robbie into having a baby.

But the year that had been so bountiful ended with a shudder. The hopeful company returned to New York during Thanksgiving week for an unprecedented experience: they would open two new plays with separate companies, in consecutive weeks. Within a fortnight the first play had opened and closed, and the Group was reeling with the knowledge that the other play seemed doomed to failure.

Weep for the Virgins opened first and was trounced by the critics. Audiences did not respond to its slice of sleazy, cannery-row life; particularly fine work by Evelyn Varden, Ruth

Nelson, and Phoebe Brand went down the drain. Julie played Hap Nichols, a raffish suitor in the home of three gum-chewing girls of the movie culture. He gave an incisive, comically resourceful performance that John Houseman could remember in detail thirty-five years later: "Julie had such energy, and a magnetism I don't believe he understood. I had seen him before, but *Weep for the Virgins* made me aware of a special quality he had. There was a natural tendency to watch him when he was on stage, at the exclusion of the other actors. He wasn't upstaging them, he didn't have a star complex; but the star quality was unmistakable."

The Group was not intimidated by the failure of *Virgins,* but *Paradise Lost* was another matter. The reviews were not nasty, but they weren't polite either. They were not "money notices," and the Odets-watchers were in a mood for something bigger than life. What they got was an eloquent but conventional social tragedy—a good man watching his business and family fall to ruin. The Group waged a game fight for the life of *Paradise Lost,* but threw in the towel in February, 1936. After its close they hastily contracted to stage *The Case of Clyde Griffiths*—Dreiser's *American Tragedy* in stylized, Greek tragedy motif. Julie played a very small role. It was Lee Strasberg's first directional venture since *Gold Eagle Guy* and the production was praised, but it opened and closed in March.

In an earlier, less jaded time, the Group members might have made financial sacrifices to save the play, but the events of that December reopened old wounds. The Group's most precious asset—its unity—was in jeopardy. It sustained a considerable jolt when Clifford Odets, stricken by the debacle of *Paradise Lost,* announced that he was accepting an offer from Paramount to go to Hollywood and write the screenplay of *The General Died at Dawn* for Gary Cooper and Madeleine Carroll. Lewis Milestone—Hollywood-based, but long a friend of the Group and a sometime financial supporter—was the director, and that seemed to excuse Odets's defection, especially as it was only a temporary thing. The Group was more agitated that Joe Bromberg, without even hinting, had signed a 20th Century-Fox contract and had also packed off to Hollywood.

That it was 1936 and an election year was part of the problem. Oracles who had said the Group Theatre could only be as healthy as the theatre's Left movement could cite the collapse of the Communist Party as an important event in national political life. The party had pointed to 1936 as its year of truth, but already the radicals were lining up behind Franklin Roosevelt to withstand what initially appeared to be a vigorous revival of Republican conservatism. Some of the card-carrying members, Odets and Kazan among them, were denouncing their Communist Party affiliation to support Roosevelt. Julie no longer aspired to a party card; when membership was in vogue he had sought it as a status symbol, but a card had been denied him because he was young and not yet proven trustworthy. He had even courted the party's blessing by helping stage a Lenin Memorial program for the Young Communist League. Now even Joe Bromberg, who had championed the propaganda power of the theatre, was content to go to Hollywood and be a rich, capitalistic supporting player.

To preserve its continuity, the Group toured *Awake and Sing* through several eastern cities and on to Chicago during the spring of 1936. Robbie accompanied Julie on what they declared was their belated honeymoon; but for the Group, perhaps, the honeymoon was over. The tour, with Bob Lewis replacing Bromberg as Uncle Morty, was successful, but not to a degree that distress and conflict were calmed within the company. By summer, the Group had arrived at a familiar crossroads, certain that the coming season would be either its best or last one.

They rented a theatre and lodgings at Pinebrook Club Camp near Nichols, Connecticut, following the standard plan of rehearsing three plays for presentation on Broadway in the fall season. Odets promised to bring a new play with him upon his return from Hollywood, and a John Howard Lawson drama was also slated—*Marching Song,* for which Julie was likely to be assigned an important role. The third project would be a departure: a panoramic war play by Paul Green, with a complete score by that most brilliant of refugees from Hitler's Germany, the composer Kurt Weill.

The Garfields had a glorious time at Pinebrook. The weather was idyllic—there was ample tennis, badminton, croquet, and handball—and Group camaraderie was resurgent. Otherwise, it was a disastrous season marked by disappointment, anxious waiting, and false starts. The Group decided not to go through with the Lawson play, or he chose to withdraw it from their care; alternate versions of the disagreement flourished. Odets returned from Hollywood and rented a farm adjacent to Pinebrook Camp, and got to work on the script of *Silent Partner*. Significantly, it would make no noise: notoriety seemed to have put Odets in a muddled state and this was reflected in his writing. The Group decided his play could not be made ready for summer rehearsal. That left only the Green-Weill collaboration on *Johnny Johnson,* perhaps the Group's most ambitious undertaking and certainly its most expensive one. Out of need for keeping the company busy, the directors put it into rehearsal before it was ready. The production was hastily shaped at the tag end of a wasted summer, Strasberg replacing Clurman as director during the early going.

Johnny Johnson kept its November date in the Forty-fourth Street Theatre (a cavern that Clurman decided was not in the best interests of the play's gentle intimacy), but it did not have theatrical form and discipline. That came in the weeks following the opening. In its polished state *Johnny Johnson* struck a chord; but it was too late to save the ship. The press had been respectful, but no less indifferent than the play's first audiences. Later, the word of mouth was encouraging and the audience began to build, but not to a point of meeting the complicated production's break-even mark.

In historical terms, *Johnny Johnson* is one of the best-remembered jewels of the Group legacy—perhaps the American theatre's most beguiling pacifist statement—a legend after its own time. The play included more than fifty speaking roles; and Julie's contribution, although small, was extraordinary. Got up in a Kaiser Wilhelm mustache, he played a German sniper in a churchyard scene. He terrorized the homespun ex-tombstone cutter, Private Johnny Johnson (affectingly played by Russell Collins), by pointing a rifle through a hole in his shield—a statue of Christ. The enemy soldiers discover their spiritual brotherhood in an ironic dialogue, and the sniper peels off his mustache to reveal himself as a sixteen-year-old boy. Before their return to battle, the young German's embrace of Johnny yielded a touching moment in the theatre. It stirred the hard-hearted George Jean Nathan to report that "Jules Garfield appears to have some ability in both comic and dramatic acting."

Johnny Johnson closed in January, 1937. The Group attempted to get the Odets labor play, *Silent Partner,* into rehearsal in New York, but dissatisfaction with the script stalled the project; and it was scrapped when a petulant Odets returned to Hollywood to write another screenplay for Lewis Milestone. Odets thought Julie should capitalize on the Group's layoff by accompanying him to Hollywood to get a taste of movie-acting. Julie might have considered it, but Robbie was firmly opposed to the idea. She was determined that they would stay in New York despite the Group's uneasy destiny.

Without a production to keep them occupied, the Group members thrashed out their problems and decided on a complete reorganization. The three directors submitted resignations as a formal gesture, but agreed to participate in the development of new plans. The actors elected a grievance committee to formulate the sore points. The official line was that the reconstituted Group Theatre would be back on the boards in the fall. But gossip around Shubert Alley was that the Group was indeed dead, and not likely to rise again. Certainly its actors were free to seek other employment.

Some did go to Hollywood. Even Morris Carnovsky tried the films, taking the Anatole France role in Paul Muni's *Zola* vehicle. Walter Wanger, who was producing *Blockade* independently, with Milestone as director and Odets as writer, hired Harold Clurman as an artistic associate. Wanger really wanted to contract the entire Group Theatre to appear in his pictures, and there was a premature report that he and Clurman had made such an agreement. But the Group actors reaffirmed that their commitment to one another was only for the stage. Clurman stayed in Hollywood several months, applying Stanislavsky principles in his coaching of the John Robert Powers models for Wanger's projected *Vogues of 1938* musical. When the models walked, it was supposed to have *meaning* for them. Clurman's real mission in Hollywood was to watch over the erratic Odets who, he felt, still represented the Group's theatrical future.

Like Franchot Tone before him, Odets had fallen in love with a sovereign star of imperial M-G-M. Luise Rainer, the tiny Viennese whose movie career began so promisingly, had an impetuousness to match Clifford's own, and they married suddenly. It was a stormy union that amplified Odets's cantankerousness, and he had a falling out with Walter Wanger. Odets quit his scripting assignment—an action that pleased Luise Rainer, who believed her husband should be writing *plays*. At Clurman's suggestion, Wanger engaged John Howard Lawson as Odets's substitute, and Lawson turned *Blockade* into Loyalist propaganda for the Spanish Civil War.

In New York, Jules Garfield emerged as one of Broadway's more employable actors. He did not have to go job-hunting. In café meetings and phone calls he received overtures for varied acting assignments. Scripts were delivered to him, speculating on his interest. The Theatre Guild's Philip Moeller offered Julie a part in *The Masque of Kings,* explaining that Julie had been personally favored by the playwright, Maxwell Anderson. Then Marc Connelly dangled the male lead in a comedy he was directing—Arthur Kober's *Having Wonderful Time.* Asked for advice, Morris Carnovsky told Julie to take the job that offered the most money, and suggested it was a good time to take on an agent. Julie was a sometime drinking companion to the Russian-born Arthur Lyons, who had gone into the agency business; and Julie's tenure as a Lyons client began promisingly with Lyons getting him under contract for *Having Wonderful Time* at $300 a week.

Marc Connelly, vaguely appreciative of Julie's stage work since *Counsellor-at-Law,* had seen in his *Johnny Johnson* stint the blend of comedy and pathos required of the juvenile lead in *Having Wonderful Time.* For a play that was a warm, exuberant visit to a Jewish summer camp in the Catskills, Julie was a natural. He was the best-paid and also the best-known player in a large cast populated mainly by unknowns, none billed as stars.

The advance sale was small; the out-of-town tryout did not go well; and when *Having Wonderful Time* opened at the Lyceum Theatre on February 20, 1937, the thinking was that only the critics could save it. They did. The play was cordially received, and favorable word of mouth built it into a surprise smash hit. When the movie rights were sold, Julie received an unexpected salary increase of ten percent, owing to his agent's foresightedness.

The female lead was Katherine Locke, younger than Julie, although they had known each other years earlier on "the rounds." Herbert Ratner, a minor Group actor, was in the cast, and the unknown Sheldon Leonard showed comical promise in a secondary role. The distinctly personal success was Julie's and now George Jean Nathan cited him as the *best* of the young actors with comedy skill. Yet other cast members wearied of Julie's repeated reference to "the way we do things in the Group." Marc Connelly's casual staging method left Julie to his own resources and he tried to apply an "intellectual" approach to a role that hardly required it.

In an offstage scene with Katherine Locke—only their voices heard, with a suggestion of lovemaking amid the shrubbery—the dialogue went this way:

> SHE: Ouch!
> HE: What's the matter?
> SHE: How long since you shaved?
> HE: Since noon, why?

The exchange got laughs until Julie decided he wasn't *feeling* the lines properly; they were becoming automatic. With each succeeding performance his pause before "Since noon" became longer, and the laugh was lost. Katherine Locke asked why he waited so long to answer her, and Julie said, "Well, you ask how long since I shaved and I have to *think* about how

long since I shaved, don't I?" The cast kidded him about the
Group's dogma, and when he started picking up his cue, the
laughter came back.

When the Group gave Julie a party to celebrate his success,
he received more scorn than congratulation. They kidded him
for representing the commercial establishment. They derided
Having Wonderful Time as commodity theatre: it lacked social
significance. It was pap, it was pulp, it was popular—all the
things the Group wasn't. And Julie's performance, they said,
was superficial and full of mannerisms. He was hurt. After all,
Clurman was in Hollywood teaching models how to move, and
nobody was criticizing Clurman.

Perhaps the Group feared the loss of Julie to the conventional Broadway that obviously coveted him, and they also
regarded the fashionable theatre jealously in spite of themselves. *Having Wonderful Time* represented that theatre.
Arthur Kober, the playwright, was one of the sophisticated
New Yorker writers. Marc Connelly had written successful
comedies with George S. Kaufman as well as other estimable
works on his own (including *Green Pastures*), and was one of
the wits of the durable Algonquin Round Table. Connelly's
multitude of friends were famous or rich or both. They all
came to see the play, and a good many wanted to meet Jules
Garfield: Dorothy Parker; Cole Porter; George S. Kaufman
and Moss Hart; Howard Lindsay and Russel Crouse; Richard
Rodgers and Lorenz Hart; Bella and Sam Spewack. Julie met
George Gershwin backstage only a few months before the
composer died.

Elmer Rice, boasting that Julie was his own discovery, introduced him to S. N. Behrman and Philip Barry, and their
interest in Julie made him aware that he held options on success outside the Group Theatre. His allegiance to the Group
was not threatened, yet he was dazzled by this other kind of
theatre person, the sophisticate. His new friends, he decided,
were not so much different from his Group companions as
they were better dressed, but he also enjoyed their exotic
conversation. Julie was beguiled by real wit such as he only
aspired to, and he knew he was overmatched by a special

new acquaintance, Oscar Levant. Their association flourished mainly at Club 21 and Sardi's, and Julie devised a Levant impersonation to rival his Paul Muni cartoon.

Another effect of *Having Wonderful Time* was to increase, not diminish, the interest of the movie people in Jules Garfield. Art Lyons, Julie's new agent, prodded their interest and did not understand his client's reluctance to entertain the big money. Albert Lewin wanted to use Julie in a picture in the coming fall. Julie liked Lewin, who had been Irving Thalberg's lieutenant at M-G-M and had entered independent production after Thalberg's death; but Julie still cited the Group as his first obligation in the fall. Both Paramount and Warners invited Julie to make screen tests in New York, and he made a brief test for Warners that he never saw but which was apparently well-liked. They wanted to talk contract, but when Julie said he would want to have time off for stage work, Warners would not agree to that. But he liked telling people he had "turned down" a movie offer of probable lucrative dimensions.

The late summer marked the return from Hollywood of Harold Clurman; of Clifford Odets with Luise Rainer; and of an uncompleted but promising Odets script, *Golden Boy*. The Group members reassembled as if by magic, almost the entire body. There was talk of a fall production of *Golden Boy,* pending the company's satisfaction with its own reorganization. Julie and Robbie attended the meetings that throbbed with renewed dedication, but were marked by more than the usual amounts of shrill argument and name-calling.

The actors who were gainfully employed outside the Group were asked to give their decisions on availability for a fall season. Athough *Having Wonderful Time* promised continued healthy business, Julie said he definitely intended to return to the Group, but he wanted to be an actor, not a slave. He was cheered for that. The actors' committee read its forty-eight-page manifesto, largely an attack on the three directors and their rigid policies. One complaint was that it had been impossible to get any work done for all the high concern over the members' *souls*. Some of the actors had become so philosophical in their Stanislavskian dedication that their real purpose in acting had been cast aside for solitude and meditation.

The committee judgment was that an actor should not be expected to *die* for the Group, or be ridiculed for accepting outside work when the Group wasn't keeping the actor busy. Art Smith said that if Julie and Robbie Garfield wanted to have a baby, they should not have to seek permission from the Group administrators. That drew applause, and when Julie grinned and said, "Can you excuse Robbie and me for about fifteen minutes?" there was laughter to relieve a tense session.

Specifically cited was the *Winterset* incident that occurred before Julie joined the Group. Maxwell Anderson's play, destined for recognition as an American classic, had been offered to the Group for production, but Anderson had insisted that Burgess Meredith should play the leading role. Meredith wanted to join the Group; but when the three directors in their interview said, "Mr. Meredith, do you love the Group Theatre above yourself?" he did not hesitate in saying no. Anderson withdrew *Winterset,* it was produced elsewhere with great success and Meredith heading the cast; and now the Group actors wanted assurance that such foolish mistakes would not occur in the future because of the Group's own ill-advised dogma.

Lee Strasberg and Cheryl Crawford heard all the grievances and then made separate official departures from the Group. There was a report that they would go into production together and would employ some Group actors, but nothing came of it: they went their individual ways, both successfully. Harold Clurman, however, accepted the conditions specified by the actors, and emerged as sole managing director of the new-look Group. An executive committee was formed and it included Clifford Odets.

During the previous summer at Pinebrook Camp, Odets's rapport with Julie had been strengthened by a continuing dialogue about the prizefight game. The friendship may have derailed the *Silent Partner* project, because Odets found excuses for not working on the play the Group awaited, and gave increasing thought to a drama about a poor boy who could hit hard. Julie's exaggerated claim of prominence in the Golden

Gloves impressed Odets, who conceived a drama in which the central character would have an artistic gift in conflict with his fighter's compulsion. The new idea obsessed him, and in Hollywood it caused him to lose interest in the *Blockade* project. There was never any doubt in Odets's mind who would play Joe Bonaparte in *Golden Boy;* nor in Julie's.

But rather than being the solution to the Group's problems, Odets suggested the problem personified. *Golden Boy* needed a third act and Odets was coming apart at the seams, bereft of confidence. The long Hollywood experience, with only a marginally successful screenplay and a tempestuous marriage to show for it, had brought him to the brink of destruction. He was convinced that his first tumultuous celebrity had been a fluke. Before it had struck, he had written rapidly like some obsessed angel, pausing betimes to shout, "God, this is terrific!" or an equivalent conceit; but now he sat at the typewriter transfixed, often unable to write at all. In *The Fervent Years,* Harold Clurman wrote of conniving to have Kazan and Luther Adler hover about Odets at all times, protecting him from distraction to see that the play got written.

Luise Rainer was only part of the problem. Like her husband, Miss Rainer rather resembled an early-extinguished comet. For her work in *The Good Earth* she was expected to win a second successive Academy Award; but by the time the prophecy was fulfilled, she was considered washed-up in pictures. All of her subsequent pictures had failed at the box office and with the critics, and Louis B. Mayer would not forgive her for marrying "a rotten Communist." Miss Rainer had not been really interested in a film career, and now she hated Hollywood. Odets and the theatre were the antidotes she sought, and now she hoped to act in Group productions. But there was no role for her in *Golden Boy,* and in her idle state she was a deterrent to Odets's efforts to write. The Group found little chores for her. The $3000-a-week movie actress seemed content to read and evaluate foreign-language scripts in the Group office for no remuneration while her husband worked in isolation. But Odets, following the lead of the American public, was tiring of Luise; and unwisely, he sought solace in Frances Farmer, who was even less stable than himself.

She was his own filmland "discovery," although Harold Clurman also thought Frances Farmer's early screen work had stamped her as an actress of promise. She loathed Hollywood, and in the film colony was perhaps the most disliked among the legendary "difficult" actresses. Odets believed she needed the Group Theatre and vice versa, and he conceived the role of Lorna Moon in *Golden Boy* in Frances Farmer's image. Clurman, who logically expected to direct *Golden Boy,* accepted Odets's claim that Miss Farmer's movie name would simplify the task of obtaining backing for the production. And Odets told Frances Farmer she would be playing opposite Jules Garfield. He alerted Julie to be prepared to make love to a really luscious dame on stage.

Frances Farmer went East in the summer of 1937 to play in *The Petrified Forest* at Connecticut's Westport Playhouse. Weekend partying at Westport now kept Odets from finishing the play. He and Miss Farmer were loud and brazen revelers, and soon Luise Rainer withdrew from the festivities with the admission that her marriage was over. The Group meanwhile accepted Frances Farmer's husband—Leif Erikson, an able young actor—in a package deal, and by the time the *Golden Boy* script was completed to everyone's satisfaction, backing for the production had been obtained as well as a November booking at the Belasco Theatre.

Julie was the first person to read the final version of *Golden Boy,* before it won Clurman's blessing. Odets said Julie's positive reactions always rode over his own doubts and gave him courage to deliver a script to the exacting mind and eye of Harold Clurman. Julie thought *Golden Boy*—about the young violinist who goes against his father to seek his fortune in the ring—was just about the greatest play ever written. The character of the Italian boy, Joe Bonaparte, was Jules Garfield reincarnate.

When Julie informed Marc Connelly that he would be leaving the cast of *Having Wonderful Time* to return to the Group Theatre, the newspapers expanded the tidbit and re-

fueled the legend of the Group's shabby grandeur. He re-
portedly was forsaking his high-salaried assignment to work
for the Group standard of forty dollars a week. (The figure
was underquoted: Julie's Group salary was seventy-five.) But
Julie silenced second-guessing within the *Having Wonderful
Time* ensemble by saying he was going to be playing a role
about as great as Hamlet, in a play Shakespeare would have
been proud to have written.

Then came the crusher. Julie heard from Michael Gordon,
the Group's technical director, that Clurman wanted Luther
Adler to play the boxer lead in *Golden Boy*. Julie sought a confrontation with Clurman but got drunk instead, and Robbie
urged him to see Clifford Odets for confirmation that he was
still the choice. Odets, riding a trajectory of high emotion, told
Julie it was no joke—Clurman was insisting on Adler, and
Clurman would have to have his way since he had already
"given in" to Odets on the matter of Frances Farmer. Relations between Clurman and Odets had become strained, but
Odets still trusted Clurman to deliver the best production
Golden Boy could likely obtain. And because Odets was beset
with financial problems but was also an investor in his own
play, he needed to protect his investment with Frances Farmer's "name." He also confessed to being in love with the
actress, and said he intended to marry her as soon as they both
were free to do so.

Pulling himself together diplomatically, Julie went to Clurman and pleaded to be allowed to play the role that Odets had
written for him. Clurman said it wasn't that he didn't think
Julie good enough, but that he thought Luther Adler (his
future brother-in-law) would be better. It was a view not
generally shared within the Group, and not even Luther Adler
thought playing Joe Bonaparte was such a hot idea. Carnovsky,
Kazan, Bud Bohnen, Bob Lewis—all took up the argument
for Julie, but Clurman wouldn't budge. Nor were the Group
actresses happy about the state of things, especially since they
were being passed over in favor of a movie actress for the leading female role. That Frances Farmer more nearly resembled

a leading lady apparently held weight with Clurman, although Luther Adler hardly approximated, in this case, the leading man.

Adler was ten years older than Julie and did not physically suggest a prizefighter, or the raw handsomeness Odets had endowed in the character. These were irrelevancies in Clurman's view, and it was apparent that Clurman really doubted the extent of Julie's talent. Despite the shining work in *Awake and Sing*, Clurman saw Julie's theatrical flair as primarily a comic one. With that in mind, he wanted Julie to play Siggie, the fighter's cabbie brother-in-law—a colorful supporting role written with Elia Kazan in mind.

Marc Connelly sympathetically suggested that it was not too late for Julie to reverse himself and stay with *Having Wonderful Time*. But to do that would mean severing ties with the Group. Julie held to his word and accepted the Siggie role, but he was both disappointed and deeply hurt. Robbie's own sense of injustice left her mainly displeased by Odets's behavior. But she had earlier warned Julie not to count on the Bonaparte role prematurely, and the disappointment did not alter her own fierce devotion to the Group. She felt that Julie, at twenty-four, could look forward to many roles in many plays, and she accepted his reduced salary without complaint.

Defending his choice of Luther Adler, Clurman said in *The Fervent Years:* "Garfield was obviously the type, but he had neither the pathos nor the variety, in my opinion, to sustain the role." Obviously Julie's popular hit away from the Group counted against him, for Clurman found him "monotonous and mannered" in *Having Wonderful Time*. Clurman saw Joe Bonaparte not as a fighter, but as "simply a sensitive, virile boy," but that hardly advanced his case against Julie.

History's judgment, of course, is against Clurman, and the *Golden Boy* disappointment is thought to have affected Julie permanently. Richard Schickel, in his book, *The Stars*, synthesizes the thinking: "Among his (Garfield's) grievances was the Group's absurd failure to cast him as *Golden Boy*, relegating him to a minor part where he could watch the miscast Luther Adler do a part for which Garfield was born. The

Group may have polished Garfield's talent, but its lingering effect on him was to create doubts about the value of his work, the reality of his talent. Its influence robbed him of the chance to enjoy the movie stardom which a part of his personality craved."

Julie's grievance was not directed personally against Clurman, toward whom he felt considerable indebtedness; or against Luther Adler, who had become one of his closest friends. He tackled the Siggie role with dedication, even enthusiasm. Clurman found Julie totally selfless toward the Group, and his "warm, engaging nature" more pronounced. Stella Adler, too, found Julie less reticent, more responsive, and sincere as ever; she gave him special tutoring in "the method"—the Group's modification of the Stanislavsky system.

Golden Boy opened during Thanksgiving week at the Belasco Theater. It pleased the critics and was an unqualified commercial hit: after years of adversity, the Group was solvent. For all of Julie's happiness over the company's welfare, the turn of events only increased his bitterness over what might have been his foremost personal triumph. In a generously praised production, Luther Adler received perfunctory approval and Frances Farmer was judged not yet ready for major stage work. Conspicuously successful were Julie as Siggie and Phoebe Brand as Anna, his wife, for giving a touch of comic relief to the drama. Carnovsky was Papa Bonaparte with a thick Italian dialect; Bohnen was Tom Moody, the fight manager; Lee J. Cobb, who joined the Group after Julie, was Mr. Carp, the neighbor; and Elia Kazan was the gangster Eddie Fuselli, who tries to corrupt the prodigy.

The Group's most successful production was not, however, its happiest one. A most discordant note was the hectic affair between Odets and Frances Farmer, whose marriage to Leif Erikson had evaporated. Odets seemed to derive pleasure from belittling Frances before the company, then rushing her romantically when they were alone. Even the usually tolerant Julie resented this, but Odets said he couldn't help himself—it was the "real thing."

In her posthumously published autobiography, Frances Farmer recalled that Odets would charge into her dressing room before a performance, lock the door and prop a chair against it, and undress and proceed to make love to her. Then he would taunt the compliant girl for being so lustful, and accuse her of perverted desire. He would change suddenly, apologize childishly, and make love to her again but more gently.

Frances Farmer would blame Odets for her chronic alcoholism and other problems that kept her in mental institutions for eight years. In 1937 even an amateur psychologist could see that Odets was shredding the twenty-three-year-old actress emotionally, most critically when he jettisoned her in midstream. Luise Rainer had gone to Europe but was sailing back, and the Odetses would try a reconciliation. Odets notified Frances *by mail* that they should not see each other again in privacy, and briefly he dropped out of sight. He had been the buffer against what Frances thought was the Group's unified hostility toward her, but now she looked into the crowd for a friend and found Jules Garfield . . . and he gave her solace.

Besides being the most attractive male in sight, Julie was her own age and was still obviously nursing—and attempting to conceal—his disappointment in being passed over for the Bonaparte role. Julie and Frances became clandestine drinking companions, sharing sympathy. Frances also had a sense of mission—to save Julie from Hollywood. The Group actors knew that Julie continued to receive feelers from filmland, and before the *Golden Boy* opening Julie had told Art Smith he would probably be heading West if the play failed. Frances Farmer was not happy on the stage and the inevitable return to films filled her with dread. She told Julie he should never let himself get talked into a movie contract, and he said he didn't intend to.

Then Robbie became pregnant. This development gave Julie excited pleasure; it was what they had wanted. But reality stared him down, and for the first time Julie was worried about being broke. He and Robbie had been buoyant paupers, even thrilled by a steady progress that was giving them a better living than they had known, and a beginning of "nice things." They lived frugally enough, and his *Having Wonderful Time* salary pulled them out of debt. But they had almost no savings, and the approach of fatherhood forced Julie to think about security.

He requested a salary increase and the Group administrators agreed to twenty-five extra dollars—not on hardship grounds but because, with the play doing so well, he was entitled. But his new status hardly approximated the big money; in Julie's mind that could only be the despised Hollywood. Since taking on an agent, he had not been able to purge his thoughts about the movieland alternative.

During the early run of *Golden Boy,* Julie got to know Arthur Lyons's partner—a fabled, hard-drinking Irishman named John McCormick: not the great tenor, but one who had been a prime mover in Hollywood until he drank himself out of prominence in the industry. McCormick had been production head of First National Pictures before its merger with Warners, and had married Colleen Moore after guiding her to stardom in silent pictures. He managed a spotty success as a talent agent mainly because he still had convivial ties with some of the veteran Warner executives. He knew of Max Arnow's attempts to add Jules Garfield to the Warner talent roster. Arthur Lyons had failed to deliver Garfield because of Julie's insistence on a time-off clause that would allow stage work. McCormick believed he could get Warners to go along with such an arrangement; after all, he reasoned, they always *say* they want to go back to Broadway, but never do.

When Warners came through with a firm and generous offer that included the stage clause, Julie did not immediately confide in Robbie. First he consulted Harold Clurman, who said essentially what Elmer Rice had said five years earlier: Julie should put the movies out of his mind during what should be his period of *growth* as an actor. Odets echoed Clurman; besides, he told Julie, there was likelihood of a *Golden Boy* production in London, so perhaps Julie could play Joe Bonaparte after all. Julie didn't even mention the Hollywood prospect to Carnovsky or other veteran Group actors, or to Frances Farmer: he knew what they would say.

He did not expect, however, that Robbie would be allied with the Group against him. She was. The money he was making in the theatre was ample for their needs, Robbie felt, and she had no intention of leaving home to have a baby in a strange place. And because Julie had a way of deferring to her in all things, Robbie doubted that he would go through with the Hollywood business. But he did.

Julie signed the contract in Warners' New York office—the standard featured-player agreement, seven years with options, plus that special concession to Julie. He did not tell his fellow actors what he had done, but they found out immediately and their reaction was fiercer than he had expected. That same evening's rendition of *Golden Boy* had an uncommonly melodramatic shading. Julie's first scene was with Carnovsky and Cobb, playing the oldsters whom Siggie was playfully agitating. Their hostility came through the dialogue, and "they glared at me as if they wanted to kill me"; and right after the final curtain, they tore into him.

Carnovsky was livid. He was also hurt because Julie, who sought his counsel in many things, had kept silent about *this*. When Julie protested that, all things considered, he didn't see that he owed the Group anything, Bud Bohnen gently suggested that Julie owed the Group *everything*. The actors called a special meeting to protest Julie's action and to discuss the disposition of his *case*. Julie felt like the victim of a special Inquisition. The actors seemed determined to prevent his taking a film contract, by any forceful means. Told repeatedly that he wouldn't be forgiven if he sold out to the movies, Julie said, "You forgave Franchot Tone, didn't you?" Actress Dorothy Patten shot back, "That was different!" Julie said he couldn't see just how it was different.

Franchot Tone, in the semi-official Group version, was one of life's tragic figures, anxious to return to the Group and never reconciled to having left it. They would not see his pictures which, they said, insulted his talent. Julie had seen a lot of Tone's pictures and thought he was terrific, especially in *They*

Gave Him a Gun. And he could not see how the rest of it added up to tragedy. If Tone was less than a major film star, he was a securely established player and a popular one. He earned better than a hundred grand a year and had married Joan Crawford. They had a mansion and a great swimming pool that Group people enjoyed unsnobbishly when they visited Hollywood. If what Franchot has is misery, Julie said, then I should be so miserable. In a scolding lecture, Julie heard again that only Franchot Tone's generosity had pulled the Group through one financial crisis after another. Julie said all right, he intended to do the same thing. If he made a lot of money in pictures, the Group would have a fair share of it. His antagonists were not pacified.

They changed tactics. He got the chill treatment. Their hostility was measurably reduced only when Julie confessed that he regretted the decision. He said if he had to do it over again, he wouldn't sign that contract, but he would lie in the bed he had made for himself. He protested that he had held out for the time-off clause, and he was indentured only for a year. But as time approached for Julie's departure, most of the *Golden Boy* company carried on as if they were never going to see him again. He completed his obligation to the play in a state of dejection.

Elia Kazan, recalling the Group's militant show of disapproval, suggested that the Group did not fear that Julie would fail in pictures, but that he would succeed too well. "It all tied in with *Golden Boy*. Had he played the lead, as we all sooner or later realized he should, no picture company could have dislodged him, not at that time. We were all very upset, but we weren't being fair to Julie. Carnovsky was full of righteous indignation, but hell, he was making more than double Julie's salary, and wasn't half as good-looking."

Harold Clurman theorized in *The Fervent Years* that Robbie Garfield, who "had developed a sense of justice, a stiff-backed resistance to the thought of being taken advantage of," had felt that Julie's innocence was being exploited by the Group, and was responsible for his decision to go into pictures. Clurman cited four cases of unhappy wives speaking of the Group "as they might of a co-respondent in a divorce case." But Clurman's logic was in error here, as Julie informed him after the book's publication in 1945. Robbie remained opposed to Julie's movie deal, and would make good her vow to remain in New York. About joining him in Hollywood, she adopted a wait-and-see attitude.

Julie would later tell columnist Sidney Skolsky that it was their first real quarrel. "Robbie and I had fights before, the harmless little ones that everyone has, but nothing serious. This was pretty serious, all right. But then we got to talking about things we could do with the extra money, like travel to Europe, which we both wanted to do. Not on the Queen Mary, but maybe on a tramp steamer."

He stayed in *Golden Boy* right up until his reporting time at Warner Brothers. There was no party afterward, no presentation of gifts—the traditional little ceremonies he had observed and might have expected. He went out for drinks with some of the younger, newer actors—Karl Malden, Curt Conway, Martin Ritt. He drank a little too much Scotch, becoming sadly nostalgic about the people he said he loved—Carnovsky, Kazan, Bohnen, Meisner, Art Smith, Lee Cobb, and all sorts of people named Adler. He started crying and there was no stopping him. It was no help that Frances Farmer, who was being called back by Paramount to make a picture opposite her estranged husband, spoke of Hollywood in a way that made it sound like some unexplored corner of Hades. When she asked Julie why the hell he'd agreed to the contract, he said: "I just reached a point where I had to do something on my own. Other people were always making decisions about me, and for me. So I thought, it was a way of being my own man."

For the cross-country drive Julie had bought a rusty-fendered, 1933 Chevrolet coupe. He offered Frances Farmer free transportation to California, but she said she thought she'd destroyed enough marriages for one season. Just as well: the car was too small for all the things Julie intended to carry with him. He named the car "The Cramps." It was a sputtering thing, but it got him to Hollywood safe and sober. And during his week of solitude on the road, nothing was on Julie's mind so much as a desire for quick failure in the movies.

VI

In the Warner Style

There were four Warner brothers. They were Polish Jews, born around the world during a disorderly family migration that ultimately deposited them in Youngstown, Ohio, at the turn of the century. The Canadian-born Jack was the youngest son and the favorite of his brothers—Harry, Sam, and Albert. The Warners failed in one business scheme after another, whether it was butchering hogs or operating a bicycle shop. Then Harry Warner worked the family into the new motion picture game, starting with the purchase for two hundred dollars of a ninety-seat theater in New Castle, across the border in Pennsylvania.

The brothers graduated into regional distribution, soon operating a Pittsburgh exchange. To eliminate the middle man, they organized Warner Features in 1913 and began to produce their own pictures. They were still only minor operators when twenty-five-year-old Jack Warner opened the modest Warner studio at Sunset and Bronson in Hollywood, in 1917; but from that point the brothers waded ever deeper into moviemaking waters. Almost too deep. For although the twenties was a boom period for the solvent movie companies, Warner Brothers Pictures resembled a failed enterprise. The marginal profit earned by its program pictures was often erased by losses sustained on the prestige films of Mr. John Barrymore, the only Warner star of consequence. Warners went deeper into debt to buy out the last survivor of the movies' stone age—the Vitagraph company—which had seen better days, but whose theater holdings the brothers desperately needed.

But it was soon apparent they had overextended themselves, and in their despair they adopted a clumsy apparatus that had been unsuccessfully peddled at every healthy studio. Calling the device the Vitaphone, Warners began experimenting with talking pictures. Barrymore's *Don Juan* in 1926 was accompanied by a synchronized musical score, and Warners issued novelty short subjects featuring mostly singers and musicians, popular and classical. The Vitaphone failed to create a commotion and looked like another bad investment until Al Jolson sang a handful of his most diverting songs in the first part-talkie, *The Jazz Singer*. It was a sensation in the fall of 1927, but the ruling studios remained complacent, confident that the Vitaphone would pass like any other fad. But Warners persisted and turned the business inside out. Within two years the rest of the industry capitulated. Talking pictures were permanently established, and Warners became a giant, acquiring in the process the assets of the sprawling, beleaguered First National company.

The First National package included a huge modern studio in Burbank. For several years movie patrons would be confronted by the Vitaphone and First National emblems, as well as the Warner shield, but it was one enormous moviemaking activity under Jack Warner's supervision. During the early thirties, Warners became Hollywood's top-volume producer. That the company had survived in the first place said something about the tight ship run by Jack Warner.

Where other companies were spendthrift, Warners emphasized frugality. Film was not wasted; the director tried to "get it in one take." Lean production schedules were rigidly adhered to. Warner employees worked harder and for lower salaries than they might have drawn elsewhere. There was neither fat nor deadwood on the studio payroll, and everyone was in a hurry. This spirit spilled over into the product.

Jack Warner was not a "creative producer" on the order of Irving Thalberg and David Selznick, but he had a knack for nurturing people who had the faculties he lacked. Hal

Wallis and Darryl Zanuck, boy wonders like Thalberg and
Selznick, began as minor studio functionaries and moved up
fast. Zanuck was put in charge of the Warner Hollywood
studio, with Wallis running the Burbank operation. And when
Zanuck struck off on his own in 1933, Wallis became executive producer of all Warner film activity.

The lavishness that typified M-G-M and Paramount remained a contrast to the Warner way of doing things. Partly
it was a matter of economic shrewdness, but it also embodied
a moviemaking philosophy. What was evolving was a unique
Warner style.

The M-G-M view of life was essentially gorgeous, whatever
its pitfalls. It was a glamorized world of collar-ad men and
ultrafeminine ladies. In this milieu a poor shopgirl could somehow maintain an apartment that was luxuriously appointed
beyond all logic, and show off a wardrobe that sophisticated
lady movie patrons were challenged to emulate. This was life
not as it *was,* but, according to M-G-M, life as it eternally
should be. Warners took quite a different view. Large, expensive sets simply did not get built at their studios prior to the
arrival of Errol Flynn. The settings were intimate, intensified
by low-key lighting. Warner films were blacker, harsher, and
photographed in higher contrast than the pictures of other
companies. And the nervous rush that characterized studio
activity paid off: the films were supercharged with energy,
the physical tempo was brisk, the dialogue unusually fast. The
pacing of a Warner film seldom relaxed, and editing was
strategic.

It figured, then, that a Jules Garfield would be more coveted
by Warners than by another autonomous company with a
fixed, illustrious image. Warners viewed humanity less senti-
mentally than its competition. The Depression emphasized
this. The Warner product had a socialist orientation that dif-
fered from the Hollywood norm. And Warner players were
less pretty and more credible.

Discounting the brief, freakish success of the anachronistic
George Arliss, Warner stars of the thirties were grim urban
types, forceful lowlifes who belied Hollywood elegance. Neither

Edward G. Robinson nor James Cagney conformed to the standard specifications of the leading man; and while Barbara Stanwyck and Bette Davis had the advantage of distinctive appearance, "pretty" was not a description that came immediately to mind. The reliable second-rank players—Joan Blondell, Warren William, Aline MacMahon, Ricardo Cortez, and the ubiquitous Glenda Farrell—were hard-boiled eggs in the Warner salad. Even the Busby Berkeley musicals held to a cynical viewpoint: the chorine heroines were frankly seeking a cure for hard times, and willing to compromise for it. They were *Gold Diggers,* and it was easy to identify with them.

It followed that the gangster picture would become a Warner specialty, for the Depression had given a new dimension to crime, and Warner movies were rooted in working-class sociology. There was social significance in—and controversy over—Mervyn LeRoy's *Little Caesar* and William Wellman's *The Public Enemy,* the titles that trumpeted the era of the gangster picture. And the socialist urging so prevalent on Broadway found a Hollywood habitat in such Warner melodramas as *I Am a Fugitive from a Chain Gang; A Cabin in the Cotton; Two Seconds; Black Fury; The Black Legion;* and *They Won't Forget.* The sanctimonious folk who decried the influence of the gangster epics also applauded the Warner liberal arguments for social responsibility. But crusading was not the issue. Mervyn LeRoy said he never looked for social consciousness in any script—just a corking good story. Getting out hard-hitting entertainment was the Warner business.

By 1938 the domestic film industry had achieved stability and Warners was on the threshold of its greatest prosperity. But there was discontent among the troops. A Warner contract director was expected to complete three, four, or even five pictures in one year. Stars and featured players worked year-round for salaries many felt did not reflect their value to the studio. The company produced sixty pictures a year plus occasional featurettes, yet the contract list showed less than a hundred players. M-G-M, Paramount, RKO, and especially 20th Century-Fox regularly scouted and signed novice players on rank speculation, but Warners seldom contracted a new screen player unless a definite plan had been worked out for building the performer. Reliance on central casting kept the Warner overhead down.

Jules Garfield came into the Warner fold at a significant time, both for the studio and for the movie industry generally. The new stars who had gained dominance with the beginning of talking pictures had been prominent for most of a decade and now were old stars. The studios were beginning to hear it from the distributors: the marquees needed some new names, the screen some new *faces*. In 1938, Warners signed up a battery of youngsters, experienced and otherwise, and set about "building" them as movie regulars. It would be more economical than granting exorbitant new contracts to the reigning stars when their current terms were completed, and such action could also keep the old stars in line. By signing enough Jules Garfields, Warners expected to have few or no replays of the annoying recent experiences with Bette Davis and James Cagney, their most valuable stars.

In 1936, Bette Davis, feeling overworked and underappreciated, walked out on Warners and tried to stake out a new career in England, only to lose a bitter lawsuit and return to Warners where, however, she would subsequently be treated with more respect. At about the same time, Cagney quit the company because he found a legal technicality that justified it—billing below Pat O'Brien, which was against his contract. Cagney was gone for two years and now was back at the studio, but with more clout.

Julie did not consider himself a threat to Cagney or any other established player, and neither did his employers. There is no clear accounting of what they did think of his potential. Although he was decidedly attractive in a rugged way, Jules Garfield was not conventionally handsome and was not in the monolith of the matinée idol.

He was too short and he was Jewish. These would have been formidable deficiencies at any other studio. But the only two male players of Jewish extraction to emerge as major stars during the talking period were in the Warner stable—Edward G. Robinson and Paul Muni. And both Robinson and Muni conspicuously lacked height; as did both Cagney and Humphrey Bogart, another Warner player and one not then regarded as star material.

Neither Hal Wallis nor Jack Warner can offer a clear accounting of how Garfield was recruited. Between the time of Lew Stewart's initial overture in 1933 and the actual signing nearly five years later, several studio executives and lesser functionaries got into the act of getting Garfield, although no one seems to have had strong feelings about him as a star prospect. Max Arnow left the job of Warner casting director in 1937, but was on record as recommending the hiring of Jules Garfield shortly after *Having Wonderful Time* opened. He felt that Garfield would fit neatly into a gang ensemble, as an interesting and younger contrast to Allen Jenkins, George E. Stone, and the others. In time, Steve Trilling, Arnow's successor, would be credited with Garfield's "discovery"; but so would Hal Wallis and each of the three surviving Warner brothers.

Upon arriving in Hollywood, Julie was greeted warmly by Joe Bromberg, who helped him find a place to stay. Shunning an expensive hotel suite or a fashionable bachelor apartment, Julie took a single room in a boarding house on Sycamore Street in the heart of Hollywood. He telephoned Robbie to say he'd arrived safely. After that he would watch his pennies carefully, hoarding "diaper money."

Unescorted, he checked into the Burbank studio on a rainy spring morning and was intercepted by Bryan (Brynie) Foy, who had responsibility for the studio's low-budget features. Foy said, "You'll probably be working for me in the beginning, because practically everybody does." He led Julie through several offices, collecting Hal Wallis and lesser executives en route, and finally the group entered the chambers of buoyant, dapper, forty-five-year-old Jack Warner. The studio chief threatened to break Julie's hand with his greeting.

"We expect great things of you, Jimmy," Warner beamed. "I understand we're going to be calling you James something-or-other, so I thought I'd throw a Jimmy at you."

The first fracas was over his name. Julie liked the name

that had sustained him on the stage for nine years and he fought to retain it. When he was turned over to Bob Taplinger, the publicity chief, Taplinger showed him the draft of a publicity release that would introduce an actor named James Fielding to the Warner contract list. The blurb said Fielding had been with New York's famous Group Theatre, and had earlier been known as Jules Garfield.

"Don't I have any say in this?" Julie asked.

One version is that Jack Warner had vetoed the surname as well as the Jules part, saying, "What kind of name is Garfield, anyway? It doesn't sound American." Julie said it was American enough to have been the name of a President of the United States. They decided he could remain Garfield, but the Jules would have to go; so his name would be James Garfield.

"But that was the President's name! You wouldn't name a goddam actor Abraham Lincoln, would you?"

"No kid, we wouldn't," a studio official admitted, "because Abe is a name most people would say is Jewish and we don't want people to get the wrong idea."

"But I *am* Jewish."

"Of course you are. So are *we* . . . most of us. But a lot of people who buy tickets think they don't like Jews. Well, they certainly like Eddie Robinson and Paul Muni, but we'd have a hell of a time trying to sell them Emanuel Goldenberg and Muni Weisenfreund. Look, kid, the people are gonna find out you're a Jew sooner or later, but better later. If you stick and they like you, they won't mind. But if we say right off you're a Jew, they ain't gonna like you. And Jules is a Jew's name."

Julie said he knew a singer named Jules Bledsoe who was colored. And the studio man said, "Then we'd sure as hell better change your name, since we don't want anybody calling you a nigger, either."

John Garfield was Julie's own suggestion as a compromise. The argument ended; everybody liked the name. It first appeared in a single paragraph in the *Hollywood Reporter*, belatedly noting Julie's arrival in filmland. It rated a somewhat longer mention in Louella Parsons's column, which described the newcomer as a "fiercely talented" graduate of the famous Group Theatre, parroting the Taplinger publicity line. For an entire week Julie was the property of the publicity department, getting photographed in every kind of pose and costume. He also assisted the writers, whose mission was to develop an "angle" on John Garfield. He didn't like what they had prepared in advance, some of it being rank fabrication; somebody had decided unilaterally that Julie had gone to Cornell. That part was corrected, but none of the early studio biographies made note of his being Jewish. Or short.

Julie gave the boys plenty to work with. In his first days in Hollywood he liked nothing so much as talking to reporters, publicists, and anyone who seemed interested in finding out things about him. He said he didn't expect to be in Hollywood very long and was saving his money; his limited wardrobe was adequate for his needs. The flacks saw the '33 Chevrolet that had become a curiosity piece in the studio parking lot, they saw the unpretentious boarding house where he stayed, and they had their angle: John Garfield was a nonconformist, an actor devoted to his craft and determined not to "go Hollywood."

But a *talking* nonconformist. Savoring the spotlight, Julie advertised his liberal politics, his allegiance to the Loyalists in the Spanish Civil War, his abhorrence for the Hitler regime in Germany, and his devotion to the artistic ideals of the Group Theatre.

Joe Bromberg and Clifford Odets, the latter having returned to Hollywood with Luise Rainer, were among those who suggested to Julie that he might be talking too much. Julie's standard rejoinder was, "I pay taxes, don't I? I've got a right to be heard." Apparently they heard him in Washington, because his name was added almost immediately to the Dies Committee list of Hollywood names with possibly subversive politics. Recruited by Walter Wanger, Julie joined the Hollywood Anti-Nazi League, which Congressman Martin Dies called a "fascistic-type group," although its roster included reputable people such as Rupert Hughes, Ernst Lubitsch, Eddie Cantor, Paul Muni, and the Fredric Marches.

Julie was flattered by association: he would join almost *any-thing*. He put his name on a petition advocating the boycotting of German and Japanese goods in America. He became a member of the Hollywood Independent Citizens Committee for the Arts, Sciences, and Professions; in a later and different era it would be accused of political subversiveness.

There was a lot of liberal lobbying going on in Hollywood, and Julie started attending meetings that were usually well represented by people he had known or worked with on the stage. He had ample time for such activity because, he complained, he wasn't very busy as an *actor* in pictures. He did have an inordinately long wait; but then a call from Bryan Foy told Julie his first job would be in *Girls on Probation*. All right, it was only to be the B picture it sounded like, but he would take the male lead; and just to be started out in leads meant that the studio thought a lot of him. And Julie supposed Warners did, for his likeness joined an array of framed "new faces" along the studio executive suite walls. There were also poses of Craig Reynolds, Patric Knowles, Jeffrey Lynn, and Willard Parker; and of Virginia Dale, Linda Perry, Gloria Dickson, Doris Weston, and Jane Wyman. The photos were also collected in a studio trade ad under the label, "Ten for the Top."

When Julie arrived at the studio, the list of official Warner stars numbered fourteen players—nine men and five women. But it was a deceptive inventory: several were lame ducks of one kind or another. Marion Davies, for instance, was still on the roster, although she had faced a movie camera for the last time. Nor would Leslie Howard make another film for Warners; and two longtime studio worthies, Joan Blondell and Dick Powell (then married to each other), would leave the company before the year was over. And Warners was quietly washing its hands of its "second Boyer"—Fernand Gravet—who had failed in two efforts at the studio, and was dispatched to M-G-M, where he would fail again as Johann Strauss the younger before sailing home for France.

The serene but lispy Kay Francis was the highest-paid

player on the lot, but she was washed-up at the box office. She had refused Warners' bid to settle her contract, and her penalty was to complete her contract by working only in B pictures. Warners even announced this publicly—an unprecedented slap in a star's face. But with a long-range plan that did not include Davies, Blondell, or Francis, Warners obviously had need of new and potent female stars. Aside from the reigning Bette Davis, the only certified distaff star was the young Olivia deHavilland—pretty enough, but not yet suspected of the considerable talent she would reveal in years to come. For the future, studio hopes were pinned on a Paramount discard whose Texas accent still posed a problem—Ann Sheridan—and on the sisters Lane, Rosemary and Priscilla.

The male stars included the veteran powerhouse trio of Muni, Robinson, and the prodigal Cagney; the superathlete and stud of renown, Errol Flynn; and serviceable commodities named Pat O'Brien and George Brent. A coterie of near-stars included Humphrey Bogart, still only a functional "heavy"; Warners' all-American boy, Wayne Morris; and the marvelous all-purpose character actor, Claude Rains. From the acting standpoint Warners obviously was a man's studio, yet the high command acknowledged some worry about its lineup. The front rank was taking on an elderly aura, with Robinson, Muni, and Leslie Howard all in their mid-forties. Indeed, it was the sudden and enormous popularity of the relatively inexperienced Errol Flynn that nudged the studio toward an all-out youth movement. Flynn and Wayne Morris were under thirty, and so were all of the male hopefuls contracted during Steve Trilling's first season as casting director.

The group included Dennis Morgan who, under his proper name of Stanley Morner, had flunked out of M-G-M; Eddie Albert, who started at Warners with John Garfield, almost to the day, and was also from the stage; William Lundigan, rebounding from Universal; Ronald Reagan, a former sportswriter and lifeguard; and the very pleasant Jeffrey Lynn, who carried the studio's highest hopes. Lynn ("rhymes with Flynn . . . looks like him, too") was getting a calculated buildup as a can't-miss "star of tomorrow." But today's star of tomorrow could as quickly become yesterday's hopeful. Shortly after Julie's arrival, Warners dropped Willard Parker's option; some years later, Parker would bob up on the Columbia list. Two of the studio's busiest ingenues, Carol Hughes and Beverly Roberts, got their walking papers when it became apparent that stardom was not their destiny; and even Ruby Keeler was cut adrift after a 1937 studio decision to discontinue musical features. The contract list was in constant revision. Some players who were less than stars were fixtures at the studio. As familiar to movie audiences as the people who led off the billing were such reliable supporting players as Frank McHugh, Allen Jenkins, Alan Hale, and a grand old trouper, May Robson.

During those early days at the studio while he remained unassigned, Julie would often believe he was being "mentioned" for this or that picture. These were publicity "plants" in the gossip columns, bent on familiarizing the public with the John Garfield name. He was pleased to read in the Louella Parsons column that he would support Cagney and O'Brien in *Boy Meets Girl,* an "important" picture already before the cameras; but he wondered why he hadn't been told. He called the studio and learned that Louella had garbled her information. It wasn't *Boy Meets Girl* but *Girls on Probation,* which merited only a three-week shooting schedule. Julie was disappointed, except that he was interested in Jane Bryan and was to be her leading man in *Girls on Probation.*

Considered the studio's most promising ingenue, Jane Bryan had been brought along carefully, exposed in several of the better Warner pictures over a two-year period. Now the studio wanted to see if she could "carry" a picture. Julie also heard that none of the incumbent Warner stallions had been able to get Miss Bryan into the sack. That provided an interesting challenge.

He met Jane Bryan and liked her. But they also gave him a *Girls on Probation* script, and he didn't like *that.* It wasn't fashioned by a Clifford Odets, obviously. Couldn't somebody try to make it better? Dave Bromall, an assistant director and one of Julie's first friends at the studio, said it wasn't worth the worry. If a B picture turned out well, that was fine, but it didn't matter: all the B's returned a profit anyway, and the studio used its B pictures to give new players the feel of movie-acting. Bromall assured Julie that his performance would be judged on its own merit, and that the studio chieftains would be watching it.

Then, as the picture was getting ready for a three-week production schedule, Julie was told he wouldn't be in *Girls on Probation* after all. Another picture had been postponed, putting Ronald Reagan at liberty. So Reagan would play opposite Jane Bryan, and the studio would find something else for Garfield, possibly something "bigger." Following a report that the studio brass liked some publicity shots of John Garfield in trunks and boxing gloves, there was an announcement that *The Patent Leather Kid* would be remade to showcase him in the ring, and on the battlegrounds of the First World War.

Julie remembered the picture: a First National vehicle for Richard Barthelmess in the late silent period—very exciting. He noted that from the time the papers gave lead play to the resurrection of *The Patent Leather Kid,* people at the studio treated him differently, particularly the young girls employed by the studio and now inclined to fall all over him.

So he was confused when he was ordered to report immediately to the sound stage where *Secrets of an Actress* was already midway through its hurry-up schedule—Kay Francis bitterly playing out the string. Watching Miss Francis and George Brent work, Julie was appalled. It was apparent that nobody cared about the picture; they were just trying to get it in the can. Julie was to play only a small role, but it was a chance to see what he could *do.* They weren't going to give him billing, and that way he could still be "introduced" in *The Patent Leather Kid,* the same procedure that had been applied to Wayne Morris in *Kid Galahad.* Julie was given a script and told to learn a scene. Next day at the studio he was told that since the picture was running over schedule, they were trimming the script, including all of his part. He felt a sense of relief. So would it be *The Patent Leather Kid?* Well, not yet, Brynie Foy told him; they didn't even have the dialogue—after all, it had been a *silent* picture, and making it as a talkie was still only an idea, but good publicity for John Garfield.

Julie had been "announced" for a battery of pictures, but hadn't faced a camera. But the summons to *The Sisters* was for real, and he was not displeased. *The Sisters* was one of the studio's more ambitious films, bringing together the studio queen and the crown prince: Bette Davis and Errol Flynn. Adapted from a best-selling novel, *The Sisters* had the San Francisco earthquake for its climax. Anita Louise and the busy Jane Bryan were playing Bette's younger sisters, and Julie was to be enlisted as a suitor.

Before his assignment to *The Sisters*, Julie had met Bette Davis at the studio and carried on a colorful conversation with her. They spoke a common language, one often identified with sailors; and it pleased Julie that Bette Davis, whose acting he admired, had a better idea of what the Group Theatre was than most people around the studio. Errol Flynn, on the other hand, seemed completely unimpressed by Julie's credentials and addressed him as "Group"—a derisive nickname that caught on briefly.

What gave *The Sisters* an aura of importance was its director. Handsome, Russian-born Anatole Litvak was an international success and *Mayerling* had been his artistic passport to Hollywood. There he conquered filmland socially, wooing and winning one of its leading actresses—Miriam Hopkins—who, perhaps not coincidentally, would soon replace Kay Francis on the Warner star roster. Litvak's first Warner credit was *Tovarich,* a prestigious success, and now he rivaled Michael Curtiz as the Warner director *par excellence*. Litvak was impressed that Julie could converse about Stanislavsky and that he had studied under the late Richard Boleslavsky. What Litvak did *not* have was a good ear for American dialect and regional inflection, or Julie would not have been assigned to his project.

Outfitted in Edwardian costume, Julie faced a movie camera for the first time since he had watched Cagney and Keeler tapping away in *Footlight Parade*. He thought his first scene went well enough; but after some discussion between Litvak and some other people around the set, the director announced they'd have to do the scene over. That annoyed Errol Flynn, who apparently thought acting was drudgery. Again the scene seemed to go smoothly, but again a little huddle followed. Irving Rapper, the dialogue director, found Julie's inflection unmistakably New York, and unalterably modern. Litvak suggested that Julie modify his dialogue to erase the more obvious wrong notes, but in a dry run Julie became tongue-tied, losing his lines and his sincerity. Next day he heard the verdict. He wasn't "right" for the part, so he was out.

Julie blamed his teeth. Before leaving New York for Hollywood, he had his teeth capped, and soon afterward they began to give him pain. Joe Bromberg sent him to a good Hollywood dentist who performed temporary work but felt that in time the entire job would have to be done over. Julie believed that if the job had been done correctly in the first place, he could have rid himself of the Bronx accent that was limiting him.

"That was probably the lowest moment in my professional life. All those years I'd been knocking Hollywood, saying it wasn't good enough for me. Then all at once, I couldn't meet its standards. When I heard who was doing the part—Dick Foran, for God's sake—I knew I was the flop of the year."

He was shocked and disappointed; but he found that in Hollywood, there was an antidote for such affliction.

"I was in Hollywood a week before I got laid," Julie said. "I don't know, that just may be a record."

It happened before he was aware of it. In four years of marriage in New York, Julie had overcome nearly every temptation to stray. But the tinsel of the film colony got to him. The girls were different, and Hollywood to Julie was a wilderness of girls. Sex was out there in the open, staring at you. It seemed to Julie that every starlet was competing for the title of Easiest Screw. He had a wife, he told them. Well, did that matter? It didn't matter to *them*. The wife was back there in New York, wasn't she?

Years later a writer friend of Julie's said: "This town got a little the best of him. It wasn't any one girl. It was *girls*. To be fair about it, he didn't chase them, not at the start. They chased him. Trouble was, he had married young, hadn't sowed his wild oats. Julie was easy pickings."

Playing the mattress circuit, he was an instant star, and certainly a desired object. The ruffled curly hair, the sleepy squint, the sensual mouth: all preliminaries were positive. He had a sense of guilt but low resistance, especially in a town where he was both lonely and depressed.

He poured out his guilt to Clifford Odets, but the playwright offered small comfort. Odets had his own problems— writing scripts that didn't get filmed—while the prospect of salvaging his marriage to Luise Rainer seemed about as promising as the shape of her career.

Luise may have been the first star to win two Oscars, but Odets said M-G-M was trying to get rid of her. They were still billing her as a star but the roles were getting smaller and the scripts thinner, and by mutual agreement something called *Dramatic School* would be the last. That Odets might write a play for her to act with the Group seemed a remote possibility at best. Nor was it likely that Franchot Tone would make good his often expressed vow to take Joan Crawford to New York for study and acting with the Group. The Tone-Crawford marriage also was ending. Both Odets and Tone counseled Julie to make every effort to bring Robbie to Hollywood or else go back home. They honestly did not know how to contend with the sex thing in Hollywood, but Franchot Tone said if there was a way, perhaps its name was fatherhood.

None of the Group alumni seemed content in Hollywood. Stella Adler, who went to Hollywood before *Golden Boy* was staged, was neither comforting to Julie nor comfortable to be with when they had a drink together. She had heard all the arguments about Julie's defection and told him it wasn't fair to Clurman that he had left; soon afterward Stella returned to New York, and later married Clurman. If Bromberg was the one most blissfully resigned, Alan Baxter was perhaps the most unhappy. Considered the Group's most promising leading man when Julie was an apprentice, Baxter had jumped to the movies to play opposite Sylvia Sidney in *Mary Burns, Fugitive*. His performance had the critics searching for superlatives, but the picture did poor business and Baxter's subsequent Paramount projects weren't as strong. The studio finally dropped him, and now Baxter was shuttling from one studio to the next, working regularly but typecast as a thug, never in leading roles or distinguished fare. Liquor was Baxter's solace.

Julie said that wouldn't happen to him. He had made up his mind to quit after his year was up, and he'd give them every reason not to pick up his option. All he wanted was the paycheck, and he was saving most of the money. But Clifford Odets said, "Julie, if you stay in pictures a year, you'll stay in them always. Failure isn't in you. You'll succeed, go up, whatever. Better than Franchot, better than anyone who's been in the Group or is in it now. The big challenge is in handling it when you get it."

The inactivity that seemed to have spanned months was only a stretch of a few weeks. Julie's stock had not really fallen. Anatole Litvak told Hal Wallis that Garfield was obviously an able actor who only needed to be cast properly. Bette Davis told the front office that the Garfield boy was good and that she hoped to get him into one of her pictures. And Paul Muni, noting the name of a boy he'd worked with on the stage on the studio's new contract list, suggested that Julie play Porfirio Diaz in the projected superproduction of *Juarez*. Warners agreed, although shooting for *Juarez* was still months away. They told Julie to be patient for a while longer, but he wondered how he could be patient if his wife was going to have a baby. He wanted to make a picture in a hurry, then get back home to Robbie.

Julie said to a group of writers lunching in the studio commissary, "Don't any of you birds write the kind of parts a punk from the Bronx can do?" One of the writers, also called Julie, aroused Garfield's interest by mentioning a good secondary male role in *Because of a Man*—a lousy title, he admitted, but Errol Flynn insisted on it, and Errol was the star. Julius Epstein said that the supporting part, properly cast and performed, could take the picture away from the lead actors.

"Who's directing?"

"Michael Curtiz. He doesn't like the assignment. Neither does Flynn."

"They don't like your script?"

"Let's say they don't like the casting gimmick. You see, all these dames are really sisters . . ."

In 1937, Warners employed America's most popular choral group, Fred Waring's Pennsylvanians, as window dressing for an inane Dick Powell musical called *Varsity Show.* Because two sisters from Iowa were the prettiest girls in the ensemble, they were selected for ingenue service to the collegiate story line. They were Rosemary and Priscilla Mullican, and their older sister had been in Hollywood for years—a minor actress known as Lola Lane. So they took Lola's professional surname and registered a mild hit in *Varsity Show,* then separated so each could test her own wings. Warners put Priscilla into *Men Are Such Fools,* a limp programmer with Wayne Morris and Humphrey Bogart, and gave Rosemary the primary focus in *Gold Diggers in Paris*—fifth, last, and weakest in the Warner series of dames on the make for the take. With some powerful publicity by Louella Parsons, the Lane girls became "hot copy." The oracle foretold careers of prominence, especially for the blonde Priscilla, who became instantly popular. But around the studio the notion persisted that selling the girls as a single entry was the best commercial tactic. So the story department was instructed to dig out a property about sisters, that sisters could play.

Warners owned a Fannie Hurst story out of *Cosmopolitan,* called *Sister Act.* It concerned not two but four sisters, all living in fairly deep suds with their widower father. Lenore Coffee's script was gathering dust until Julius Epstein inherited it for revision in the plural Lane image. He was also ordered to fatten up the principal male role for Errol Flynn. *The Adventures of Robin Hood* was the season's box office champion, so a Flynn picture seemed the best possible exposure for the Lane girls. Flynn's *Robin Hood* director, Michael Curtiz, was assigned *Sister Act* and expressed contempt for the property in a few poorly chosen words. Then Flynn himself backed off, saying he wouldn't touch the retitled *Because of a Man* until his role was stronger. He sailed away on his yacht and remained pointedly out of touch with the studio, although sets were built to accommodate an exacting production schedule.

Julie Epstein admitted to his own overriding interest in the subordinate role of a tragic young composer. He shaped the character for Van Heflin to play, for the studio had hopes of building the then-unestablished Heflin toward stardom in a new category, the "character juvenile." But Katharine Hepburn's *Philadelphia Story* stage venture tied up Heflin. Julie read the Epstein script and knew he had found the role he wanted, even though the picture was being kicked around the studio like a soccer ball—and in fact, came very near to being canceled.

The title reverted briefly to *Sister Act* before it was changed to the more lyrical *Four Daughters*. That was because Errol Flynn was no longer involved. Jeffrey Lynn replaced him, making *Four Daughters* a curiosity project—a Curtiz picture *without stars* was unheard of.

Curtiz had been with Warners since the silent days and directed most of the studio's quality films. He was considered a consummate technician—a master of lighting, composition, and every trick of narrative camera. But his players were often left to their own resources. Curtiz was not concerned about character motivation or interpretation. If his players were Davises or Cagneys, the resources were sufficient. An inexperienced cast might betray his ennui with actors, so a Curtiz film always had top stars.

The starless lineup assembled for *Four Daughters* was not inexperienced. Claude Rains would play Adam Lemp, the musical father of the musical girls, accent on the classical. May Robson, in her sixth decade of continuous acting, came aboard as the crusty housekeeper aunt. Frank McHugh and Dick Foran were among the girls' suitors. Lola Lane—why not?—was brought in to play with her sisters. And the fourth daughter would be Gale Page, an ingenue with dramatic flair, but whose unhappy destiny would be permanent identity as "the fourth Lane sister."

When Julie heard that Eddie Albert was likely to get the Mickey Borden role, he began to lobby with Curtiz, Wallis and everyone who counted—including Henry Blanke, Wallis's associate producer who relented after much pestering and told Julie he could have the part.

It was a mildly controversial bit of casting. Many around the studio thought John Garfield was undistinguished in looks, voice, and manner, and he was already a subject for light ridicule as an amateur Left-wing politician. But Julie said, "Hell, you got me under contract, you've got to put me in a picture sometime!" And he really wanted this part. He liked listening to music, and told Joe Bromberg he felt he could "put on the music arranger like an old suit of clothes."

Shooting was underway before Julie was confirmed for the Mickey Borden role in April. The character made a delayed entrance, but was of strategic importance to the picture's second half. From the beginning there was widespread interest in the Borden part, where there was only apathy for Felix Dietz—the thankless role Jeffrey Lynn would play, but with whom all four girls would somehow fall in love.

Julie memorized his entire role before facing the cameras. Curtiz was amazed and annoyed. Julie said that was the way you were trained in the Group Theatre, and from that point Curtiz addressed him merely as "Group" or "Mister Group." Julie's outgoing charm did not woo Curtiz, an actor of sorts and an egotist. A Hungarian trained in the French and German cinemas, Curtiz was multilingual and capable speaking flawless English but had little inclination to do so. Butchering the language with cunning, he challenged Sam Goldwyn's capacity for generating comically quotable publicity. Julie's judgment was that the well-advertised Curtiz personality was phony, and he was not certain of the director's talent. The Mickey Borden characterization was entirely Julie's creation, and he felt his director should make a better show of interest in what his actors were doing. Once again the dialogue director was Irving Rapper, whose confidence in Julie's work enabled him to concentrate mainly on Priscilla Lane and Gale Page, both of whom had to do a lot of weeping.

Other actors teased "Group" for worrying too much about his characterization, but Julie was unruffled. Out after hours with Joe Bromberg, he said, "I've got to find someone to hang this guy on. He's a gloomy musician." Bromberg suggested using Clifford Odets as a model, since Odets was a kind of musician after all. Julie said he'd even thought of that, "Except that Cliff's not always gloomy, and Borden can't be anything else."

Bromberg jokingly suggested that Julie could do his impersonation of Oscar Levant, and that provided the key.

"Yeah, Oscar's a mystifying son of a bitch, and a musician to boot." Julie reasoned that even when Levant was funny, he was woeful beyond the legal limit. He decided that among other things, Mickey Borden would be a compulsive coffee drinker and a chain smoker who talked while a cigarette dangled between his lips.

Four Daughters proceeded on a reduced schedule; the budget had been trimmed so it had a "small picture" aura, despite the retention of Curtiz as director. The project merited no special attention and studio jesters called it the Warner answer to the Dionne quintuplets. The little Canadian girls had been successfully exploited by 20th Century-Fox.

To Julie's surprise, making the picture was an entirely pleasant experience. His letters to Robbie were sales pitches on California. He said the movie game wasn't as lousy as they'd heard, and he had made many new friends.

An unexpected benefit was his association with Claude Rains, whose performances for the Theatre Guild Julie had admired. Their socializing began and ended at the studio, but they were usually seen together during idle moments on the set. Rains consistently gave rich performances on film, but his heart still was on the stage he had abandoned. He and Julie talked about actors and the differing styles of their craft; and when he felt he had won Julie's confidence, Rains offered a tip that brought Mickey Borden's character into a better screen perspective. Informally rehearsing an early scene, Julie asked, "How'm I doing?" and Rains said, "Rather theatrically, I believe." There was a difference between acting on a stage and before a movie camera. As Claude Rains explained, "You were addressing May Robson as if she were seated in the last row of the balcony. The movie critics will like that—they approve of anything done big. But if dramatic truth is your aim . . ."

Julie muted his scene, and when it was shot Rains assured him he was right on the button, adding, "And I notice it's rubbing off on Priscilla." The youngest Lane girl was a better actress in her scenes with Julie than the earlier shooting had indicated. Julie said Claude Rains "taught me things some people never learn about acting in films. He warned me about Mike Curtiz and his mania for close-ups. That's when you have to underplay. No two screen directors are alike, so an actor must always make adjustments."

Mickey Borden was a suicide, laid to rest before the picture's concluding scenes. During the final days of filming, Julie was only an observer on the set. The tension that had gripped him while he was on camera evaporated, but uncertainty returned like an old rash. There was the customary party on the set after the final takes in June, and Julie accepted perfunctory congratulations from studio personnel at every level. But there was no air of special accomplishment, other than Claude Rains's hunch that "We have a nice little picture."

Julie briefly entertained a sense of insecurity because he wasn't being rushed into another assignment, as were all of the other *Four Daughters* players. Priscilla Lane and Jeffrey Lynn were set for leading roles in *Yes, My Darling Daughter,* an expensive property based on a stage success. Gale Page was at work on another picture even before *Four Daughters* was completed. And Michael Curtiz wouldn't get a day's rest: he was to begin principal photography on Cagney's *Angels With Dirty Faces* immediately. Julie told everyone he would soon be going into *Juarez;* but that project still lay in the distance, and it was possible that Warners could drop its option on John Garfield before the picture rolled. Nor was he consoled to

learn that *The Patent Leather Kid* had been shelved indefinitely; later, as *Knockout,* it would help launch Arthur Kennedy's career as a Warner hopeful.

Warners wouldn't keep a contract player waiting very long.
Now the idea was to see if John Garfield could "carry" a
picture—meaning, a *little* picture—and Julie was assigned the
lead role in *Blackwell's Island,* one of Bryan Foy's B pictures.
The shooting was to be completed in just sixteen days, after
which Julie would be given a vacation to await the baby with
Robbie, in New York.

The *Blackwell's Island* script seemed professional enough
for a routine melodrama. It was about a crusading reporter
who gets himself railroaded to prison in order to expose conditions there. The director was Bill McGann, a sort of short-
order cook at Warners, grinding out one B after another.
Rosemary Lane was the girl cast opposite John Garfield.

Disenchantment set in quickly. "This isn't acting," Julie said
while *Blackwell's Island* was being filmed, "this is what's
called racing with the clock." Again he sensed that no one
really cared about the finished product. Preparing the picture
seemed to have no connection with drama, and the only compensation was that part of the shooting would be done in New
York, actually at Blackwell's Island. He was homesick not only
for his wife, but for the theatre and for New York itself. His
attitude toward Hollywood was becoming contradictory.

During one of his visits to Hollywood, Harold Clurman
assured Julie that yes, he could return to the Group at any
time; the bad feeling would blow over as it always does, and
all would not only be forgiven, but forgotten. Still, Julie could
be ruled by pride. He did not nibble at a near-offer to play
Golden Boy in London—the Bonaparte role this time. And
he didn't want his hoped-for eventual return to the Group to
occur sooner because he had *failed* in pictures. Not even if it
was a season of the chickens going home to roost.

Everyone seemed to be rejoining the Group. Clifford Odets
and Franchot Tone, each about to be divorced by a different
M-G-M star actress, were both returning. After six years in
pictures, Tone would act in *The Gentle People,* a role that the

playwright, Irwin Shaw, had hoped Jules-John Garfield would do. And Odets had a new play called *Rocket to the Moon*— designed, he said, to make Morris Carnovsky the theatre's next sex symbol.

Among theatre people it was said there was nothing wrong with working in Hollywood for money so long as you said you hated the work and the place. Julie could disparage Hollywood on cue, but he liked it more than he would admit. What he liked about the place was what made him fear it; he sensed that it preyed on his weaknesses.

The publicity line was that John Garfield did not want to "go Hollywood" and that he hadn't; but somehow Hollywood had gotten to him, in a big way.

The sociology of the film colony was unique. In the years just before World War I, a huge new industry mushroomed almost overnight. A quaint, almost conservative factory town grew around it. The studio payrolls were dominated by artisans and laborers whose life-styles tended to the ordinary, rather opposed to the well-publicized shenanigans of the stars who were the window dressing for the canned entertainment the factory yielded.

Middle-aged Jewish businessmen carved out the industrial structure, but the people who served up the entertainments— the directors, players, and other artists—comprised a mix from all over the country. They were all astonishingly young— mostly high school dropouts with adventuring spirits. The early movie queens were teen-aged girls far from home, unshackled from the moral scruples of parents and community. They matured with the industry but youth recycled, as new waves of girls and boys sought fortune and fame as movie stars. Failing both, they could settle for a good time, burning the candle at both ends.

The star system dictated its own social order, as it did on the stage. Popular and high-salaried stars tended to meet socially and carry on as bluebloods remaining true to their class. Persons with steadier careers in supporting roles did not speculate on an upward ladder but had a sedate little society of their own. But the largest, boldest, most desperately glamorous stratum was the unestablished multitude: girls and boys under "starlet" contracts, and even greater numbers of kids in town still angling for a start, trying to be noticed. They all lived above their means, going into hock for the stylish clothes and trappings that imitated the Hollywood life-style. Even as the Great Depression lingered on, hard times were masked by the optimism of would-be stars ready to celebrate tonight the good fortune they would surely obtain tomorrow.

It was an orgiastic whirlpool and John Garfield was pulled into its vortex—the proverbial boy who, after years of being deprived of sweets, finds himself locked inside the candy store. He was nagged by guilt from the start, but sex in its infinite variety was irresistible to him, and he had an overpowering appetite. Later on he would confide in friends, seeking to cure his affliction or perhaps merely to purge an obsessive guilt. He said that if Robbie had gone to Hollywood with him the first time, things might have been different. But loneliness gnawed at him, and yearning for Robbie only made him easier prey. In a professional community where the importance of virility was blown all out of proportion, John Garfield soon became a closet-talk legend.

The immediate objects of his pursuit were the generally acquiescing girls new to the studio contract list. But it didn't stop there. There were carhops and hatcheck girls pretty enough to be in pictures, and that was why most of them had come to Hollywood; they were a positive influence in building Julie's confidence.

As a new player in whom Warners had earnest hope for the future, Julie was tapped by the publicity department for interviews with writers and columnists, including some who exercised considerable clout in filmland. One of the more enterprising gossip columnists was a then-young, oversexed British lady whose startling autobiography, published many years later, gave a rather pathetic account of her brief physical affair with an actor who, while not named, was unmistakably John Garfield.

They shared an interest in Shakespeare, although the col-

umnist suspected Julie knew little about it. He told her that
he and some friends were going to record a scene from Shakespeare and invited her to join him. She felt he was basically
shy, but she sensed his magnetism and accepted the recording
date. After the reading they all went to a restaurant where
Julie proceeded to make "whisper love" into her ear. They
left the others at the restaurant and Julie took her home. Inside
her front door, he "had me face to face as I imagined a puppy
would if he could. He made love like a sexy puppy, in and out,
huffing and puffing in quick gasps." It was over as soon as it
began; he worked fast and it meant nothing. There was early
and lasting agreement that quantity and not quality was Julie's
strong suit as a lover.

While *Four Daughters* was still in production, word filtered
up to the Warner offices that they had another stud on their
hands. The studio hierarchy, from Jack Warner on down,
always accepted Errol Flynn's well-reported capers with whim-
sical tolerance, but they were of a different disposition toward
a nice Jewish boy with a lovely wife who was pregnant besides.
They counted on Julie persuading Robbie to come to California, where hopefully she would keep him in check. Meanwhile,
the publicists continued to fabricate stories about John Garfield's breezy independence, indicating that the least likely
place to find the new actor would be at a Hollywood party.
Julie, who was likely to show up at any open party he knew
about, was frequently amused by the yarns, such as one in
which he supposedly said he would never be caught in formal
attire, anywhere. After all the commotion over his untailored
life-style, he thought he'd cause a sensation by putting on the
ritz.

He went to the wardrobe department and ordered white tie
and tails. The clerk said a dress suit wasn't on his list for *Four
Daughters,* but Julie said they'd just added a scene. He got
into the fancy clothes and then mounted a bicycle and pedaled
all over the studio, trying to attract attention and surprise. The
only reaction came from a studio guard who said, "Out all
night *again,* Mr. Garfield?" Julie said, "You can't make a high
class guy out of me this way, but it sure helps." He returned

the dress suit to wardrobe, and soon afterward purchased a tuxedo for himself. Recalling that Clifford Odets and Luise Rainer had said, "You'll dress well in Hollywood because everyone does," he decided to have some suits tailor-made for the first time in his life. He chose a dark, pencil-stripe fabric that became his favorite and a Garfield trade mark. He had caught a glimpse of stylish Hollywood, and a part of him wanted to be a part of it.

In sending Julie to New York for some atmospheric shots for *Blackwell's Island,* the studio hoped he would persuade Robbie to return with him to California, where her presence might keep him in check. But it was an uneasy homecoming. In letters and occasional telephone calls, Julie had kept Robbie posted on the professional aspects of his exile, with no mention of his partying. But too many people who knew both of them were in Hollywood, and word of Julie's carousings got back to Robbie in New York before he did. He was apologetic, and was given the satisfaction of forgiveness. But despite his protestations of renewed faithfulness, the fabric of their marriage was permanently scorched, baby or no baby.

Anyway, Julie boasted, he had "earned diaper money" out there. Now he and Robbie could occupy a nice apartment with a nursery. The baby was only a matter of weeks away.

Location shooting for *Blackwell's Island* occupied Julie for only a few days, but what followed was anything but a restful vacation at home with Robbie. The first report came in on *Four Daughters*: its sneak preview in California had been received with maximum enthusiasm. The word was that John Garfield was the hit of the picture, and soon the Warner home office had him lined up for promotional interviews with both stage and screen reporters.

The Manhattan preview was sneaked just after the Labor Day weekend, ten days prior to its opening. There was an official Warner Brothers contingent in attendance, but Julie and Robbie chose to remain incognito. They paid their way in, and separated inside the theater. Robbie took an orchestra seat and Julie sought hunched seclusion in the balcony. He thought his performance "not as good as I'd hoped it might be, or as bad as I feared it would be." He could tell that the audience liked the picture—nobody coughed—but did not know what they were thinking about *him*. He wondered what Morris Carnovsky would think of the Mickey Borden portrayal. Robbie knew what *she* thought. Immediately recognizing the strength of his performance, she sensed something of the sensational reaction that would occur upon the film's release. It wore down her grudging resistance; she was thrilled. That seemed to settle the big question. Robbie decided that after the baby came, they would go to Hollywood as a family group.

News of the *Four Daughters* opening in Hollywood confirmed that the picture was going to be a sleeper and that Garfield was the whole story. And in mid-September the New York critics merely iced the cake, so taken with the picture's charm that they overlooked its syrupy center. It was described as bittersweet, beguiling, inspiring, enriching; but mostly it was heartwarming, they said. But all of the superlatives were wired into the Garfield performance, which the critics saw as the core of the picture and the reason for its being. Fannie Hurst said the picture had "outgrown my simple story and acquired a life of its own." She added that the Mickey Borden characterization was John Garfield's, not her own. Julie was hailed as the sensational new "find"—not of the year, but of the decade.

He was besieged by New York reporters. He said, "Never will I get such a reception again. My future performances will always be compared with my role of Mickey Borden. It's a handicap I don't look forward to." He also said all the talk about his raw sex appeal scared him. "People will go to see me with chips on their shoulders, daring me to prove I'm as good as the critics claim I am." But he was delighted and effusive, saying all the right things: "When an actor doesn't face a conflict, he loses confidence in himself. I always want to have to struggle because I believe it will help me accomplish more. Hollywood is a marvelous medium, but you can't take many chances there and I believe the more successful an actor becomes, the more chances he should take. An actor never stops learning."

Garfield mini-biographies began to appear in the newspapers, giving the Group Theatre some lively free advertising and the American public the rags-to-riches yarn it always savored. Up in the Bronx, Julie's father was a minor celebrity and Angelo Patri was almost a major one. All of his teaching theories had been realized in John Garfield. Patri joyously contacted Julie with a request that he address the P.S. 45 graduating class. Julie said he would do it. Afterward he would try to make a visit with his old principal an annual event, but always accompanied by photographers.

Julie said it was good to be among brothers again. The Group people accepted his movie triumph as his vindication, and Julie was telling reporters that he wanted to act for the Group again and that his contract permitted it. There was talk of *Heavenly Express*: for years the Group had held Albert Bein's play, and the principal role of a likable troubador ghost was one Julie thought he'd like to play. He could not conceal his pleasure in knowing that what *he* wanted to do had become important to the Group. That importance could also be expressed in new ways. To help finance Odets's *Rocket to the Moon,* the Group accepted a thousand-dollar "loan" from Julie's first movie earnings.

Again, Julie and Robbie were consumed by activism, and if the Depression was passing, the radical movement had a sharp focus on the civil war in Spain. The Group as a body supported the Loyalists' losing struggle against the Franco fascists. Frances Farmer, on tour with *Golden Boy,* met the Spanish ambassador in Washington and agreed to kick off a campaign to aid the children who were victims of the Barcelona bombings. Miss Farmer got Julie over to Brooklyn for a money-raising dance, and his topical movie fame helped make the event a financial success. The adulation of his new fans left Julie beaming; this was the part of being a movie star that he most liked.

The Group members, while respectful toward Julie's performance, did not rate *Four Daughters* a work of art. But they were not oblivious to its popularity. Soon it was evident that it was close to a smash hit—the kind of strong audience picture that would benefit from word of mouth. It advanced the careers of most people identified with it, although the widespread opinion was that Garfield carried the picture and everyone in it. *Time* called him "the sole positive charge in an otherwise negative cast."

The story told of the coming of age of four sheltered, musically gifted daughters of a kindly minor conductor. Two young composers enter their lives: steady, reliable Felix; and Mickey, one of life's losers. One critic called him fate's whipping boy. Mickey was bitter and disillusioned, yet intrinsically gentle and warm. The youngest sister marries him out of pity, but Mickey remains vulnerable to despair and tragedy.

The definitive scene occurred in the Lemps's living room with Mickey playing his own composition at the piano—defiance written all over him and a cigarette hanging from his lips.

"It's beautiful," urges the sister played by Priscilla Lane. Not removing the cigarette, Mickey says, "It stinks. It hasn't got a beginning or an end. Only a middle." When Ann Lemp suggests he could add a beginning and an end, Mickey says, "What for? The fates are against me. They tossed a coin—heads I'm poor, tails I'm rich. But they tossed a two-headed coin."

His screen image was born.

The bountiful fall harvest of 1938 included a Garfield daughter. They named her Katherine and she was indeed a healing link. Julie's fascination with his infant daughter seemed to surpass even the customary foolishness displayed by fathers toward their firstborn. As soon as mother and daughter were able to travel, the Garfields went to Hollywood.

It was more than just an option renewal. Warners revised Julie's contract—designating him a star player rather than a featured one—for seven years *without* options. In *Four Daughters* he had been billed seventh, but the studio was fashioning a name-above-the-title "vehicle" and the title told the story: *They Made Me a Criminal*. Julie was effusive about the new agreement. He wanted all his friends to know that even after his agents took their cut, he'd clear a hundred grand the first year.

While they looked for a place to live, the Garfields were guests of Arthur Lyons at his manicured Sunset Boulevard estate. That was Robbie's introduction to the glamour life. There was an enormous swimming pool spanned by a bridge, and a small sailboat floated in the water. The house was casually elegant. The host, behaving as if Robbie were his primary responsibility, paraded in guests by the couples—old friends of the Garfields and new acquaintances—hoping to make her feel at home in the film colony.

One couple already friendly with Julie was a local journalist and his wife. Unbeknownst to Robbie, the woman had already withstood Julie's attempt at seduction following a private luncheon at the studio—a meeting arranged by the husband as a favor to his wife, who was one of the early John Garfield fans. The woman immediately took a strong liking to Robbie, in whom she detected an anxious insecurity that could not be masked by Robbie's extreme prettiness. She helped Robbie locate a modest, smartly furnished two-bedroom apartment in Hollywood.

It suited the Garfields' idea of comfort. Robbie could enumerate the dreary residences she had occupied with her family and then with Julie, and allow that she would be living as a queen. The move to the apartment was easily managed; she said they were never going to be "things" collectors. Robbie hung a large salami in the kitchen and inscribed "We live here" on it—to remind them, she said, of their humble station. They agreed on a weekly allowance of fifteen dollars for Julie's lunches and cigarettes; that way they could build a savings account quickly. But Julie satisfied an old ambition to take drum lessons, and he and Robbie also bought a large Capehart phonograph and an ample supply of records, both classical and popular. When Julie came home tired, relaxing to music was his favorite pastime.

Julie bought an almost-new car and then went out and bought the books he was accustomed to borrowing: Stanislavsky's *An Actor Prepares,* all of the Jack London books in print, and a life of Freud. His external interest in books suggested a faith that mere possession would enhance his intellect. He bought more books than he read, and he read more than he absorbed.

Robbie was the real reader, but books and baby together couldn't contain her nimble mind. She was prodded by compassionate responsibility toward other humans, and saw Julie's financial security as a benefit to her own mission. Robbie would become an indefatigable fund-raiser for liberal causes. Julie's name would prove useful for raking in funds, and he would play host when Robbie held meetings in their apartment and their later homes. Their friends said Robbie was too energetic and independent to be content with a back seat while Julie was in the limelight; in pursuing her own interests she would not be put down as the nobody-wife of a movie star. In *their* New York, the theatre had been an adhesive for their mutual crusade, but Hollywood was *his.* Away from the collective existence that had characterized the Group, they became competitive. Friends observed that Robbie felt a pressure to retain her own identity.

She showed little inclination to visit the Warner Brothers studios, where everything had changed for Julie. He was a fussed-over object, no longer able to nose around the lot inconspicuously. Everyone knew who he was and that pleased him inwardly. The working girls around the studio who previously had given him an approving once-over now held the stare longer in homage to a new and rugged star. Julie reveled in attention and Robbie understood his need for it; and she understood better than he that his vault to sudden fame was not accidental. She counted on his first starring picture being a popular hit, although she did not dispute Julie's suspicion that it was close to being lousy.

Some years earlier, *The Life of Jimmy Dolan* had been a routine Warner program picture with the younger Douglas Fairbanks. It clicked at the box office because it combined elements of prizefight and gangster pictures. Later it was dusted off as a likely showcase for Errol Flynn, then put back on the shelf when costume pictures became the Flynn password. *Dolan* was tailor-made to put the newly-formulated John Garfield image into focus. It could be filmed and released in a hurry while *Four Daughters* was fresh in the moviegoing memory. The obligatory new title was *They Made Me a Criminal;* and a callous, mechanical attitude toward the production aroused Julie's suspicions.

The director was the least likely candidate—Busby Berkeley, creator of those excessive dance sequences for a score of Warner musicals starting with *42nd Street.* In those days Warners hadn't thought highly enough of Berkeley's ordinary abilities to give him a dramatic trust. He was a *dance* director, and there would be a Mervyn LeRoy, a Lloyd Bacon or an Archie Mayo to guide the story line. But Warners stopped making musicals while Berkeley still held an expensive contract, so they had him direct nonmusical pictures that were not, however, of the caliber given to a Curtiz or a Litvak. Julie was bothered by the rumor that Berkeley was given *They Made Me a Criminal* because he was a fast worker—maybe that meant careless.

He also heard that Jack Warner had ordered a sequel to *Four Daughters* and wanted Julie available to act in it as soon as a script was ready. A sequel? Julie wanted to know how that was possible, since his character had been killed off. He was told that could be easily remedied; maybe Mickey Borden had a twin brother all along. The studio had Julie Epstein and *his* twin brother, Philip, at work on the project. Hearing that Garfield was agitated, Jack Warner said he should be pleased that he was becoming a full-fledged star in only his second picture.

"Which one do you mean?"

"Why, the thing you're making," Warner said. "Whatever we're calling the Jimmy Dolan picture."

"Yeah, well, I seem to recall having already made a second picture. What about *Blackwell's Island?*"

Julie's recollection was better than Warner's. The studio chief knew they'd shot a picture by that name but had forgotten some of the small points, such as who was in it. He emphatically did not like the idea of John Garfield having made a B picture. It might jeopardize the big things the studio had in store for him. Had anyone seen the footage? Was Garfield any *good* in it?

The studio people who had screened the final print rated *Blackwell's Island* a dandy little action picture and endorsed Julie's furiously-fast performance as something more likely to fortify his standing than diminish it. But Warner wanted it released as an A picture and said it would have to look like one first. He recalled all the prints just as they were going out to theaters for second-feature duty on double bills. An additional $100,000 was pumped into the budget, and Michael Curtiz was called in to direct some new scenes and reshoot some others. Julie discovered how busy a movie actor could be, commuting from one set to another—a reporter-convict in the morning and a fugitive-boxer in the afternoon. He said it was not really conducive to character immersion: Stanislavsky would not approve. And while both pictures were filming, *Juarez* finally went into production.

Even as his energies churned to a hard schedule, Julie welcomed the partying side of Hollywood life. In later years the Garfields would not be in the film colony's regular partying mass, but 1939 would find them attending many functions. Robbie enjoyed the affairs much less than Julie, but he justified their attendance with cliché logic. It was important to get some relaxation, to unwind from the grinding production ordeal; it was important to be seen, to make contacts and friends while you were new in the business. But Julie was really only an impressionable young stranger, decidedly starstruck. One of their first oversized galas was hosted by Darryl Zanuck at his stables, and Julie couldn't get enough of ogling Barbara Stanwyck and Robert Taylor, then the most publicized filmland romance. Robbie showed little interest in celebrities and while Julie flitted through a crowd, she would withdraw into the company of a few persons with whom she was already acquainted. When Robbie was ready to go home, Julie would only be getting the feel of the turf.

They Made Me a Criminal, a January release in 1939, certified John Garfield as a dominant personality—one who could carry a picture. It was a very ordinary movie and Julie did not plumb the depths of his character as he did in his screen debut. But it was reliable formula stuff and a money-maker from the start, proof that Garfield already was some kind of movie *name.*

Echoing some negative feedback from the Group—again they were saying his performances were becoming mannered —Julie said he was disappointed with *They Made Me a Criminal* and found his own performance hollow. In later years he would deprecate the picture at every opportunity, yet Clifford Odets believed Julie adopted a defensive posture against his most severe critics, who were also his friends. Odets said *They Made Me a Criminal,* like other pictures of Julie's honeymoon period in Hollywood, was mainly a pleasant experience for him. He particularly liked working with the Dead End Kids, the only actors he knew, besides himself, who had come out of the New York slums. In the picture they were orphans on the ranch where the boxer goes into hiding after being framed in a gang killing. Julie thought two of the youths— Billy Halop and Gabriel Dell—were true actors not unlike the very young Jules Garfield. For the screen version of *Dead End* in 1937, Sam Goldwyn had imported six boys who had been the adolescent life of the stage success. They stayed in Hollywood, first under a Warner contract; and as later studio itinerants they degenerated into decidedly elderly, low-camp teen-agers.

Also in the picture were Ann Sheridan, in the early city sequence, and blonde Gloria Dickson later, at the ranch. Gossip had Julie carrying on with first one girl and then the other, in a way that established the customary pattern of relationships with his leading ladies. Sexual affairs were of the moment, not of the heart, and almost always would terminate with the completion of the picture.

Although Julie thought Claude Rains, as a hounding detective, contributed the strongest performance to *They Made Me a Criminal,* the reviewers concentrated on John Garfield almost exclusively, and again they were generous if no longer surprised or excited. That was also their response to *Blackwell's Island,* which Warners shrewdly released right after *They Made Me a Criminal* played its first-run engagements. Whatever Michael Curtiz may have done toward enhancing *Blackwell's Island* was not easily seen, but the box office return exceeded expectation and Garfield rendered a level of authority not commonly found in a B picture.

Even the most professional of the reviewers (and certainly Julie himself, as well as his Group critics) seemed to misunderstand what the audience recognized clearly: that a role of Mickey Borden stature was not necessary to prove that John Garfield was an entirely new kind of movie actor.

It came through in *They Made Me a Criminal* and to no lesser extent in *Blackwell's Island.* Julie's work was spontaneous, un-actory; it had abandon. He didn't recite dialogue, he attacked it until it lost the quality of talk and took on the nature of speech. The screen actor had been dialogue's servant, but now Julie switched those roles. The critics may have misrepresented the Mickey Borden portrayal—overpraising it in terms of interpretation—when all along they were merely being bowled over by the uniqueness of the Garfield style.

The hint of hesitancy in Julie's vocal delivery before the movie cameras was less a mannerism than an aspect of the nervous energy that clawed at him while he was acting. He did not, he insisted, ever *try* to stammer as a means of developing characterization—not the way James Stewart could stammer so well if it could benefit his acting. Ever since Angelo Patri made Julie aware of the tendency, he had tried *not* to stammer. Talking fast was part of that effort. But talking fast was also a virtue at the pace-smitten Warner studio, where it could separate the Cagneys and the Robinsons from the

George Brents. And with Julie, the nervous excitement that gave a snap to his speech also put a positive charge in his body. Like Cagney, he was an exceptionally mobile performer from the start of his screen career. These traits were orchestrated with his physical appearance to create a screen *persona* innately powerful in the sexual sense. What Warners saw immediately was that Garfield's impact was felt by both sexes. This was almost unique.

Few star actors were equally *liked* by men and women patrons. Clark Gable came close, but a part of the masculine audience persisted in despising Gable, perhaps only jealously. Gary Cooper won the ladies first, then the men fell into line; and with Spencer Tracy it was the opposite case. Cagney scored a sexual bulls-eye with a good part of the female audience, yet it was the men who held him as a champion. If John Garfield would not have a career of comparable length and breadth, nor be as hysterically worshiped, he nonetheless would command the entire patronage in the movie house perhaps as no one before him had done. Jack Warner and Hal Wallis realized this, but Julie himself did not. Had he sensed his own strength, he would not have fought to stay in *Juarez*.

When the shooting commenced, John Garfield was no longer on the cast roster. The Porfirio Diaz role was vacant, Julie learned, because the role was not of size or importance commensurate with his new status. Julie said he didn't care about the size of the role, or the billing. John Huston, one of the *Juarez* writers, had given him a script in which he'd recognized the kind of picture he said he came to Hollywood for —not like the crap they were giving him. Paul Muni was Julie's ally, demanding that he play the young Diaz, most of whose scenes would be shared with Muni's Benito Juarez. So the casting was reconfirmed.

Juarez was a super-A that expressed itself in platitudes close to Julie's heart. It espoused freedom for the little guy, especially freedom from foreign domination. Although the most practical of the major companies, Warners would indulge itself occasionally in an extraordinary pursuit of prestige—disastrously with *A Midsummer Night's Dream,* but successfully with the earlier Muni biographical films, *The Story of Louis Pasteur* and *The Life of Emile Zola*. All of these projects were administered not by Curtiz but by William Dieterle, a refugee from the German cinema with something of Curtiz's technical command, but a greater concern for dramatic truth. And Dieterle would direct *Juarez*.

The cast flowed over with top professionals. Besides Muni and Bette Davis (who had no scenes together) and the ubiquitous Claude Rains, there were Joseph Calleia and Henry O'Neill from Julie's early stage period, as well as Brian Aherne who, as Maximilian, had a long scene with Julie, confronting Diaz in prison. There was also Gale Sondergaard, who had come to Hollywood a few years before when her husband—Herbert Biberman, Julie's early mentor—started directing minor pictures. Miss Sondergaard only came along for the ride but soon emerged as perhaps the most serene villainess in film history, and certainly the most distinctive one. Also in the *Juarez* ensemble was the young Mexican, Gilbert Roland, a sincere actor disenchanted with the shape of his career. Later Julie would say Roland should have played Diaz.

In the daily production rushes Julie approximated the ideal —a likely handsome Mexican giving an able silent performance—but when the sound track came into play there was a discordant ring to Julie's Bronx-Mexican accent. Some thought was given to replacing him with another actor, but that was ruled out on practical considerations, one being the rising Garfield popularity. His name in the supporting cast would help at the box office, bringing in people who might otherwise scorn a serious biographical film. Those were also people who didn't care how Julie might sound, and would not be aware of his bad accent.

Showing up in his Diaz costume in the studio commissary, Julie was saluted by his Jewish writer friends as "the all-Mexican *schlemiel*." He parried their jibes, confident that *Juarez* would be a great picture. He said William Dieterle was his kind of director, and Dieterle's craving for authenticity enabled Julie to regain the dozen pounds he had lost by working in three films in quick order, and sometimes simultaneously. He was down to 140 pounds when he started shooting the prison scene that required him to eat and talk at the same time. Dieterle said the food *had* to be Mexican corn, and in midwinter it could not be found except at a University of California agricultural experimentation station. It cost four dollars an ear (plus mailing expenses) and Julie boasted of having eaten hundreds of dollars' worth of corn in almost one sitting. He was filmed eating Mexican corn over a three-day period, dozens of ears a day. He was gratified that it was all for art, but it would have been beneficial if Dieterle had been as knowledgeable and exacting about authenticity in Mexican speech.

Midway during the *Juarez* schedule, the Garfields returned briefly to New York on a summons from Dinah Garfinkle. Julie's father was thought to be mortally ill and wanted to see his son. The visit had a tonic effect on David Garfinkle, who was only beginning his long struggle with terminal cancer. Julie was shocked by the wasted man's appearance. His father told him not to worry, he was going to be all right; but Dinah confided that it was only "a matter of time." Julie's visit had an effect of perking up his father. David Garfinkle improved, and death did not come until 1942. Julie rhapsodized about life in southern California and about pictures as important as *Juarez*. This time the prodigal son had made good with his talents, and the fact that *everybody* recognized him was exhilarating for Julie, who had just given James Cagney and Spencer Tracy a keen battle in the New York Film Critics' balloting for the 1938 best performance citation.

And he had been nominated for an Academy Award. The Academy had settled on a distinction between leading and secondary roles, so Julie was up against less formidable competition, and upon his return to Hollywood he learned that he was favored to win. When Walter Brennan's standard character was cited for *Kentucky,* the thinking was that the film colony was not yet ready to honor a stage recruit with upstart tendencies. Julie gave one of his more convincing performances concealing his bitter disappointment, while the *Juarez* set crowded over with photographers and reporters paying homage to the certified best actress, Bette Davis, who had been *Jezebel* to the life.

In May, *Juarez* opened in major cities as a roadshow attraction—meaning payment in advance for reserved seats. The picture received a strange critical reaction, a mixture of huzzahs and disparagement. A generation later, it was both a consensus classic and a secular disgrace. *Juarez* was a curious hybrid of a Franz Werfel play and a minor novel that dealt only with Maximilian and Carlota; and it never lost the appearance of two vaguely related movies in one piece. Bette Davis hated it, and this showed through her Carlota, which contained fine moments nonetheless. Paul Muni's appearance seemed not so much a performance as a pose: the actor held his face rigid as though his superb Juarez makeup was about to crumble. The unexpected result was that the character of Maximilian threw the whole picture off balance; it was by far the most interesting thing about the film, partly through Brian Aherne's splendid performance. On one point there was general critical agreement: John Garfield's performance was the picture's worst, and was less than a disaster only because the part was not large. It wasn't entirely a matter of Bronx-Mexican speech. Perhaps any actor would have failed in a role with some of the worst idealistic dialogue written for the screen.

In the scene with Maximilian:

> MAXIMILIAN: If my generals are to be believed, you are the best soldier in Mexico.
> DIAZ: I do not fight for glory, but for liberty.

Or,

> MAXIMILIAN: I want your help in bringing peace to Mexico.
> DIAZ: Only one man can bring peace to Mexico—Benito Juarez.

And,

> MAXIMILIAN: Tell me more about Benito Juarez, that he inspires men such as yourself. Tell me, General Diaz.

DIAZ: He was President of Mexico, and ruled it justly and well, till traitors and land owners and speculators brought the French to depose him and put you in his place. You: Maximilian von Habsburg! And now he seeks to liberate his people, to educate, to uplift them through *democracy!*

One ironic press notice said John Garfield played with just the sort of gullible patriotism out of which future dictators—such as Porfirio Diaz—are born.

The *Juarez* debacle helped establish guidelines for the John Garfield screen image, in terms of what the actor should *not* do. The producers agreed that he would be exploited in contemporary roles exclusively—no more period stuff—and that they would reflect something of his own background. They decided that he was a solid talent, but a distinctly limited one that could be ideally tailored to the kind of pictures that were the studio's stock in trade.

There was, of course, the gangster picture, always urban in atmosphere; and always anchored by actors who, besides being vivid urban types, had strong, distinctive personalities —Cagney, Robinson, and the still-minor Bogart. But with expert command Warners also dispensed admirable social dramas by adhering to the melodramatic framework of the gangster film. This genre included some of the better Muni titles—*I Am a Fugitive from a Chain Gang; Black Fury*—but more characteristic were such entries as *They Won't Forget,* probing legal injustice and mob violence (a school teacher, convicted of murder but probably innocent, is lynched by a mob), and *The Black Legion,* depicting moral corruption in an organization obviously patterned after the Ku Klux Klan.

These were major projects, but produced without popular stars—indeed, without stars at all. Claude Rains (*They Won't Forget*) and Humphrey Bogart (*The Black Legion*) were at that time only featured players. Such pictures usually were somewhat more successful with the critics than with the public, verifying the wisdom of *Variety* that the hicks would nix any pix about the sticks—certainly if they were grim movies with uncompromised endings. Warners felt such pictures would have more commercial energy if they could focus on a popular star who would be acceptable to the public as a *loser*.

Cagney and Robinson were winners. They played mobsters or hoods who were pretty much in charge of things, directing the traffic, masters of circumstance and seldom its victims. Cagney at his most terrifying still exuded a breezy glamour, and Robinson, in spite of his tight-fisted gang ruler image, was almost comically vulnerable, say, to the wiles of a *femme fatale*. If in the Cagney or Robinson vehicle the hero would "get his" in the final reel, he remained a hero nevertheless— grinning through his last breath, or experiencing some righteous reawakening; and often, particularly in Cagney's case, not getting killed off at all, but emerging regenerated and able to lead a useful life.

John Garfield was just what the studio had been looking for—a common denominator for the social drama and the gangster melodrama. He was a creature of circumstance and its chosen victim—a born loser, like Mickey Borden. Millions of moviegoers could identify with this boy, as they had in *Four Daughters*. But that was a domestic drama, such as Warners would likely do only infrequently. The melodramas addressed themselves to the working-class audience that had made Warners a powerful company, and they would endure as the studio specialty. In them John Garfield could die and die again, with lamentation on his lips for the chance in life he never had. The people would never be able to get enough of that.

The Loyalists collapsed; Franco's forces laid Spain's republic to rest. The non-aggression pact between Soviet Russia and Hitler's Germany then proceeded to knock the props from the Marxist movement within the American intellectual community. There were new players on the international chessboard, and the controversy at home was involvement versus isolation. Yesterday's radicals now were defending the New Deal against reactionary elements—Father Coughlin, the America Firsters, and certainly the Bund meetings that tainted the cities with organized hatred.

When Julie arrived in Hollywood he was surprised and

fascinated by the proliferation of social-awareness organizations and proceeded to give his name and other forms of support to the liberal causes. That support was reinforced vehemently by Robbie, who worked for the Finnish Relief Fund and was on a committee urging the boycott of Japanese goods. (For her part, she refused to wear silk stockings and silk underwear.) The Garfields were assimilated socially by a left-wing fraternity dominated by writers, but also enlisting directors and a few actors. The circle included some of Julie's oldest acquaintances—the Brombergs, the Bibermans—and was loosely presided over by the director Lewis Milestone and his wife. This group was not likely to be mentioned in the fan magazines or the daily gossip columns, and this became a problem for the studio publicists, who wanted to get their boy planted in the journals but were confronted by Robbie Garfield's aversion to synthetic publicity. Soon the Garfields were in the "uncooperative" category. A publicist might set up a magazine layout and then lose it because Julie said he didn't want people coming to his house and prying into his private affairs. On such occasions he deferred to Robbie's wishes.

Julie was hardly one to scorn a little publicity, and sometimes he pursued it actively. Now he lobbied to write a guest newspaper column (ultimately ghostwritten by a studio publicist under the Garfield byline) in which he refried every movie-loving platitude ("The screen can bring entertainment to millions, the theatre only to a few."). He wouldn't refuse a publicity junket that included a choice assortment of Warner starlets, as when he went to Kansas for the premiere of *Dodge City* and challenged the picture's star, Errol Flynn, to a duel of an unusual nature.

Julie was gracious with reporters at the studio and at other public places. At Chasen's or the Brown Derby he was always talkative, enjoying himself and exuding a charm that could not conceal his vanity. He was addicted to poker and likely to get into a game at almost any party, forsaking Robbie for a smoke-filled room. Knowing few people in the community, Robbie would wait uncomfortably, trying to "fit in" until Julie won or lost. But Julie would pacify his wife with expensive surprises. Robbie was vulnerable to jewelry, and one of his first peace offerings was a large opal ring with an opulent filigree. He gave her luxurious pearl earrings, and it was typical of him not to notice that they were made for pierced ears. So Robbie had her ears pierced, rather than return the jewelry. But Home, Julie said, was a retreat. He and Robbie were anything but reclusive, but their guest list included few names from Julie's own studio. Julie was always a likely bet to bring guests home for dinner without warning, and Robbie learned to be prepared for that.

Robbie learned that it was necessary to keep the refrigerator well-stocked with food. Julie had a strong appetite, and said it always helped him not to have an empty stomach. But having had to cook for himself as a youngster turned him against kitchen chores, and he expected Robbie to do the cooking for him and for his guests, no matter how many.

Sometimes they hosted meetings of their political action groups, and soon they needed a larger place to live. With a friend's assistance, Robbie combed the Hollywood hills and San Fernando Valley, finding in the latter her "perfect place" —a white colonial two-story house, with a swimming pool and a white picket fence surrounding it. The owner was Helen Mack, a movie player Julie had known earlier, when she attended the Professional Children's School in New York. She had furnished the house in Early American, and Julie shared Robbie's enthusiasm.

To get to the Warner studio from his new residence, Julie regularly made a long drive to Burbank along a Ventura Boulevard that was never crowded in those days. His habit of picking up hitchhikers for company boomeranged when a youth stole some things from his car when Julie stopped to make a phone call. But for the first time since their wedding, the Garfields now occupied a real home.

Jack Warner still wanted a *Four Daughters* sequel. The New York office was demanding one, and John Garfield had to be in it. Julius and Philip Epstein got the assignment. Because Rosemary Lane was the only daughter not endowed with a man of her own in the fadeout of the first picture, the initial suggestion was to pair her off with a new Garfield paraphrase of Mickey Borden. The Epstein brothers, who abhorred any notion of a sequel, negotiated an uneasy compromise. They wouldn't write a sequel exactly, but would put together a script that could be filmed to look like one. There would be four sisters for the Lane girls and Gale Page to play, plus a good part for John Garfield who, this time, would lead off the billing. Searching through actually hundreds of story properties owned by the studio, both the previously-filmed and the never-touched, they came up with *Fly Away Home,* a good play that had starred Thomas Mitchell on Broadway and had been bought for Edward G. Robinson. It was a family play in which the wandering ne'er-do-well father turns up after a long absence, like Enoch Arden, and finds his wife not only divorced but about to remarry; whereupon he proceeds to charm their children, whom he has never known.

In the Epsteins' film adaptation, the prodigal father more nearly resembled Rip Van Winkle: the length of his absence becomes twenty years rather than the play's ten; and this renders him ever more mysterious and compelling to his "children" who, of course, are all fully grown, and all daughters (instead of mixed), and number four (instead of three). Claude Rains would play the father, and besides providing equivalent *Four Daughters* roles for John Garfield and Jeffrey Lynn, the Epsteins devised characters for Frank McHugh and Dick Foran, and again worked in May Robson as the family maid. Necessary additions were Fay Bainter as the mother and Donald Crisp as her businessman fiancé.

Julie liked the feel of this picture, and this time the enthusiasm was shared by Michael Curtiz, again the director. The Epsteins' script was a more cynical but a richer and truer transcript of life than *Four Daughters.* But they all loathed the title, as copious as it was inaccurate, but dictated by the front office: *Daughters Courageous.*

The Garfield role was built with star-part substance, and as an inside joke obviously alluding to *Juarez,* the Epsteins made his character Spanish—but a vagabond from the Bronx. And as a smart show of defiance, they fashioned in Gabriel Lopez a role that was a stunning contrast to Mickey Borden.

Lopez is a born survivor. So is Jim Masters (Claude Rains), cut of the same cloth and sharing Gabriel's wanderlust. They represent free-spirit nonconformity in an environment (the Masters household) of socially acceptable behavior. When Jim Masters realizes he cannot reclaim the wife he still loves but must yield her to the stuffed-shirt reliable, he conspires to prevent the marriage of daughter Buff to the unpredictable Gabriel, in whom he sees his own failings. Masters and Lopez leave town on the same train, seeking new adventure together. The Warner front office, missing the cynicism of the Epsteins' script, thought the ending the conventionally "happy" one that had been dictated; but many in the audience were disappointed, unless their taste was for the tragic.

Whereas Ann Lemp in *Four Daughters* married Mickey Borden out of pity, the Garfield character in *Daughters Courageous* simply dazzles the youngest daughter with the power of his raw sexuality. Gabriel's combination of toughness and innocence is established in a courtroom scene in which he is an accused con man who has tried to sell one of Moby Dick's teeth to the beach tourists. Admonished by the judge that Moby Dick is a creature of an author's imagination, Gabriel hesitates, looks around for support, and finding none, stammers, "Well, he made him seem very real to *me*." Buff Masters (Priscilla Lane) falls in love with this very different person. Physical seduction is implied not so much by the script as by the Garfield/Lopez persona. He really loves this girl; it is in his nature to *take* her. Not schooled in the niceties, he asks only to be accepted for what he is. Out on the town with Buff, he is broke but she gives him money to play the pinball machine. Then: "Buy me a beer?" Buff isn't certain: "Are you serious?" "I'm *thirsty*."

Certainly Gabriel could make Buff happy in a way the pallid young townsman played by Jeffrey Lynn could not—in the way the later Stanley Kowalski fulfills his Stella. But Gabriel cannot be held down: Buff must choose between her way of life and his. As it turns out, *Daughters Courageous* is the realistic alternative to a remarkably similar later play and movie, William Inge's *Picnic,* in which the girl leaves town with the drifter.

Julie rated *Daughters Courageous* as one of the half-dozen or so, among all his films, that were successfully realized, and preferred his Gabriel characterization to the Mickey Borden part because it was more varied. But the picture was not the major hit Warners had counted on. It had a favorable press and did well enough at the box office; but many moviegoers, so diet-regulated toward formula, were disappointed that it was not a true sequel. Meriting distinction as one of the American classics of the late thirties, it is all but forgotten today. Michael Curtiz liked to call *Daughters Courageous* "my obtuse masterpiece," and he meant obscure; but the picture is interestingly obtuse.

Comparing the receipts and also the reactions to *Daughters Courageous* with *They Made Me a Criminal,* Warners was more than ever convinced that its new star should be confined to the melodramatic film.

VII

From Rogues to Riches

After completing *Daughters Courageous* in May of 1939, Julie returned to New York for another visit with his ailing father and to keep his speaking engagement before the June graduating class at P.S. 45. Angelo Patri's creed was still in evidence: "Get the students to do for themselves." Art projects crowded the hallways, but Julie saw that the large plain school had barely changed since he left it.

The eighth grade graduates were thrilled by the presence of a famous alumnus, and it was standing room only in the small auditorium. As the featured speaker, Julie said once again that but for the influence of P.S. 45, he could have ended up dead or in jail, as so many of his early friends were. And he reaffirmed his love of the theatre over movies.

"I must be in the theatre, otherwise I'd die. I'm young and the theatre is a place to learn things, a place where the actor is sometimes allowed to take a chance. If it hadn't been for this school, I would never have found out. No matter where I am or where I live, I will always act. Acting is my life."

While Julie was savoring the students' applause, Angelo Patri appeared on the stage, dressed as always in bright green, and presented Julie with a leather case. "Here's something you forfeited seven or eight years ago," he said. "We feel it's coming to you now." Tears came into Garfield's eyes as he accepted the principal's gift.

After the ceremony Julie signed autographs and returned to the rented Cadillac he had parked on the street. The aerial, the lights, a door handle and some chrome stripping had been gouged off for souvenirs. Shaking his new leather case, he shouted to the kids that had followed him, "There's a point where adulation stops and highway robbery begins!" He hoped the parts would be returned. Nothing was, and the bill for his car rental was astronomical.

Julie was in awe of anybody's literary flair. He fancied that he was becoming a writer himself. His guest articles cropped up often in newspapers. He always consented to such requests, and particularly liked to write for the Brooklyn *Eagle* since it was "the paper most of my relatives read."

His fascination with writers amused and amazed the writers themselves. Their genuine fondness for him did not prevent their making Julie the butt of their diabolical wit. He was a hero worshipper by nature, but in his view writers were much bigger than life. He became friendly with John Steinbeck and William Saroyan. Among screenwriters, Harry Kurnitz and Herman Mankiewicz were buoyant drinking acquaintances, and both could rival Oscar Levant for the cruelly funny squelch. But Julie's basic fraternity was with the Warner contract writers—daily at table, and occasionally in their homes.

The Warner commissary was the studio's social hub and people gravitated toward their own kind—technicians to technicians, actors to actors, and so on. But Julie dined with the writers, whose acid sprays at his expense did not diminish his appetite for their company. His naiveté and gullibility (acknowledged in less euphemistic terms by his antagonists) were everyone's joking matter.

Phil Epstein, an accomplished mimic (especially in Jewish dialect), never tired of generating diabolic comedy at Julie's expense. He would get Julie on the telephone at home, usually to issue some kind of preposterous proposition; yet Julie rose to the bait on every occasion. Once a cadre of Warner writers had to struggle to stifle their laughter while Phil Epstein toyed with Julie by remote control, pretending to be a stranger to southern California—one who had been advised by "liberal connections in the East" to seek John Garfield's aid.

"Mistah Garfield, my friends tell me you can advise me on getting a nice hotel but one that is not, you understand, too expensive?" Julie enumerated some respectable hotels that were not the prohibitively luxurious ones, but all seemed much too extravagant for the distressed caller. Julie named some less elegant apartments, but the poor fellow on the other end of the line still felt they were out of reach "for a man with a large family with him." He became more plaintive, working for (and getting) the sympathy of John Garfield, who was flattered that those "liberal contacts in the East" held him in such esteem. But no, Julie did not know of any close friends who might be temporarily out of town, whose houses could be occupied on a gratis basis by a family that grew larger by the minute.

"Mistah Garfield, my friends tell me you have a very nice house that is perhaps not very crowded." Julie said yes, it was a nice house; he and Robbie were very proud of it. The man had heard that Robbie was very nice, too, and was also spoken of highly by the liberal interests. He would like to meet her. "Mistah Garfield, may I bring my family to your house for only a few days? We will be no trouble, and we'll help with the housework. My friends in the East say John Garfield is one person that will never let down a liberal comrade."

Warner writers were a distinct breed. The argot of the fast-paced movie screen was an American sublanguage of their invention, and they had more autonomy than writers at other studios. A Warner director might throw the script away; but while it was being written, the author was his own man. They put in regular hours at the studio because Jack Warner demanded it, but their kind of work was practically impossible in the ambiance of the studio, so they socialized on the lot, and wrote their scripts at home.

If Julie approached a quorum of studio writers with "Fellas, let's have ourselves a real intellectual discussion," Phil Epstein would say, "Sounds fine, but who's going to represent *you?*" His friendly tormenters, besides the Epstein twins, were Casey Robinson, Jerry Wald, Norman Reilly Raine, Robert Buckner, Richard Macaulay, and one of Julie's devoted friends in years to come, Robert Rossen. Politically they were on the Left and furnished Julie with liberal platitudes and epigrams that would sustain him in cocktail-hour conversation. Julie was a squirrel hoarding vagrant bits of opinion, and one writer said, "That dumb kid has more ideas about everything than Father Barber."

The writers tripped Julie on his own fraudulence, especially on literary matters. He pretended to have read *everything,* and would bluff his way in table talk—on Stendhal, say—until through devious questions the writers proved Julie's total ignorance of Stendhal's work. Julie coveted association with the literati in the belief that their sophistication would surely rub off onto him.

Malapropisms were his undoing, but a delight to his listeners: Julie described a studio executive as a congenial idiot, and Bob Rossen corrected him. "The word's *congenital,* Julie. A congenial idiot is what *you* are." Julie would say obsolescence for absolution, or credos when he meant kudos. But beneath the pretense there was genuine thirst and the writers sensed this.

They also sensed the personal magnetism that had captured the nation's moviegoers, and every Warner author wanted to write screenplays for Garfield. His first movie performance had helped move Julie Epstein from the second line of filmwriters into the front rank. Screenwriter Seton Miller said Garfield was a talent you didn't write down to—you did your best to write up to it. And Bob Rossen said that just knowing Julie was going to play a part inspired a writer to create better dialogue.

The writers tolerated Julie's pretense and his tendency toward prevarication because his personality was as beguiling as any con man's, and also because they thought he was on the verge of becoming the top dramatic actor in Hollywood. And oh, how he wanted to believe them!

In the fall of 1939 Warners splashed color spreads featuring a new lineup of sixteen stars (including some with questionable credentials) in the trade publications. New but of established background were Miriam Hopkins, Merle Oberon, and George Raft; and newly certified as stars were Ann Sheridan, Jeffrey Lynn, and the late-blooming Humphrey Bogart. Among the new featured players of whom much was expected were Geraldine Fitzgerald, Joan Leslie, Brenda Marshall, Anthony Quinn, and a pudgy comedian named Jackie C. Gleason.

The stars were ranked so precisely that Julie knew exactly where he stood with his employers; he was number five among the men, and eighth overall. The lineup: Muni, Flynn, Cagney, Davis, Robinson, Hopkins, Oberon, Garfield, deHavilland, Raft, Pat O'Brien, Priscilla Lane, George Brent, Bogart, Lynn, and Sheridan. The three veteran actors ranked above Garfield were all within a few years of completing their Warner contracts, and none intended to renew. Errol Flynn usually adorned a different sort of picture, so Garfield symbolized the continuity of Warner melodramatics.

The trade display featured some future Warner films, including a still of Garfield and his Priscilla, hands linked and running (apparently for their lives, but possibly from bad reviews), in *Dust Be My Destiny.* Warners had bought two Jerome Odlum novels, intending both as Garfield vehicles. *Dust Be My Destiny,* a tragedy of fugitive innocence, was to follow the first Odlum property—*Each Dawn I Die,* a more pretentious elaboration on the *Blackwell's Island* theme of the honest reporter railroaded to prison. The plan was for Garfield to costar with James Cagney, and since the Group Theatre people had rated Cagney the best actor in pictures (and had lobbied to return him to the stage), the prospect pleased Julie. But then Warners signed George Raft, once a popular gangster star despite only marginal ability; and in the campaign to restore him, they cast Raft as the hood kingpin and switched Cagney to the reporter role that Julie was to have played. Once again he was yanked from a picture in which Jane Bryan was the leading lady.

Garfield and Cagney would never make a picture together after all. Perhaps more strangely, they would never become friendly. They saw one another across the lot or at various studio functions; but in their life-styles, political thinking, and private behavior, they had little in common. The versatile and more widely liked Cagney was not likely to put in a good word for Julie, professionally or otherwise.

The turn of events left Julie grumbling; he had even suc-

ceeded in getting Alan Baxter, the one-time Group actor, cast
as the primary villain in *Each Dawn I Die*—his best part in
years. He was less successful in getting Margot Stevenson, a
New York actress-friend, cast opposite him in *Dust Be My
Destiny,* which became his next project. The studio signed
Miss Stevenson to a contract but put her to work in another
picture, possibly worried that Julie's interest in her was more
than professional. Once again Priscilla Lane was the girl, and
Bob Rossen whipped the established Garfield and Lane images
into a strong social statement in his first pass at the *Dust Be
My Destiny* screenplay. Julie was plain Joe Bell, who ran off
with Mabel, daughter of the keeper at a work farm where Joe
was doing time; then was hunted down as the keeper's suspected murderer. The ending called for Joe and Mabel to be
shot to death. But because a forthright tragic resolution had
been the commercial undoing of a recent and similar picture—
Fritz Lang's *You Only Live Once*—Warners decided to give
Dust Be My Destiny a happy ending. Rossen refused to write
one, but other minds conspired an end-of-picture revelation
that Mabel's father died of heart failure after all, thereby setting Joe and Mabel free.

Julie thought the picture dramatically sloppy. The director,
Lewis Seiler, was proficient in terms of action for its own sake
but had little interest in and less mastery of what Julie called
personal drama. The critics gave *Dust Be My Destiny* a sound
whipping and tore into the cliché manifestations of what they
now recognized as the standard Garfield screen character. Yet
Warners was satisfied with the picture's commercial return
and Julie heard that the studio planned to continue his tandem
casting with Priscilla Lane for perhaps half of his assignments.
Together they were assigned to *The Roaring Twenties;* and
while Julie could moan that it was yet another melodrama, it
promised to be special for its kind, with the cast listing Cagney
and Bogart. Bob Rossen's script called for both of the veteran
toughies to be wiped out in the carnage of the conclusion, with
Garfield still alive to get the girl. Then Rossen reported that
he had instructions to rewrite Julie's part for Jeffrey Lynn to
play. The new Garfield assignment was called *Invisible Stripes,*

with Julie cast in a colorless subordinate role as George Raft's younger brother. The bloom was off the Hollywood rose. Julie said he wouldn't do *Invisible Stripes.*

He said he wanted to play characters of different types. Didn't the studio ever do any comedies? A studio spokesman said no, he didn't have to make a picture if he didn't want to, but the studio didn't have to pay him, either. And John Garfield was taken off salary.

In accepting his first of many suspensions, Julie joined a roster of distinguished Warner dissidents. Cagney, Davis, Flynn, deHavilland: often they accepted their chores only grudgingly, but at other times they would not compromise their professional decency. When Bette Davis, with her first Oscar under wing, was summoned to dress up a thing called *God's Country and the Woman,* she refused flatly and was replaced by an obscurity named Beverly Roberts.

Suspensions were a seldom thing at 20th Century-Fox, rare at M-G-M, and almost never occurred at Paramount; but at Warners they were commonplace. The Warner actors earned their salaries on relative merit, but they were the most effectively pigeonholed actors in town. However reluctantly, they were true to type. Jack Warner, Hal Wallis, and the satellite producers—Henry Blanke, David Lewis, Robert Lord, Robert Fellows—honestly believed they knew what was best for their chattels. "If we let *them* cast the pictures," Steve Trilling said of the actors, "we wouldn't have a single box office star except Rin-Tin-Tin, who never doubted us."

When Warners placed an actor on suspension, a characteristic ruse was to offer the embattled player another property that was distinctly inferior to the one he had rejected. There was no intention of casting a valuable player in an obviously weak vehicle. But Julie was gullible, and when they offered him *The Angels Wash Their Faces* he took them at their word. Julie scanned the script (a sequel, unimaginatively titled, to Cagney's socko gangster picture *Angels With Dirty Faces*) and found he would be doing straight-man stuff to the Dead End Kids and getting in an occasional clinch with Ann

Sheridan. He said he'd rather stay on suspension and play tennis.

His angry discontent had been incited not so much by his Warner assignments as by the studio's refusal to loan him to Columbia for the *Golden Boy* film. With Rouben Mamoulian directing and Barbara Stanwyck cast as Lorna Moon, *Golden Boy* was Columbia's prestige venture of the season, and an industry-wide search was initiated for an "unknown" to play the title role. Julie heard that it was mostly a publicity gimmick—that Columbia would like very much to have Garfield do the part that may have actually been written for him. Still smarting from Clurman's snub two years earlier, Julie ached for the screen assignment and got the Lyons agency working toward a deal. Flesh-trading was a favorite studio pastime, and Warners cast covetous glances at Columbia's Jean Arthur, who could nicely accommodate the *No Time for Comedy* picture Warners planned. Warners would have settled for a one-for-one exchange, but Columbia was said to be holding out for other concessions and no deal emerged. Columbia went with an unknown player after all, and a considerably younger one—William Holden, whose screen career began as Joe Bonaparte. But Julie thought Warners could have been more persuasive with a little effort.

His suspension ran into weeks. *Invisible Stripes* was reoffered, but he angrily said, "Get Bill Holden to do it"; and Julie was surprised indeed when Holden was borrowed from Columbia to play George Raft's kid brother. (Not long afterward Julie got himself into the running for the male lead in the *Our Town* film at RKO and again lost out to Holden, who was much the better choice.) The next suggestion was a remake of *20,000 Years in Sing Sing,* but Julie said he'd had his fill of jailbirds: "Parole me!"

He rather favored another projected remake. Warners wanted Julie to take the male lead in its second version of the play *Life Begins,* to be retitled *A Child Is Born.* It was a grim thing but promised a change of pace, and Julie was fairly dazzled by the leading lady. She was the lovely Geraldine Fitzgerald, whose studio service had begun nicely in Bette Davis's

Dark Victory, and the new picture was calculated to raise her to stardom. Julie agreed to the assignment, partly because Rossen was writing the script. But Rossen was aghast. "Sure, they'll give you first billing to protect the investment, but the girl has all the lines. You're better off taking the Sing Sing thing." So Julie reneged, and almost inevitably, Jeffrey Lynn became Miss Fitzgerald's leading man.

Julie ran off a print of *20,000 Years in Sing Sing,* the 1933 Curtiz film with Spencer Tracy and Bette Davis, and agreed to do it, "provided you don't change the ending." In the original, Tracy went to the electric chair to cover for Davis, who had shot and killed the real villain—defending Tracy, to be sure. The Hays office accepted that ending only because the Tracy character was a convicted murderer in the first place, although a reformed one, and not on Death Row. Warners had no intention of altering the ending, so Julie was taken off suspension. The title for the remake became *The Castle on the Hudson.*

Julie was warned that his performance would be compared with Tracy's. Such a prospect could frighten many a young actor and Julie was determined not to copy the Tracy version. In *20,000 Years in Sing Sing,* Tracy played a rather affable thug who managed a weak little smile at his unhappy conclusion. Julie chose to face the chair with a steely defiance, as if he could discourage the electric current with gritted teeth. The picture was produced with some care (Anatole Litvak directing in a lean, forceful style) and Julie plotted his characterization under the precepts of the Stanislavsky method. He was disappointed that the critics tended to dismiss the picture and say Garfield was only going through the motions—dispensing a performance as he would a piece of pie at the Automat. But the paradox held: the picture did good business and reaffirmed the Garfield magnetism. His stardom was no longer tentative.

Julie desired growth as a performer above anything else, but with each new variation on what was essentially a single role, Warners seemed bent on determining the limitations of his talent rather than investigating its farthest horizon. He felt challenged to avoid becoming an anthology of personal mannerisms. He needed the kind of intense study the Group had offered, and a chance to prepare a role thoroughly, even to become lost in it. He enlisted Joe Bromberg's help in working out a complete mythology for a character to be portrayed. Some of the players he worked with were derisive of Julie's method, and Alan Hale in *Dust Be My Destiny* revived "the Group" as a personal nickname for Julie. He parried their barbs good-naturedly, but dissatisfaction was grinding into him. Julie was at odds with himself; he wasn't at all certain that he *liked* making movies, but it was obvious enough that he enjoyed being a movie 'star.

On stage, Julie sensed an audience that dwelled out there in a blackness, and *they* peaked his nervous vitality. But on a movie set he might be photographed while responding to lines fed by an off-camera girl wearing slacks; and at other times he could not muster his best concentration while the camera and the hot klieg lights trained on him, with people moseying about on the perimeter of the set.

The conflict often made him tense in a way that didn't help his relationship with Robbie, although she was sympathetic. She did not object to his going on suspension at a loss of salary. Sometimes she even advised it, and he sought her counsel in professional matters. There was no love lost between Robbie Garfield and Julie's Hollywood employers. Julie still advertised Robbie as his severest critic, and perhaps she had always been that; but their closest friends observed that Julie's career was becoming their only mutual interest, where in another day they had shared many other avenues.

The Garfields were living well. Money was going into the bank. They were buying plenty of books for Robbie to read and Julie to *try* to read. Robbie had bookshelves built into every room in their house, including the bathroom. Julie liked to collect books, but Robbie was the real reader, whose practice included reading in Hebrew. She sought to teach Julie, who was willing to consider reading in Hebrew for the literary content but was repelled by memories of his father's religious posturing and said he wanted no part of any formal religion in any language.

The inevitable "big break": the young Garfield as the office boy of the *Counsellor-at-Law* Chicago production, with Otto Kruger in the title role.

Perhaps the Group Theatre's finest hour: Clifford Odets's *Awake and Sing* (1935) featuring, from left, Garfield, Morris Carnovsky, Stella Adler, J. Edward Bromberg, Art Smith, Luther Adler and Sanford Meisner.

The Group Theatre at Pinebrook Camp, Connecticut, in the summer of 1936. Julie is in the second row behind Bob Lewis, who cradles the Garfield legs. Others in the front row from left: Lee Strasberg, Sanford Meisner, and Harold Clurman. Elia Kazan is seated directly behind Garfield. Robbie Garfield is in the back row with a flower in her hair.

Garfield and Phoebe Brand (above left), enacting brother and sister in *Awake and Sing*, were a "team" in three Group productions. A serious moment for Katherine Locke and Garfield (above right), in the successful romantic comedy of 1937, *Having Wonderful Time*.

Four Daughters (1938). Garfield's notable screen debut, with Priscilla Lane and May Robson.

They Made Me a Criminal (1939). Garfield in a scene with Billy Halop, in the picture that formulated the image of the sympathetic fugitive.

Blackwell's Island (1939). Rosemary Lane visits Garfield in the Big House.

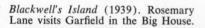

Juarez (1939). The all-Mexican *schlemiel:* Garfield as Porfirio Diaz.

Daughters Courageous (1939). Claude Rains and Garfield act brilliantly together in an unjustly neglected Curtiz film.

The Castle on the Hudson (1940). A Sing Sing inmate scorns his new wardrobe.

Saturday's Children (1940). A domesticated Garfield exchanges sympathy with Roscoe Karns.

Garfield returns briefly to Broadway as a rather unusual Angel of Death in *Heavenly Express* (1940), with Harry Carey and Aline MacMahon.

Flowing Gold (1940). Garfield's helpful attempt to rehabilitate Frances Farmer's troubled life and career.

The Sea Wolf (1941). A classic of its kind, teamin Garfield with two players h admired both professionall and personally—Ida Lupin and Edward G. Robinson.

Tortilla Flat (1942) M-G-M's conception o Steinbeckian lowlifes: Spencer Tracy, Hedy Lamarr and John Garfield.

Air Force (1943). Garfield, George Tobias, Harry Carey, Ray Montgomery and a B-17 as their leading lady.

The Fallen Sparrow (1943). Sinister doings with Walter Slezak and Maureen O'Hara.

Pride of the Marines (1945) splendid Garfield performance Marine hero Al Schmid.

The Postman Always Rings T (1946). Cecil Kellaway introd Garfield to his wife (Turner). You figure out the

Nobody Lives Forever (1946). Perhaps Garfield and Geraldine Fitzgerald are toasting their freedom from Warner Brothers, after eight years apiece.

Humoresque (1946). While Garfield fiddles, Oscar Levant plays piano and Joan Crawford—seated immediately behind Levant—falls in love.

Body and Soul (1947). Contrasting scenes from the definitive Garfield film: at table with Joseph Pevney, Anne Revere and Lilli Palmer; and in the ring with Canada Lee, who's just hit the canvas.

Gentleman's Agreement (1947). Garfield and Celeste Holm in Elia Kazan's Oscar-winning film. A generation later, their performances are the picture's best.

We Were Strangers (1949). Garfield is revolting in South America with Jennifer Jones.

Under My Skin (1950). ●
field and Orley Lindgren
father and son in a Heming
story.

The Breaking Point (1⁇
With Juano Hernandez i▸
Have and Have Not as Her
way wrote it.

Garfield as the young Peer Gynt with Mildred Dunnock, and as the aged Peer, with Karl Malden in the 1951 Broadway offering of Ibsen's classic.

He Ran All the Way (1951). Shelley Winters watches him with yearning pity in the grim scene that closes the Garfield screen career.

The *Golden Boy* revival in 1952: Garfield and Lee J. Cobb.

Although material worries were behind them, both Robbie and Julie sensed that the days when they were dowdy-poor had been happier. Professional satisfaction often acted as a barometer for marital bliss, and it also worked the other way. The frustration of Warner servitude began to tell. If he was secure in a role and stimulated by it, he more nearly approximated the devoted husband, the beaming father, and the naturally attentive male who was, besides, a creature of engaging good humor. But now he was seldom inspired by his workaday labors.

He was smoking three packs of cigarettes a day and riding a little heavy on the Scotch. He did not go to seed physically because tennis and handball kept him in solid trim at 150 pounds—ample for his short, stocky frame. He got plenty of exercise, but not enough rest.

The work had turned out to be harder than anything he'd expected. He said the one thing an actor on the stage knew least about was how grueling a screen actor's life could be— and at Warners, very often *was*. (Joan Blondell once reported that she made twenty-seven films in a thirty-two month period, six days a week without any kind of break.) Julie worked from September, 1938, until August, 1939, without a vacation or even a brief furlough, always on time for the 6:30 morning call, every day except Sunday. His reward was suspension from salary for refusing to make inferior movies.

Even while Julie was sitting out his first suspension, the old Warner magic created a strong illusion of a working John Garfield. The Epstein twins finally capitulated to the front office demand for a sequel to *Four Daughters,* and the inevitable *Four Wives* also "featured" John Garfield merely by means of repeating his Mickey Borden footage out of *Four Daughters,* in a flashback sequence. During the 1939 Christmas season, many a marquee advertised "John Garfield in *Four Wives"* ("Only *four?* And whose?" said Oscar Levant), and at that time nobody knew anything about residuals.

Actors, being no different from other people, found ways to drown despair. Some could do it with booze, others by making violence. Julie's opiate was sex. It was nothing more, he said, than a nasty habit, much like smoking; and it meant no more to him than that. It was just a thing he *did*. But he smoked in the open, in the presence of wife and family and friends. The other habit he tried to keep private, like an adolescent boy in a clothes closet. Sometimes he was a good enough actor to bring off innocence with conviction, or to earn forgiveness with a fervent promise to reform. But if he could deceive Robbie even for a while, he did not deceive himself. Guilt ground into him, but he was helpless. Sex was a necessary compensation for other failings.

He was suspended again. *Flight Angels* wasn't a melodrama, but Julie decided it wasn't much of anything else either, and said no. He sacrificed his salary for a few weeks and then took his problems to Henry Blanke, the Warner producer whom he trusted most.

"Know what they thought of me on the stage? That I was a so-so dramatic actor, not really smart enough, but a hell of a comic. Harold Clurman thought that. And Lee Strasberg. Get a part that needed the funny juice squeezed out of it, they asked me first. I've made eight or nine pictures and haven't cracked a joke yet!"

Blanke said the trouble was that Julie was too successful as a tough. If he was not in the top ten at the box office, he was pretty much a commercial sure thing nonetheless. "What you have to do is come a cropper two or three times. Fail at the ticket office as a hood, then they'll let you do comedy."

Julie said that if Warners could give Edward G. Robinson an essentially comic picture without causing the actor to abandon his standard character (as in *Brother Orchid,* with mobster Robinson masquerading as a monk in the monastery he's pegged as a hideout), and if Jimmy Cagney could work so much rich comedy into his every picture no matter how sinister . . . well, why couldn't John Garfield? Blanke said the difference was that Robinson and Cagney weren't fate's whipping boy. Julie thought it possible that fate's whipping boy could be put into a realistic situation out of which some natural comedy could grow freely. "I need three dimensions and right now I've got only two . . . but I'm working toward just one."

According to Henry Blanke, neither Warner nor Wallis was without sympathy toward Julie—they were only trying to protect the studio's investment in him. But time on suspension helped nobody, and Warners preferred a contented Garfield to an inactive one. They invited Julie to look over the inventory of scheduled projects. Within certain boundaries, he could choose the picture and role that would remove him from the suspended list.

Julie was only vaguely familiar with *Saturday's Children,* which Warners already had filmed twice without notable result. But the source play was by Julie's eminent good friend, Maxwell Anderson; and in the twenties it had been warmly received featuring the young Ruth Gordon. Now it was again on Henry Blanke's production schedule, this time as a proper vehicle for elevating the studio's best ingenue, Jane Bryan, to full stardom. The male lead had not been cast.

"It has *now,*" Julie said, on learning that the Epstein brothers were doing the screenplay. They warned him not to appear overeager. His doing the part should be *their* idea, and Julie should have Warners believing he was doing them a favor—giving grudging assent to what was secretly his own idea. While Julie was playing this old studio game with the executives, the Epsteins started building the male role to scope equal or better than the girl's. Soon Julie was being *begged* by his employers to accept *Saturday's Children:* he could take costar billing above Jane Bryan, while the studio prepared a really *good* vehicle for him. Julie hemmed and hawed and "reluctantly" consented, saying it would be nice to finally work with Jane Bryan after so many false starts, including his stint in *The Sisters* that hit the cutting room floor.

Then Jane Bryan quit the movies. She wanted to marry and have babies, and her husband-to-be didn't want her to go on acting in pictures.

"But she can't just quit," Julie said. "She's on a contract."

"You sound like the old man," a studio worker said. "Sure Jane can quit. She's breaking her contract. She don't need the money. Sometimes it means giving something up, like a little money . . . but *anyone* can always just quit."

Warners could not dissuade Jane Bryan, whose career offered the sharpest contrast to Julie's meteor-like ascendance. She had been groomed for stardom slowly and cautiously over several years, but at twenty-two she knew what she wanted. Soon she would be almost completely forgotten by the moviegoers, and would never pursue the "comeback" that is customary for the retiring ingenue. Rarely does a young film star give up the pinnacle at the moment of attaining it, although in the same season another newly certified star—20th Century-Fox's Andrea Leeds—also walked out of pictures and never came back.

Jane Bryan's departure almost canceled *Saturday's Children*. Edmund Goulding, a director skilled at shaping star vehicles for actresses, was given another assignment. But in their anxiety to get Garfield back before the cameras, Warners gave Julie extraordinary license to locate his own costar, and he also conspired with the Epsteins to pick the director.

"I suppose they were going to put Priscilla in the picture," Julie wrote Clifford Odets, "and that would have been all right, except they would start jamming her three sisters into the frame, and that wouldn't be all right." He got the studio to borrow Anne Shirley from RKO. She was a bright girl whom he'd met socially: her politics were liberal.

Julie and the brothers Epstein plumped for the unheralded Vincent Sherman to direct. Sherman, who had acted with Julie in the Chicago company of *Counsellor-at-Law* and in the Group's *Paradise Lost* a few years later, had come to Warners as a dialogue director for the minor efforts packaged by Bryan Foy. When a couple of Bogart B's came off the assembly line with more sheen than they required, they were released as major features and sent Bogart's stock rising. Hal Wallis decided to give Sherman a full shot as director for another one with Bogie, and *The Return of Dr. X* emerged a sleeper. So Sherman had come into favor just when *Saturday's Children* advertised a vacancy. Getting Vincent Sherman slotted made the picture one of Julie's happiest experiences at Warner Brothers.

Claude Rains took the third starring role, as the girl's father; and of Vincent Sherman, Rains said, "This man is precious . . . one of the best directors of actors I've worked with." (Four years later, in another script by the Epsteins, Rains would be a magnificent *Mr. Skeffington* opposite Bette Davis, with Sherman directing.) Julie, too, said he had been directed by foreigners and by studio hacks, but not before by anybody who saw a moviemaking problem from the actor's point of view.

Sherman respected Julie's method of preparing for a role, and before turning on the camera, they thoroughly dissected the character of Rims Rosson—an adventurer trapped into marriage and stifled by its confinement, despite his love for the perky, optimistic Bobby. *Saturday's Children* was shaped for fewer camera settings and longer takes than were customary, but James Wong Howe was an important collaborator with a fluid camera: actors moved in and out of the frame and the scene had dramatic continuity, but a pressing tempo of action, for the frame itself was mobile.

Years later, Julie Epstein would reflect that in *Saturday's Children* Garfield more nearly played his real self than in any other film: Rims was an awkward, gullible, likable fellow—an idealist and a dreamer, but unsure of himself, and a loser. The performance was one of which Garfield himself would always be proud, free of the identifiable mannerisms. Julie's Rims had his own way of talking, and was a more literate sort than the recent run of Garfield jailbirds; it was a restrained characterization that suggested a power to explode. To make the character more distinctive, Julie decided to wear glasses. James Agee thought this imparted a reality to Garfield's innate sexiness.

When *Saturday's Children* approached completion of production earlier than scheduled and therefore under budget, Vincent Sherman was warned to slow things down: if you undercut the budget, it would be smaller next time. So the

Epsteins pretended to "pad" the script and Sherman went along with a time-consuming gag that was engineered at Julie's expense. In order to express the intimate nature of newlyweds, they decided to add a scene in which Bobby would give Rims a bath—a very affectionate sort of bath, in a tub. That way, they told Julie, a lot of people in the audience could identify with the young couple, and even get aroused in a way that would enhance their interest in the drama. A bathtub set was rigged up; and in what John Garfield assumed could be only a coincidence, that was the day the publicity department lured a battery of reporters to the studio to cover the *Saturday's Children* filming.

Affecting serious dedication, Julie did not complain. He spent the working day taking and retaking the bathing scene, and carrying on a continuing interview with the gentlemen of the press between takes. Ostensibly he was naked, wearing only a brief swim suit that was obscured by the porcelain tub. Even when Julie was confident the scene had gone well, something would have been wrong—they'd have to try it over. They had to get the bath scene *just right*. The reporters were most attentive as, time and again, Anne Shirley's hand dipped the washcloth below the waterline into the area where imagination had to rule. Retakes would be in order because Anne Shirley was blushing too obviously, or because Julie was. As the day wore on, Julie began to sense the amusement of his coworkers. After yet another session in the bathtub, he said, "Well, something was wrong with the scene, but I don't know what. Maybe this time there was no film in the camera." That broke everybody up: James Wong Howe affirmed that not a foot of film had been exposed all day. And no bathtub scene graced the final print of *Saturday's Children*.

VIII

Clobbering Those Nazis and Nips

In *The Fervent Years* Harold Clurman wrote that in the summer of 1932, "Albert Bein was bitterly unhappy because his *Heavenly Express* seemed more of a good notion to me than a producible play." Eight years later it may have been even less a good notion. Time had passed it by; it was pre-Odetsian revolutionary drama, except it was fantasy; and it stated an early-thirties sociology in hoarse, heavy voice. But over the years it was always in the inventory of "future" Group productions, and the role of the ghostly Overland Kid was one that long had intrigued Julie. In 1940, the Group could endorse any idea that would restore the exploitable Garfield name to its roster.

The Group was learning that solidarity isn't forever. It had become a fragmented body, and even among its patriots there was belief that the company had crested with the Odets plays and could never regain that pinnacle. *Heavenly Express* was a desperate move to recapture a lost grandeur. During the *Saturday's Children* filming, Julie agreed to invoke the time-off clause he had fought for in his contract, and he returned to the theatre in the Group's good graces.

He promised to say only nice things about Hollywood and Warner Brothers during the six-month absence he planned. Instead, *Heavenly Express* ran only three weeks. No disgrace, it was a total failure nonetheless. Albert Bein, who may have had more imagination than talent, had devised a play about a train ride into the great unknown. It was similar in content, if not in style, to the British seagoing play *Outward Bound,* whose inimitable Mrs. Midget might have found the passengers on the heavenly express struck all of an 'eap by an overdose of leftist propaganda.

Julie played the heavenly ghost of the Overland Kid, dead for twenty years and now functioning as "advance ticket taker representing the Almighty Vagabond." He strummed a mandolin and sang radical-minded ballads, perhaps less eloquently than a troubador named Burl Ives, who was one of the passengers. *Heavenly Express* rode the rails in counterpoint to the Group's death rattle. It was not an official Group production but was more than a stepchild—sort of a bastard child with some of the family's good traits, but clearly cursed. Kermit Bloomgarden, the Group's business manager, produced it. Bob Lewis directed, and about half the cast were Group regulars— Art Smith, Philip Loeb, Russell Collins, Curt Conway, and Will Lee. Also in the mix were Aline MacMahon, another returnee from films; Harry Carey, the spirit of movies past; and Nicholas Conte, the Richard of movies yet to come.

Julie's colorful performance was enriched by the lively sense of comedy he had been aching to set free, but even Morris Carnovsky, who was no advocate of type-casting, told Julie he was out of his element. John Mason Brown was one critic in agreement with that assessment, although the press treated Julie kindly as a rule. Brooks Atkinson said, "Mr. Garfield plays with a glow of youth and a touch of Ariel . . . altogether the most winning angel of death in the theatre."

The Group had not had a commercial success since *Golden Boy,* and a new Odets play called *Night Music* was a failure concurrent with *Heavenly Express,* and the Group's dying gasp. In its cast was a young actress named Bette Grayson, who became the second Mrs. Odets. Broke and in hock, they lived in defiant splendor on Beekman Place; and Julie forgot his own disappointment in an effort to revive Odets with the therapy of friendship. In the East with an unexpected amount of time on his hands, Julie became an easy touch for addressing anti-Nazi and anti-Japan demonstrations, and he incited some of the old fervor in the brooding Odets.

Julie said the failure of *Heavenly Express* did not cut into him so deeply. He was stimulated just to be on stage again, and he said he would be returning to New York regularly. He was redeemed by the film of *Saturday's Children,* in which his performance earned the admiration even of his most exacting Group-based critics. It opened in New York on the very week that *Heavenly Express* closed, and gave Julie the best movie notices he had gathered since *Four Daughters,* twenty months and eight pictures earlier.

Upon their return from New York, John and Robbie Garfield became once again the film colony's least known, least written about couple. Robbie wanted it that way. With small effort they could have had the fan magazine treatment regularly—for Julie's popularity, after the inevitable leveling off, held steady. He had tried handling his own fan mail, but three to four thousand letters every week persuaded him that the studio services were indispensable. It also convinced him that his popularity with the main body of moviegoers rested very little on how many interviews he granted or how many times he was photographed, here and there, with or without Robbie.

As time went by, he was increasingly here and there without Robbie. She did not participate in studio affairs except when she spoke her mind about a movie Julie should or should not make. If Julie's opinion of Warner Brothers was not high, Robbie's was clearly lower. And Julie said candidly that he wished Robbie could be compromised just a little.

Robbie had many unjoyful experiences with columnists and other members of the press. Dutifully functioning as the popular star's anonymous wife no doubt had its wearying effect, as when Leonard and Sylvia Lyons were Sunday guests of the Garfields. Sylvia wanted to take some pictures, and Julie took Kathy on his lap and he called for Robbie to get into the picture, too. But Sylvia moved Robbie out of the camera range, explaining that she wanted a picture of just John Garfield and his daughter together, and would take some full family shots later. The visit wore on; no family picture was taken.

They were not very alike. Robbie's friends found her generous, honest, and mature; Julie was childishly generous and compulsively dishonest, and above all naive. Robbie accepted things at face value and was reluctant to give trust; Julie trusted everybody and usually overrated them as well. Their friends admired and respected Robbie for her strength, and loved Julie, whose weaknesses were never concealed.

The source of Julie's trouble, a Group actress said, was also the source of his sweetness and charm: an inferiority complex of incredible depth. "Possibly the Group was the worst thing that could have happened to him, considering his particular needs. He wasn't stupid, but he wasn't particularly bright either: so in the Group atmosphere that stressed intellect and probably overstressed it, Julie *thought* he was stupid. He would have succeeded as an actor on any level except perhaps the classical. But he thought he had to be smarter than he was, and we all loved him for that. The way he tried to use big words became an inside joke and we laughed at him a lot. He took it in good stride, but I know it bothered him. And it bothered him a lot, too, that Robbie was so much keener than he was."

Robbie appreciated the financial comfort, but wanted none of the fuss. Julie, steeped in artistic sanctimony, downgraded Hollywood and said fancy cars and manicured homes and swimming pools meant nothing to him; but they meant too much. They symbolized the fame that was his spur. He liked to say, "Me? I'm little Julie Garfinkle from the Bronx. I'm just a mug."

He would also reflect that "Hollywood dangles a fortune at you, and you get softened. Money seeps through. You begin to step up the pace for more money. Before you know it, you're rich and a failure."

Actually there was more of little Julie Garfinkle in him than even he recognized, and it was what he did not want to be. He was awed by fame—his own and others'—and even more awed by brains.

He continued to be involved in every liberal or radical movement. Friends said his politics were only skin-deep, that his sincere concern for the Little Guy was more emotional than philosophical. Harold Clurman said Julie could not penetrate the depth of political thought although his wife could. Similarly, Clifford Odets believed that was why Julie always sought the company of writers; he star-worshiped their intelligence. Julie's friends now included such mainstay screenwriters as Jules Furthman and Ben Hecht, as well as William Faulkner who, like John Steinbeck and William Saroyan, was spending a lot of time in Hollywood. The Garfields were also drawn closer to the Edward G. Robinsons, and Robbie worked closely with the first Mrs. Robinson for Russian Relief during the war.

Those who were not Julie's close friends found his outspoken opinions annoying. Another male star observed that "The naive Mr. Garfield has turned into a man to cause snarls and suspicion. He stuck a chip on his shoulder, right under our noses."

Although Julie enjoyed an atmosphere of cerebral debate, he also had lowlife inclinations not shared by Robbie. He was a bar-hopper, a locker room jester, essentially a joiner; and secretly he cultivated a taste for the underside of Hollywood life that was abhorrent to Robbie.

"Julie does all the things Errol Flynn says *he* does," a Warner coworker remarked. They were a curious contrast, working off the payroll of the same studio—the Irish peacock and the East Side Kid. Flynn made a swaggering show of his sexuality, openly propositioning his leading ladies or the secretaries and carhops. He joked about his affairs for the benefit of the press, and even during the pseudo-rape trial in 1943 (when the catchphrase "in like Flynn" entered the language to stay), he flashed a brazen leer that said he was enjoying himself.

That another sex bomb ticked away at the same studio was a matter about which his fans remained ignorant. John Garfield—furtive, clandestine, quick to deny any carrying-on—was a contrast to Flynn. He wasn't a rogue, only an oversexed roustabout feeling guilty about what he couldn't control.

It may have been the "he-man" image the studio pinned on him. He said he opposed capital punishment and any form of killing, and he regularly rejected invitations to go hunting; yet he started a gun collection, which might be expected of a tough guy. And in a competitive Hollywood which placed an extraordinary premium on virility, he made an earnest bid to become number one.

Although every Garfield leading lady was an object for conquest, he mainly concentrated on the always dense residue of fly-by-night starlets and the nonprofessional girls who were not likely to leave a tracing card. An actress friend said "He had a sweet charm but an incredible inferiority complex. He wanted to think of himself as a he-man but never had it in himself to really be one. He was a good lover, and that repeatedly proved to him, at least, that he was a kind of he-man after all."

He got to know girls on the fringe of movieland, or he knew someone who did—such as the assistant director at Warners who kept a well-organized ledger of names, addresses, and telephone numbers, with regularly updated information on prices and specialty lines. Julie was to say often that "I have given Robbie reason to despise the whole business and town."

According to Elia Kazan, Robbie's posture was not so much one of tolerance as patience. Julie's friends thought he was going through a difficult phase which linked his sexual exploits with professional disappointment. They admired Robbie's capacity for forgiveness. But as time passed they doubted that she could adjust to his primary failing.

The "really big" vehicle Warners had promised Julie turned out to be *Flowing Gold,* an uninspired potboiler that had him working the oil fields with Pat O'Brien. Ann Sheridan was supposed to play the girl but risked suspension by turning it down. Olivia deHavilland also balked, so Julie went to bat for Frances Farmer.

She was back in Hollywood, her stage adventure having ended unhappily. Julie met her by accident at Hollywood's CBS studio where he kept a Lux Radio Theatre date during the shooting period of *Saturday's Children.* Frances Farmer was bitter about having been fired from the cast of Hemingway's *The Fifth Column,* which the Theatre Guild was staging on Broadway. She also thought the Group Theatre had degenerated into a pack of jealous rivals and was no longer a hotbed of genius. Tired of emulating the Group's proud penury, she decided to find a house befitting a star, and to reclaim her screen career. Julie became her house-hunting companion. Frances rented Dolores Del Rio's house, with its fabled glass roof over the bedroom.

During Julie's time in New York with *Heavenly Express,* Frances made a sleazy programmer for Paramount before the company dropped her. Then she got a part in an independently-made *South of Pago Pago*—popular hokum in which she made a good showing. Julie returned to Hollywood and they resumed their affair, although Frances again was drinking heavily and wasn't easy company. But Julie could still enjoy the view from her boudoir: the stars at night, the sunshine and blue sky by day.

And he was sympathetic. He talked Warners into giving Frances Farmer the female lead in *Flowing Gold.* He thought a good account could lead to a Warner contract that could put her real talent in focus, while stabilizing her emotionally. But Frances failed to ingratiate herself with the studio hierarchy, who offered no long-term proposition. Not long afterward she was arrested for vagrancy, as a preface to spending many years in mental institutions. When she reemerged still pretty in the late fifties, trying a comeback as a club singer, Miss Farmer pointed the finger at the Group Theatre for her emotional undoing. And when she spoke frankly of an affair with John Garfield, she became perhaps his only leading lady to issue a public admission. (It is curious that so many of Garfield's other female costars believe themselves the only one *not* successfully seduced by him.)

Flowing Gold was an awful picture that had the added misfortune of being in issue simultaneously with the glossier and far more entertaining *Boom Town,* with Tracy and Gable. Yet *Flowing Gold* was surely no worse than *East of the River* which followed, and together they would represent the low point of his film career. *East of the River* was the warmed-over tale of two boys raised as brothers, one going bad (Garfield as a racketeer and jailbird) and the other finishing first in his class at college (William Lundigan). Reversing the usual procedure,

Brenda Marshall swiveled sluttishly in the early scenes but became a dewy-eyed ingenue as the plot thickened: she played the crook's mistress, who undergoes a character transformation after falling for the nice boy. Julie couldn't finish the chore soon enough, and his lack of confidence in the script was evident in the final print. Nothing in his performance suggested a major talent, even a stifled one. One critic was to say "Garfield's and Warners' latest collaboration is a contrived, hackneyed repetition of Mr. Garfield's previous case histories of wastrels."

Despite its glowing reception by the critics, the earlier *Saturday's Children* had failed at the box office, and as a result the people who decided things at the studio no longer were in a mood for humoring John Garfield. After *East of the River* they offered him *High Sierra* and he rejected it because George Raft had already turned it down, and because he didn't want to play a man named Mad Dog Earle. It became the picture that finally secured Humphrey Bogart's claim to stardom, but once again Julie went on salary suspension.

Soon he was playing with the varsity again: Curtiz directing a Robert Rossen script—*The Sea Wolf*. Jack London's novel had been filmed at least three times already, once as a Warner early talkie, but this would stand as the definitive production. Julie insinuated himself into the cast; the plan had been to use a lesser name in the subordinate role of George Leach and to sell the picture on the strength of two stars—Edward G. Robinson and the emerging Ida Lupino. But Julie claimed Jack London as a literary hero, and he agitated to play the protagonist opposite Robinson's menacing Wolf Larsen. Rossen, sensing that Julie was not right for the actual tragic hero, the prim writer Van Weyden (played brilliantly by Alexander Knox, in his first screen role), got to work building the part of ex-con seaman Leach along the lines of Garfield's best screen image. Warners agreed to the casting, and *The Sea Wolf* came to represent forties moviemaking at its best—a triumph of nautical atmosphere and dramatic tempo. An extraordinary aspect was the electrically charged love interest without a whisper of sentimentality between Garfield and Lupino. They were the fugitive spirits of life, and Julie thought her the best actress he'd worked with in pictures. Warners agreed they were a potent team, and planned subsequent Garfield-Lupino projects.

Ida Lupino's professional pulse raced with Julie's. After several years of ingenue insipidness, she surfaced convincingly in neurotic roles and was made a Warner star. But as surely as Garfield saw the dimensions of the Cagney shadow, Lupino sensed the hovering dominance of Bette Davis at Warners and could not feel secure. Her best Warners role, in *The Hard Way,* was one Davis refused. Ida and Julie thrived on mutual respect, however; and interestingly, he thought, she alone among his coplayers usually called him John. Possibly she was only determined to maintain a certain personal distance, for at that time she was in love with Louis Hayward and was soon to marry him.

They were teamed again in *Out of the Fog,* the screen title for *The Gentle People.* It was a play Irwin Shaw ostensibly had written for John Garfield to act in one of his false-start returns to the Group, before the *Heavenly Express* production occurred. Instead, Franchot Tone had used the play for his own reunion with the Group, although the production was not successfully realized. Still, it was even less commendable on film—one of the gloomiest pictures on record—slowed to a crawl by Anatole Litvak's obvious striving for poetic effect.

As the gangster Goff (representing evil incarnate), Julie gave a flinty performance, terrorizing a pair of nice old fishermen who cannot bring themselves to kill him, although that seems their only solution. The self-consciously symbolic drama passed over the heads (or the sleep-filled eyes) of those who saw it, and the disappointing gross dampened Warners' enthusiasm for a Garfield-Lupino series. The main thing wrong, Julie said, was that everyone had overrated the property. He gave one of his most thoroughly disciplined screen performances, but it was an island in a fog the picture never came out of. It also indicated that the public wanted no part of a John Garfield presented in a wholly unsympathetic light.

In the summer of 1941 he sat out his longest suspension,

angry with Warners for refusing to lend him to Columbia to play *Martin Eden*—the vaguely autobiographical Jack London role. Columbia's Harry Cohn wanted Garfield, but Warners held back for no reason Julie knew of, other than discipline. Columbia finally gave the Eden role to the very young Glenn Ford, and that recalled the *Golden Boy* muddle two years earlier. Later Harry Cohn would say that the only two contract players ever developed successfully as leading men by Columbia—Ford and Holden—got their pivotal opportunities because he was unable to pry John Garfield from Warners.

Aware that he was making three clinkers for every good picture and not receiving proper consideration for attractive loan-out situations, Julie was settling into a state of chronic unhappiness with his employers. He also sensed that he was fighting his own losing battle, while a passive agent merely pocketed his ten percent. So he dropped the Lyons agency and became Lew Wasserman's client. And he put his business affairs in the hands of Bob Roberts, an old friend from New York, and they began plotting a course of independent film-making to commence upon his completing the seven-year sentence to Warners. Later Julie obeyed a court order to pay Lyons & Lyons slightly more than $20,000 in penalties, but he said it was worth it.

The agent switch proved timely, for Warners now sought to renegotiate contracts with all its star actors. America was walking the tightrope of neutrality while war raged in Europe, but the Atlantic Charter had confirmed her loyalties, and the lend-lease agreement had expanded them. The war had shut off most of the foreign markets, and while Warners had been issuing sixty pictures annually when Julie joined the company, the number had been cut back to three dozen. The studio chiefs took a hard look at their star salaries and decided to get tough. When Pat O'Brien, for example, came up for a new contract and demanded a raise, he was sent packing. Julie saw that he was probably in a position to engineer his own escape from Warners, but Edward G. Robinson and other veteran players advised him to use the situation to his own advantage. Instead of accepting a raise for allowing his contract to be extended, he settled for the same salary but less obligation—only two pictures a year. The new arrangement also permitted more flexibility for working at other studios. But he gained little in the way of determining what pictures he would make, and he received yet another suspension for refusing to play in *Blues in the Night,* a picture about the roots of Southern jazz. Besides reuniting him with the fading Priscilla Lane, the picture would have given him an opportunity to act with Elia Kazan, who stole the show (in what was the last of his two-film acting career).

Blues in the Night turned out better than the picture he eventually accepted, but Julie's anxiety to do a war picture was understandable. Warners had been the first studio to recognize Nazi Germany as the primary enemy, with *Confessions of a Nazi Spy* more than two years before Pearl Harbor; and while nobody was looking, the studio just stopped making gangster pictures. Melodrama remained the studio staple, but Hitler's guys were the new villains. Sometimes old scripts were refurbished with new twists; and lo! the Riffs of *The Desert Song* were raising a ruckus against the nasty Nazis. If *The Sea Hawk* was the Errol Flynn flagship of 1940, it was *Dive Bomber* a year later. Cagney was one of the *Captains of the Clouds,* Bogart outwitted stateside German spies *All Through the Night.* Garfield got the runt of the litter in *Dangerously They Live,* chasing subs and more spies. Its grade-B density submerged grade-A talents, for Raymond Massey was in the picture, and Nancy Coleman, a starlet with some talent, was introduced. Julie said he delivered an assignment, not a performance. Medium-tall Nancy Coleman remembered that when she and John Garfield embraced for the movie camera, he always stood on a little box.

John Garfield was the first major screen personality to entertain U.S. troops in wartime. Personal appearances at camps and bases eventually occupied most of the stars not actually in uniform, but Julie got into the act even before the Pearl Harbor action brought the United States into the world struggle. In the fall of 1941, Eddie Dowling collected an assortment of performers for a "Flying Showboat" to tour Yank bases in the Caribbean. Laurel and Hardy were aboard, along with Ray Bolger, Jane Pickens, Chico Marx, and Mitzi Mayfair. Dowling also sought a male film star, hopefully a young one with whom the GIs could identify, who wasn't a comic or a song-and-dance man. Julie was sitting out one of his suspensions, and beginning to take an active part in the affairs of the Screen Actors Guild; and Larry Beilensen, an attorney for the guild, delivered John Garfield to Eddie Dowling.

Julie was never without a primary patriotic cause. After the Spanish civil war, he and Robbie turned their attention to organized lobbying against the Germans and the Japanese. During the filming of *Saturday's Children,* Julie and cameraman James Wong Howe had embarrassed the studio by locking themselves into Julie's dressing room and refusing to meet some visiting Japanese geishas who were official visitors to the set. And Robbie had been in the forefront of protest against the Japanese, urging a boycott of their goods. Julie voiced a pacifist's loathing of war but was fascinated by the adventure of it, and the same impulse that made him accept such a screen assignment as *Dangerously They Live* prompted him to venture into areas where danger lived, indeed. He knew all the patriotic platitudes and shared the servicemen's delight in being "just a mug" like them. There were mosquito bites, dysentery, and other annoyances, but the tour would be only the first of many.

In November, they flew the Caribbean in a B-18. Julie recalled that the flyers broke them in easy, so as not to alarm them. "They'd say, 'Have you ever seen a parachute?' and they'd bring one out and put it on Chico, showing him how it worked. We'd get the idea, then they'd start showing us the life rafts." Their first stop was San Juan, Puerto Rico, where they received a reception "like no Hollywood premiere ever was." Julie decided the natives were as entertainment-starved as the soldiers and civilian defense workers.

He relished mixing it up with the boys, and decided that for a GI audience anything was going to pass as high wit. He'd yell, "How many are from the South?" and a throng would roar, "Yeah, yeah." Then he'd come back with, "I mean from the south of Brooklyn," and the Brooklyn boys would riot. Julie was also appreciated for contributing the only serious part of the show, reciting "The Jervis Boy Goes Down" by one of his drinking companions, Gene Fowler.

Julie later recalled that, "A surefire stunt was to pick out some feature of the camp and improvise a verse about it to the tune of a popular song. Something like, 'The Last Time I Saw Trinidad,' with a lot of crap about the camp at Trinidad. They'd love it. Or in Puerto Rico, where we had this Boca Chica drink, we'd make up something like, 'It will make you mucho seek-a if you drink a Boca Chica when you're down in Puerto Rico.' "

No matter how mundane their material, the Showboaters were an enormous hit with the servicemen. Julie's own reward was in playing again for a live audience—the thing he missed most in moviemaking. It was his idea that the film colony should do its own entertaining, since Hollywood was a natural magnet for coast-based servicemen on furlough. After Pearl Harbor, the idea evolved into the Hollywood Canteen. Julie was better at coming up with an idea than in carrying one through, but in Bette Davis he found an ally who was forceful and knew how to exercise clout within the community. They were the canteen's cofounders, and Julie proved an engaging arm-twister at booking "acts" featuring popular personalities on a gratis basis—often in uncharacteristic display. In the very heart of the filmland, GIs could gather to hobnob with movie stars who served them refreshments, or who would chat and dance with them and sometimes improvise skits. Julie even managed to break down the reluctance of his famous veteran colleagues whom the boys wanted to meet most—the Tracys, Coopers, and Cagneys. Bette Davis has recalled that during the time most of the stars were getting all dolled up for Ciro's one night and letting their hair down for the Canteen on the next, it was the Canteen everyone enjoyed most: a buoyant chapter in the social life of Hollywood, with John Garfield its ringmaster.

The Canteen was open nightly from six to midnight. A sign

paraphrasing Earl Carroll's nightclub slogan was placed above the entrance: "Through these portals pass the most beautiful uniforms in the world." Julie insisted that the Canteen was for GIs only, and no officers were allowed after opening night. Women stars danced and chatted with the servicemen. Julie and his fellow actors washed and bussed dishes, swept floors, and emptied garbage. The Canteen was the most popular drawing card in Hollywood during wartime.

Julie's gullibility caused him at least one annoyance at the Canteen. He got into friendly conversation with a private who was slightly drunk and getting drunker. They exchanged addresses. Three days later the private was invited into the Hollywood home of Sam Schuster, a well-to-do businessman. The soldier, after telling the Schusters of having met John Garfield and of how great he was, left the Schuster home. Shortly afterward Mrs. Schuster discovered that some jewelry had been taken. Obeying a hunch, the Schusters telephoned the Garfields, and learned that the soldier had gone to the Garfield house, knocked on the door, and given the jewelry to a surprised Robbie. The Schusters reclaimed the jewelry and the robber was arrested. Early in 1943, Robbie was called to court to identify the jewels. In his defense the private said he was "too drunk to remember what happened, and then I found the jewelry in my room."

The attack on Pearl Harbor occurred at a time when Julie was working away from Warner Brothers for the first time. Lew Wasserman engineered a loan to M-G-M for a picture Julie wanted very much to do—John Steinbeck's *Tortilla Flat*. Julie enlisted Steinbeck himself as a lobbyist for his services, and while Steinbeck was not officially connected with the picture, his recommendation carried weight. And Louis B. Mayer, who liked the idea of Garfield playing the lovestruck Danny, was not above blackmail when it came to getting his way: unless Warners gave him John Garfield, he might be tempted to reveal the negligence of certain Warner executives in honoring their pledges toward various Jewish charities.

Julie enjoyed most of the *Tortilla Flat* experience, sharing star billing with Spencer Tracy and Hedy Lamarr. Even more than the script itself, he savored the opportunity of working with Tracy and watching the veteran star build a performance out of little bits and pieces. Tracy had achieved the height of film prestige, but was still unreconciled to having left the stage. He and Julie formed a very close friendship during the production; but typical of Tracy, it would flicker and die after the shooting was completed.

Spencer Tracy, who had just begun his enduring secret liaison with Katharine Hepburn, surprised Julie by knowing most of the intramural facts about the Group Theatre. He said he slipped back to New York regularly to see plays, and had caught Julie's performance as Siggie in *Golden Boy*. Tracy teased Julie by addressing him as various Group-company surnames other than Garfield—Adler, Carnovsky, Meisner—and by disparaging the Stanislavsky system, which he rejected. But Tracy was amused when Julie told him that the Tracy performance in the early *Man's Castle* was much admired by the Group and had been cited in workshops as an excellent example of Stanislavsky method applied to filmacting.

While Tracy reveled in his lordly position at M-G-M, he did not share Julie's view that it was more stimulating for an actor than Warner Brothers. Tracy happily recalled his only experience at Warners—the *20,000 Years in Sing Sing* picture Julie had remade as *The Castle on the Hudson*. Tracy liked the Warner pace—moviemaking at a zip—as opposed to M-G-M, where matter ruled over mind and production slowed to a crawl. Getting the camera setups were interminable. There was much fuss with lighting and the embroidery of production detail. An actor spent a lot of time getting ready to act and a lot of time sitting around just waiting to act, but not so much time really working at his craft. Spencer Tracy was a man of extraordinary impatience.

"Christ, there've been days I've arrived on the set before sun-up, gotten into makeup and costume, and gone home at the end of the day without having shot a scene. This business is impossible!"

Other than moaning, Tracy's occupational therapy was

clowning around with Victor Fleming, the director. Julie sensed that Fleming was a master of his craft, although nothing suggested an artist. He was a contrast to the posturing Europeans Julie had worked with at Warners, and he was unlike the literate Irving Rappers and Vincent Shermans who were more typical of the M-G-M directors. Fleming, who started in Hollywood as a teen-aged cameraman, had an instinctive command of the medium, and his directorial style made moviemaking exciting for an actor, once the camera started grinding.

When Julie began his first scene for Fleming, the director called a halt and shouted: "For Christ's sake, Garfield, you have to do better than that. I fought like hell to get you in this picture, so don't make me look like a fool." While Spencer Tracy snickered in the background, Julie asked Fleming for specific suggestions.

"You want me to tell you how to act, Garfield? Hell, I don't know how to act, and I'd be making more money if I did. You're the actor, you have the reputation; now I just want you to be better."

They did the scene over and Julie was better.

"Take it easy, Garfield: don't get *too* good. A lot of your scenes are with Hedy Lamarr. She's not what you'd call unoutclassable, and we can't let that happen. Let's take it again. Be better than you were the first time, but worse than the second."

As usual, Julie was slow to realize that a humorist was preying on his gullibility. In fact, Fleming was not concerned about acting but liked to keep a picture moving. He thus would create an atmosphere in which actors could respond to his own style of pressure. Reviewing the days "rushes" (unedited exposed film without sound) was a regular thing at M-G-M, although Spencer Tracy quirkishly refused. The *Tortilla Flat* rushes excited Julie. That an essentially plotless film about leisurely, underemployed California Mexicans could fairly burst with energy told him something about Victor Fleming. He had a wonderful time making *Tortilla Flat* and some other M-G-M properties.

Julie was a live fuse turned loose in a studio where many

voluptuaries were easy setups for sexual detonation. Script girls, prop mistresses, and novice starlets at the studio's "training classes" were eager to accommodate the visitor from Warners, but most of the talk was about Hedy Lamarr. And there was a lot of talk.

She was then in the full flower of her incredible beauty, and she was also between husbands. Hedy had been regularly roasted by the critics since coming with Charles Boyer to the Casbah, but in *Tortilla Flat* she began to show real flair for movieacting, even if her speech was nobody's Mexican English—even Garfield's was better in comparison. When gossip about Lamarr and Garfield began to spread through the community, Julie explained that Hedy wasn't accustomed to playing comedy and he was out of practice himself, so they were helping one another with instruction—in her dressing room, or perhaps in his. They spent a lot of time together preparing their roles.

Not all of Julie's dressing-room encounters at M-G-M followed a pattern, however. His only private meeting with Greer Garson proved rather different, and grew into a minor legend of filmland. During the filming of *Tortilla Flat,* the picture Miss Garson would be most lastingly identified with also went into production: *Mrs. Miniver.* The red-haired English girl was fairly new to American films, but already was popular. She had been an enchanting Elizabeth Bennet in *Pride and Prejudice* and was the toast of the studio. The publicity department reckoned that a staged meeting between Greer Garson and John Garfield would provide good copy.

Julie received a note from Miss Garson saying she looked forward to meeting him and would be delighted to have him for tea in her dressing room. He was accustomed to receiving more open and less formal invitations. He also accepted as a truism the Hollywood maxim that "a girl with good manners has tail like peppermint candy." Julie thought he had the proper but vivacious Greer Garson pegged.

She greeted him with an oozing of admiration for his acting, and got about the business of preparing tea. Julie thought she was wasting time. Taking her by the shoulders, he said,

"Let's not play around, Greer, I want to fuck you right now."
Her face froze, and her suddenly glaring green eyes caused
Julie to loosen his grip. After a long pause she whispered, "Get
out!" and several seconds later she shouted it. Then she opened
the door. Julie, startled and suddenly sheepish, was getting
the old heave-ho—just as a photographer arrived to take a
Garson-Garfield picture. It never got snapped.

The Garfields returned to New York in early 1942 to be
with Julie's dying father. On his deathbed David Garfinkle de-
liriously expressed disappointment that Julie wasn't still acting
in that play with Paul Muni. Though Julie had been giving
financial support to his father and covering his medical expenses in recent years, David left no provision for Dinah. Julie
could not summon a warmth beyond obligatory sympathy for
his stepmother, but he consoled her with a promise of eighty-
five dollars a month. His father's death gave Julie a feeling of
remorse more than anything else.

Clifford Odets was at the funeral, devastated by yet another
failed play *(Clash by Night)* and hounded by his creditors.
Julie became Odets's self-appointed protector and gave him
cash to meet his obligations. Odets vowed anew to write a play
that would bring Julie back to Broadway, but his confidence
was eroding as steadily as his productivity.

During his stay in New York, Julie was an easy mark for
interviewers. Criticizing Lew Ayres's stand as a conscientious
objector, he said: "Lew made us want to show the world he
doesn't represent Hollywood." Julie praised James Stewart as
the prototype hero for screen actors in uniform. Nor did he
endorse the rumored government action to keep film actors in
the studios for purposes of national morale. "We'll go when
we're called, just like everyone else," he said. This effusive
patriotism and his pioneering as a camp entertainer prompted
a personal expression of appreciation from President Franklin
Roosevelt, and an invitation to the White House.

Julie admitted it was one of the few times he had been
"honestly at a loss for words." But the President was kindly

and tried to put him at his ease. He commended Julie for the Caribbean tour and asked him to emcee some bond-selling tours. (Carole Lombard, the first star to do so, was a tragic victim of an airliner crash after the inaugural bond rally, six weeks after the U.S. entry into World War II.) Julie agreed to help "any time, anywhere." Later Julie said, "I voted for Roosevelt both times that I was old enough. I couldn't get over meeting him for weeks and weeks. Well, that's democracy, and it's wonderful. Imagine . . . him calling me Johnny!"

John Garfield was the byline for an article in *Theatre Arts Monthly* urging stars to donate their services as entertainers for the armed forces. Julie also took an especially active role in the sale of war bonds under the auspices of Stars Over America. (It was also during the 1942 visit to New York that he helped out at the Stage Door Canteen and got the idea for its Hollywood counterpart.)

Julie expected to be wearing a military uniform very soon, and was startled by his 4-F rating after his Army physical. He was humiliated and tried to keep his classification secret. Although he was only twenty-eight when the United States entered the war, he was one of a mere handful of established male stars in his age group who did not do at least a brief stint of military service. A strong "heart murmur" had been detected.

But he and Robbie got involved with the Committee for a Second Front and other activities of the Old Left, and he continued a sort of cheerleading function in the Screen Actors Guild. His financial aid helped to establish the Actors Laboratory Theatre in Hollywood. Perhaps the Group Theatre was dead, but the cadaver was walking. The Actors Lab was an unofficial stepchild, dominated by Group alumni.

Arthur Lyons, his ex-agent, took Julie to court again in 1942, claiming that Julie owed him $4,913.33 in commissions. The arbitration board decided in favor of Lyons & Lyons and Julie made full payment but was not bitter. Lyons had alienated himself from Julie's trust by often siding with Warners in Julie's quarrels with his studio. By making final settlement,

Julie believed he was clearing the way for his eventual freedom from Warners, and already he was talking of becoming his own producer, in partnership with Bob Roberts.

Julie was also in court in 1942 to have his name legally changed from Jacob Garfinkle to John Jules Garfield. He wanted everything to be official before Katherine started school. The petition was granted and the family became the Garfields indeed, although their status as a unit was a matter of some doubt.

Wartime had a circumstantial effect of separating the Garfields, as Julie became a traveling entertainer and bond salesman, and Robbie kept busy as a home front activist in Hollywood. But even when Julie was in Hollywood for movie commitments that now were less frequent, an estrangement was evident although it was never acknowledged by Robbie or Julie. Sometimes he would stay at the Beverly Wilshire or the Hollywood Roosevelt when, ostensibly, he was living at home. The columnists ignored Robbie and sought out Julie for information. If he shaded truth, he said the "right" things.

Robbie's second pregnancy brought them closer once more. A son was born to the Garfields in July, 1943, while Julie was filming *Destination Tokyo*. They named him David Patton Garfield, honoring Julie's late father and the controversial U.S. Army general whom Julie admired. After staying up through the night with Robbie, awaiting her delivery at Cedars of Lebanon Hospital in Los Angeles, Julie reported to the studio for the day's shooting, less tired than proud. (When the grown David Garfield began his own acting career, he discovered that another player was already registered in that name with Actors Equity, so he changed his professional name to John Garfield, Jr.)

The advent of a son inspired renewed and sincere expressions of good intentions. Julie would be more attentive toward his family, staying close to the marital roost.

Tortilla Flat, released in mid-1942 during the dark early days of the war, was a prestigious rather than commercial success. It was also Julie's last opportunity to play character

comedy, and his solid work went strangely ignored in a picture that earned both Spencer Tracy and Frank Morgan the
highest praise. Julie emerged warm and likable, and not so
dumb as naive, playing the sort of fellow who would buy his
girl (Hedy Lamarr) a vacuum cleaner although her flat has
no electricity.

After *Tortilla Flat* he got in a run of pictures he mostly
liked, all of them dealing with some aspect of the war. *Air
Force* was made for its time—its patriotic substance would
look and sound a little silly only a few years later, but it confirmed Howard Hawks's authority for the masculine action-
adventure film. Julie played a gunner who successfully lands
a bomber plane after the pilot is mortally wounded. The plane
was the hero, supported mainly by proficient young players
such as Arthur Kennedy and Gig Young. Filmed mostly in an
artificial jungle, *Air Force* was tremendously popular with the
free-spending wartime audience.

So was *The Fallen Sparrow*—Julie's second loanout picture,
this time for RKO. His political views enamored him of the
story that linked Nazi villains with Spanish Fascists. He played
a Loyalist survivor of the Spanish civil war—one haunted by
the memory of a man with a limp. He was teamed with gorgeous Maureen O'Hara, whom he turned over to the law in a
climax that echoed the Bogart-Mary Astor relationship of *The
Maltese Falcon*. The Garfield performance was a fair example
of what he could now do blindfolded.

Then it was on the high seas—no, under the sea in a submarine—in *Destination Tokyo,* an entirely fictional entertainment with Cary Grant dominant and Garfield given costar
billing for a distinctly supporting chore. It was another whopping box office success. Julie's principal companion during the
shooting was his young *alter ego,* Dane Clark—formerly the
Group apprentice named Bernard Zanville, just starting in
Warner pictures.

By terms of his contract as reinterpreted during the Warner
production retrenchment, Julie owed the studio seven pictures.
He could cross off two obligations after brief and inconsequential appearances as himself in two of those star-crammed ex-

plosions of studio ego. His song-and-dance in *Thank Your Lucky Stars* misfired, although it proved serviceable for troop entertainments; and he seemed to be just standing around in the inevitable *Hollywood Canteen*. They were sandwiched around a remake of *Outward Bound* that went out as *Between Two Worlds*.

Those commitments limited his overseas activity, but he made several bond-selling tours in the East. (By the war's end, almost a billion dollars in bonds had been sold by Stars Over America alone.) Julie was on a bond drive in New England when his teeth again started to cause him real pain, making him a constant aspirin-popper. When he returned to Hollywood, Dr. David Marcus recapped his entire mouth. For several days he was in the dentist's chair twelve hours at a time, but he said, "The agony has been worth it. Not only is my smile radiant, I can smile without pain!"

Julie gloated that his role in *Between Two Worlds* had been played by Alfred Lunt on the stage and by Leslie Howard in the earlier Warner film. (The 1930 version of *Outward Bound* was one of the first talking pictures worthy of memory.) It was a fantasy about passengers voyaging from earthly life toward either heaven or hell, or perhaps both. There was a topical updating—the passengers now were victims of a London air raid—but the picture seemed awkwardly stagey as directed by Edward Blatt, whose career was brief. Julie's performance did not bristle, but most reviewers thought it the best thing in the picture. Critics in general now conceded the authority and strength of personality he brought even to a bad picture, and the Garfield name was solid enough to carry a weak entry at the box office. *Between Two Worlds* was not an "audience picture," but it made money.

It was filmed during one of those periods when Julie's nocturnal behavior was suspect, and his marital status uncertain. Rumors now implicated a very pretty girl on the studio contract list, who was romantically teamed with Paul Henreid in *Between Two Worlds*. She was Eleanor Parker, a self-promoted actress from Cleveland, and her moodiness was attributed to loneliness because her oral-surgeon husband was stationed overseas. She had a small, unassuming house where she said she merely "hung her clothes." She was driven by career dedication, a trait as likely to interest Julie as her beauty obviously would. He confessed to friends of having "fallen" for the girl. Whether she gave him a tumble was not clearly resolved, but Julie asked to have Eleanor Parker opposite him in his next picture. And although Warners had been thinking along the lines of Joan Leslie or Alexis Smith, they delivered Miss Parker because they wanted to keep Julie happy, intending to woo him with a new contract offer.

The next picture turned out to be largely Julie's own idea and one of his favorite projects: *Pride of the Marines,* the story of Philadelphia's Al Schmid, a war hero blinded in combat. Julie read a magazine account of Schmid's experience and saw the possibility of a film. He pursued the idea with Albert Maltz, a longtime friend who had come to Warners to provide the script for *Destination Tokyo,* but had been one of the interesting radical playwrights of the thirties and had written *Peace on Earth,* which the young Jules Garfield acted for the Theatre Union. Maltz came up with a treatment the studio recognized as sure-fire. But shooting was not planned until the late fall of 1944, almost a year after the project was conceived; and there was a possibility that the picture might be canceled, because war pictures were beginning to wilt at the box office as audiences sought escapist fare.

The delay enabled Julie to plan an extended overseas junket. In the spring of 1944 the State Department cleared the way for a tour to entertain the U.S. fighting units in Italy. The troupe Julie headed again was called the "Flying Showboat" and consisted of Eddie Foy, Jr., Sheila Rogers, Olga Klein, and Jean Darling. They all got to know one another quite well before Julie realized that Jean Darling was the same person who, as an especially animated curly blonde, had entertained him and had been his "secret crush" as a member of Our Gang in its earliest, silent edition. (Shortly after the Italian tour, she would create the role of Carrie Pipperidge on Broadway in *Carousel.*)

They arrived in Naples shortly after it had been taken by the Allies, but the Germans were bombing the city. Julie said, "It scared the hell out of me, and anyone who says he isn't scared is a liar." In Naples he repeatedly saw a sign reading "Al Recovero." With a straight face he said, "I thought it meant a guy running for office and I wanted to meet the gent. But in the first air raid I learned it means 'air raid shelter.' Believe me, they didn't have to tell me twice."

The troupe did not give shows in Naples but went immediately to the front. They were knee-deep in mud and their makeshift stage might be a hospital tent or the back of a truck. Only rarely did the weather encourage an outdoor entertainment. Following a custom he associated with Joe E. Brown, Julie "made a point to shake hands with every hospital case," always with first attention to the more serious cases. Later he would say, "What I saw wasn't pretty. But the morale is wonderful. The boys' one aim is to come home, and the sooner the better."

Audiences were wildly receptive wherever they went. According to then-Private Eugene Edwards, "John Garfield wasn't to want any credit, but they worked right through an air raid without any mention of it." The Flying Showboat troupe in fact would do anything that was asked of it. They agreed to an Army Staff request to entertain Yugoslavian guerrillas, an action that would be misinterpreted years later by the press and by investigating committees who saw it as a gesture of sympathy for Communism. No mention would then be made that the entertainers were obeying an Army request. Julie would recall in a later article that the detour into Yugoslavia ". . . was done under the utmost secrecy. The night we drove through the mud, we had no dinner and no place to eat it if we had. We reached some rolling country between mountains where we couldn't hide if anything happened. Finally we reached our destination at 2:00 A.M. The guerrillas' shelter was a big shack and they gave us food and vodka. We got set up and gave our show an hour before dawn. But everyone was wide awake. When we finished our show, the Yugoslavs put on their show. It was a very warm experience, but we had to return to Italy immediately."

The rugged tour lasted more than two months. The troupe spent every waking hour performing for the GIs. On the homeward return they stopped over in Casablanca to give some shows, and Julie decided that "It looks like Beverly Hills but smells bad."

Hollywood entertainers regularly praised the gallant GIs as if on cue, but Julie really felt that he was among his own fellows. "You can't imagine how wonderful those guys are until you see 'em and live with 'em. I'm going out again, as often as they'll let me, because the boys over there made a spiel as though they wanted us. They even made me feel I was good."

Back in New York, Julie telephoned several mothers, assuring them that he had talked with their sons who all looked fine. One woman told him she had been informed that her son was missing in action. Julie also kept a promise to an Army lieutenant that he would find a home for the lieutenant's wife who was being forced to vacate an apartment the owner wanted to occupy. Julie enlisted Red Cross aid and got Mrs. Ralph Bamberger squared away with housing accommodations. Unlike some do-gooder stars, he kept such actions out of the papers.

The overseas experience only fired Julie's determination to get into the war on his own. In New York he managed to pull some political strings to get his draft classification changed to 1-A. Then he entrained for Los Angeles on the Super Chief, carrying a German automatic weapon given to him by a fan after one of the Italian shows. The studio decided to get some publicity out of his homecoming, and there was a large crowd to cheer his reunion with his family at the station. He made a little speech about "boys who sit in graves they call foxholes and wait . . . they wait for Nazi bullets and maybe for a letter from home." He said he had spent his March birthday in a foxhole, and that "the closer you get to the German lines, the better everything is—the food, the mail, and the other services, even the movies." He said he'd like to hit China on his next trip, but didn't know if he would be going as a civilian entertainer, because he had been classified 1-A. Robbie was caught off guard.

He was summoned for his preinduction physical only a few days later. He learned that he had passed and would be called into service "within ninety days." But in June of 1944, during a serving stint at the Hollywood Canteen, Julie became suddenly ill and was rushed to Cedars of Lebanon Hospital. His physician, Dr. Edward Shapiro, diagnosed a mild heart attack. (The studio publicity department attributed his collapse to a sudden and severe case of the flu.) Only thirty-one and basically strong, Julie recovered quickly. He hoped the Army would remain deceived, and this appeared to be the case when he received his official "greeting" in midsummer. But his heart ailment did not go undetected, and Julie was sent home an official reject, although he claimed he had actually been inducted and then dismissed as "too old." He continued to guard his heart condition as a secret.

Nor did he obey his doctor's order to take it easy. His energetic drive remained unchecked, and he was still the hard-drinking chain smoker. He threw himself into work because he had a movie project he liked, and his consolation was that rejection from military service had assured the production of *Pride of the Marines,* which Warners would not have filmed except as a John Garfield vehicle.

Only as Porfirio Diaz had Julie depicted a real person, and Schmid would be his first and only chance to play a living one. Julie found the perfect model from which to build a performance: Schmid himself. Prior to the shooting schedule, Julie lived for several weeks with the Schmids in Philadelphia, observing the Marine closely while also building a real friendship. He marveled at Al Schmid's adjustment to blindness; physically, he had perfect control of his surroundings. Julie would blindfold himself for hours at a time and imitate Schmid's cautious but decisive motions.

Eleanor Parker's two-year marriage came to an end in December, 1944, after *Pride of the Marines* had started production. Lieutenant Fred Losee, showing no interest in his wife's career, said that "being married to a movie star may be all right for some people but not for me." John Garfield's interest, on the other hand, was obvious enough and may not have been entirely of a professional nature. But Julie had reason to sympathize with Eleanor Parker and also with Dane Clark (now the "new Garfield" was cast as Schmid's marine buddy). The increasingly complicated logistics of picture making were becoming the major obstacle to confront young film players seeking to refine their skill. The sort of conditions that had vexed Spencer Tracy at M-G-M only three years earlier now existed at every studio or location where movies were made. Julie also thought that Delmer Daves, the director who had also made *Destination Tokyo,* had to contend with much that had little to do with dramatic issues. Especially troublesome were union regulations that became ever more rigid, and craft strikes threatened by the Conference of Studio Unions—a fairly new Hollywood backstage union that many believed was Communist-oriented.

By 1945, Warners was no longer a mass production factory but a specialist enterprise producing only eighteen feature films a year. But each one required a level of fuss that only a *Juarez* would have received just half a dozen years before. The whole business was changing. But the country was prosperous; domestic moviehouse patronage was at record strength; and with the prospect of victory and peace, the spring of 1945 looked promising as never before for the movies. Stars and directors and writers would be shedding military uniforms and getting back into the picture-making harness. Hollywood still looked like the ultimate gravy train, and most people believed it would never end.

IX

Declaration of Independence

Robbie Garfield sometimes confided her doubts to friends that Julie would ever leave her. If there was leaving to be done, she would take the action. Other observers affirmed his dependence on her, and sensed that Julie was in a chronic state of precarious probation with his wife. The issue was how long she would tolerate his continued violations of that probation. Was their rags-to-riches love experience sufficient to sustain their relationship through Julie's known infidelities?

Despite gossip that occasionally linked Julie with actresses or other young women of the film colony, there was no serious speculation on a homewrecker. During a trip to New York that Julie made alone, he confided to their old associates that all of the trouble between him and Robbie was his own sorry doing. He said, "I'm crazy about that beautiful broad," implying that he did not anticipate a future without her; but the continuity of their marriage had become dependent upon their children.

Skepticism that the Garfield marriage was stable had been based on their refusal to buy a home of their own. Helen Mack returned to California to make another try at movie work and wanted to reoccupy her home, so the Garfields moved again. But now they bought a home, with little to choose from during wartime. This time they settled on a larger house on Carroll Drive in Beverly Hills. It was a silent-era mansion of elegant Spanish design, one of several owned by William Haines, the former star turned interior decorator. The house was expensively furnished without being showy, but Julie and Robbie agreed that the paintings, at least, were not to their taste and would have to go. Even the free-thinking Garfields believed that murals audaciously trumpeting nudity did not belong in a house with small children. Having given lip service to Robbie's liking for modern art, and also being in awe of Edward G. Robinson's reputation as a connoisseur, Julie began purchasing modern paintings that his more discerning friends would say weren't very good. It would also be said that some of the best art work in the house was Julie's own. Painting was an increasing pastime attention with him, and his oils often conveyed his uninhibited personality. Julie began giving his paintings to friends when he could have sold them through a gallery, but he said he painted just for pleasure and not to prove anything.

What Julie liked most about the house on Carroll Drive was the large fireplace and the exquisite glass coffee table in front of it. Love seats on either side of the table faced one another. Julie said his favorite moment of the day came when he arrived from the studio and could plop himself on one of the love seats and face Robbie, occupying the other one, to discuss the day's activities—with their bare or stockinged feet resting on the glass table.

They continued to resist becoming a household complicated by servants. They hired a nurse for the period of David's infancy, and Hilda Wane was retained as a household helper to Robbie and sometime professional secretary for Julie. But answering the door was Julie's or Robbie's job if either was home.

Kathy had the run of the place. She was an adorable child with a cheerful disposition and a proper foolishness for her father. Julie said she had inherited her mother's brains; Robbie said Kathy had her father's charm; and the little girl's beauty was quite her own. Although healthy enough in appearance, Kathy was allergy-prone and subject to occasional difficulty with breathing. Robbie became expert at keeping Kathy's allergies under control.

Julie would often recall—and later with anguish—how the five-year-old Kathy kept squeezing his hand for security when he enrolled her in kindergarten at the Gardner Street Public School in the fall of 1943. She seemed to sense her need for protection, and the Garfields had always intended to have at least one other child to give Kathy a companion. The little girl was delighted when the baby David came to live with her. Julie also remembered Kathy's tears when he left with the Flying Showboat for Italy, and her joy upon his return.

On Saint Patrick's Day in 1945, Kathy went on a holiday to a ranch that a Garfield friend owned in Vista, an inland California town about a hundred miles from the Garfields' Beverly Hills home. That was before the California freeway system made rapid travel feasible, so the plan was for Kathy to stay overnight at the ranch, in Hilda Wane's charge. That night Kathy's allergy appeared to cause her throat to be swollen and sore. Miss Wane believed that since Kathy had no fever, she was probably having only a breathing reaction to the hay she had played in during the day, and that the difficulty would pass with proper rest. But the little girl's condition was worse by morning, and Miss Wane bundled her in the car to drive her home, confident that Robbie would know how to treat the allergy. During the long trip, breathing became progressively harder for Kathy, and she was gasping desperately when they arrived at home. Robbie sensed the seriousness of the attack and immediately called Dr. Harold Jubeliere, Kathy's pediatrician. Then she began trying to locate Julie, but by the time he reached the house it was too late. Kathy died less than an hour after reaching home. None of Robbie's usual procedures for Kathy's allergy were of any help.

An autopsy failed to produce anything Kathy might have eaten that could have congested her windpipe. Death was attributed to a spasm of the glottis, related to strangulation. But a whispered rumor circulated briefly that diphtheria or some other affliction of dreaded communicability might have been the actual cause. Hilda Wane blamed herself for not rushing Kathy to a hospital upon the first signs of difficulty, but the Garfields thought she had acted logically and responsibly and asked her to continue working for them. She did, but only briefly. Kathy's funeral at the Reynolds and Eberle Mortuary in Los Angeles was a trying time for everyone, and sympathetic friends rushed to the Garfields' aid. They were confident of Robbie's stability but fearful of what Julie might do.

Julie held himself responsible, and said that Kathy's death was his repayment for having neglected her. Lee J. Cobb tried to console him. So did Lee and Paula Strasberg, whose daughter Susan had attended the ranch party with Kathy. Friends said Julie's reaction was as pathetic as it was violent: he went into the back yard carrying the automatic rifle and ammunition clip he had brought back from Italy, then loaded the gun and fired the entire clip into a wall.

Some would say the loss of his daughter had a lasting effect on Julie's personality, rendering him permanently gloomy where he had been incapable of gloom in earlier times. Yet the tragedy also brought him into a stronger union with Robbie. Julie became a better father to David, and to the little girl who would take Kathy's place. Immediately after Kathy's death, the Garfields conceived another child.

Vincent Sherman, friend and neighbor, believed the tragedy somehow made Julie a better person.

By an accident of timing fortuitous for Warner Brothers, *Pride of the Marines* was released nationally on the very week that World War II came to an end. It was a commercial smash, possibly the biggest that was by name a Garfield "vehicle," although it also gave a considerable boost to Eleanor Parker's career. Julie and Miss Parker reached an early understanding that they were not movie stars on this occasion: the Al Schmids were Just Folks, and making them that on the screen was their objective. *Pride of the Marines* was a war picture to satisfy the manly taste, and a real-life soap opera to win the ladies. The Garfield-Parker scenes carried total conviction, and Julie conveyed the healthy sexuality that blindness had not obliterated in Al Schmid. Julie said that Schmid, war hero or not, was very like himself—just a mug. The Garfield performance was nothing short of artistic achievement, yet it would not receive a nomination in the Academy Award competition despite generally weak male nominees. This indicated that an effective Garfield performance was the expected thing. He was one of the reliables of his trade.

As the postwar era began, Garfield shared approximately equal status with Bogart as the most popular and even the most distinguished of the Warner actors. There had been a radical turnover in personnel, affecting not only the actors. Hal Wallis had parted company with Jack Warner on terms less than happy, to enter independent production for Paramount. Warner now had charge of his company's product, even embellishing the trademark shield with his name. Henry Blanke and others who had been Wallis associates were accorded full title as producers. Of the "name" directors only Curtiz and Raoul Walsh still flourished, and the star lineup had been thoroughly overhauled. Muni, Robinson, Cagney, and Raft were all long gone. The Lane sisters were a vague memory. Some of the new faces—Joan Crawford's, for instance—really weren't new, and some of the older ones such as Errol Flynn's no longer rang the bell. Paul Henreid, Dennis Morgan, Jack Carson, and Ronald Reagan were bland mainstays, regularly outacted by character stars Rains, Greenstreet, and Lorre. Ann Sheridan, Jane Wyman, Alexis Smith, and Eleanor Parker were the busiest leading ladies. Flynn, Bogart, and Garfield were now the Old Guard, in concert with Bette Davis, Ida Lupino, and Olivia deHavilland. And in 1945 Miss deHavilland won a court decision against Warner Brothers that would be an industry-wide precedent, permanently changing a screen actor's relationship to his studio.

Actors had fought servitude to the studios in the courts without success for many years, and the verdict surprised them. Now screen actors no longer were obligated to their studios for time they had lost due to illness or other causes, specifically including suspensions without pay. Naturally the strongest repercussions were at Warners. Olivia deHavilland suddenly was entirely free, owing the studio no time at all. Humphrey Bogart did not owe as much time as would be sufficient to make even one picture. Some of the actors decided to follow Bogart's lead by testing their new bargaining power.

Bogart had wanted to leave Warners and other companies offered him lucrative deals. But his new bride, Lauren Bacall, had been made a Warner star, and Bogart wanted to film *The Big Sleep* with his wife and director Howard Hawks. He decided to stay with Jack Warner but the ransom was high: $200,000 per picture, one picture a year—for fifteen years. He was also entitled to make one picture a year for any other studio, if he chose.

John Garfield was sitting out his ninth and last salary suspension when the court decision was handed down. Warners quickly lifted the suspension. But since no Garfield project was ready for the camera, he was loaned to M-G-M as repayment for Warners having borrowed M-G-M's Hedy Lamarr earlier. Now Louis B. Mayer was boasting that Garfield, whose loan assignment would be the strong *The Postman Always Rings Twice*, soon would be the full-time property of M-G-M. But Warners didn't intend to let Garfield get away.

Because he had started young in films, Julie approached the peak years of his screen career still endowed with youth. Warners knew his long-term value and made several propositions amounting to millions of dollars, although none equaled Bogart's package. Soon they realized that Julie was not playing a tactical game with them for higher stakes; he really meant to break free of the studio.

Independence had become his personal panacea. He blamed Warners for all of his miseries, professional and private, even for the loss of his daughter.

Most of his friends advised him to take the best contract he could work out with Warners. They knew he planned to become his own producer, but doubted his ability to carry out the plan or to make good pictures. But while Bob Roberts went about the business of organizing a company for Julie, Warners agreed to end his contract with two pictures that would immediately follow the loan detour to M-G-M. The first was a routine melodrama, *Nobody Lives Forever,* which no one overrated; but it figured to make money and Julie accepted the assignment with a let's-get-it-over-with attitude.

The other project would certify Julie's personal redemption of Clifford Odets.

The beleaguered playwright had failed utterly to acquire a working discipline without the protective guidance the Group Theatre had offered. He had not been able to get on paper a John Garfield play or any other dramatic idea and soon he was wallowing in debt, relieved only by a trickle of old royalties or the irregular modest earnings of his actress wife, who then was rendered unemployable by pregnancy. Hearing that Odets was again on the brink of an emotional collapse, Julie sent his friend a check for two thousand dollars and a letter imploring him to come to Hollywood, where he could certainly obtain some screenwriting work to tide him over. At the Beverly Hills Tennis Club, after a few sets on the court with Charles Koerner, who headed production at RKO, Julie persuaded Koerner to give Odets a shot at scripting a good picture. When Koerner interviewed Odets, the playwright came on strong and talked his way into RKO as a combination writer-director. Then he proceeded to put together the best dramatic film the studio had made in years —the somber *None But the Lonely Heart,* in which Cary Grant delivered his most impressive serious performance, and which gave Ethel Barrymore an Oscar in her return to movie acting after a dozen years.

The revitalized Odets would never get enough of sentimentalizing over Julie for having been his only champion when he was down and out. Their kinship was recemented, and they shared in the adventure of establishing the Actors Lab at the small Las Palmas Theatre in Hollywood. Only the commitment to M-G-M prevented Julie from appearing in the Lab's initial production of Ben Jonson's *Volpone,* as he had planned. But the cast was dotted with good Group names, and the production—for which Odets was an uncredited adaptor—gave creative legitimate theatre an encouraging boost in southern California.

Then Odets, who acknowledged an indebtedness to a dated short story called *Humoresque* for his original conception of *Golden Boy,* got the idea of freely adapting the story for

Julie to do on film. Warners, still counting on Julie's inability to get his independent company off the ground, did everything possible to seduce him toward reaffiliation. They okayed *Humoresque* as his final commitment, with Odets as scripter. An oddity was that the project was an oblique collaboration by the two dissimilar persons whose written works had been pivotal to Julie's progress both on stage and screen—Odets and Fannie Hurst, author of the original *Humoresque*.

It became Warners' 1946 Christmas release, capping what was Julie's best year in many respects. It was a season of fulfillment and renewed ambition for him. Bob Roberts closed a deal making his and Julie's new company a component of an ambitious new independent called Enterprise Pictures. Or perhaps it was the best year for the Garfields in *every* way. A new daughter arrived in January, and her name had a significance of completeness: Julie Roberta. She was a charmer from the start.

Although released in February, 1946, *The Postman Always Rings Twice* was shot at M-G-M in the autumn of 1945—those honeymoon months of the postwar period when ration books were being burned and military uniforms were getting shed. Gable was back and Garson was getting him. And Julie was getting Lana Turner.

Many people both in and out of Hollywood awaited *The Postman Always Rings Twice* with uncommon interest. James M. Cain's abrasive novel, pulsating with sex, had lingered on the shelf for more than a decade because people said it could not be filmed within the thematic restrictions imposed by the Hays Office. And the Garfield-Turner teaming threatened to melt the celluloid.

In *Postman,* Julie played a layabout who wanders into a truckline café to be drawn immediately—by the chemistry of sex—toward the pretty, young wife of the old proprietor. Pretty? Lana Turner was a foremost voluptuary of the movie colony, on the screen or off it. Her glamour was at its blonde height and she was considered a major star despite not having evidenced an ability to act. Costarring with Gable, Tracy,

Stewart, and lesser stars, nothing had worked for her except commercially. But in *Postman* everything seemed to work. What was easily Lana's best performance carried the throbbing notion that she played it as if she meant it. It was well known that she fell in love too eagerly and too often, and Julie's amorous credentials were such as to invite speculation on physical fireworks even before the stars met on the set.

Lana would be photographed almost exclusively in white, reinforcing her blonde beauty as an agreeable contrast to Garfield's dark ruggedness. They started off with a teasing relationship on the set. Everyone was aware of Lana's menstrual period when it occurred because the studio supplied a registered nurse at her insistence. Seeing Lana with the nurse, Julie called out, "Hey, Lana, how's about a little quickie?" for all to hear. Lana turned on her heel and yelled back, "You bastard!" Julie and the crew found ample opportunities for laughter.

Soon there were whispers around town of something going on between Garfield and Turner, much in the manner of gossip that had linked Julie with Hedy Lamarr in his first visit to M-G-M almost four years earlier. Whatever sparks may have ignited between them were extinguished with the completion of the film, and if Julie had "lived" his role, he could chalk one up for Stanislavsky. *Postman* would be a conversation topic for its searing love scenes with the stars photographed in swimwear at picturesque Laguna Beach. Julie told columnist Ross Jackson he usually had to learn something for any movie he made—how to fish in *Tortilla Flat,* how to man a machine gun in *Air Force.* But in *Postman* his task was making love, "and that's something I didn't have to learn."

The veteran director Tay Garnett said Julie's remarkable *presence* was primarily responsible for the picture's undisputed success. Julie played a character of good instincts—aware of his criminal inclination but repelled by it—whose powerful but dormant sexuality, immediately stirred by the appearance of the Lana Turner character, makes the melodramatic story feasible. Ultimately they will kill the young woman's

affable old husband (Cecil Kellaway), who has given his cuck-
older the trust of friendship. *The Postman Always Rings
Twice,* one of the sexiest films made in America, was forcefully understated by a Garfield performance bristling with
innuendo. At the time of the picture's release Julie was
counted a "certain" Academy nominee; but the film was
ancient history by the time the nominations came up, actually
more than a year later.

When *Postman* was reviewed by *Time,* it said "The chief
players are box office naturals . . . John Garfield is so
familiar in the tough man role that his mere presence threatens the audience capacity for belief. However, too much is
beyond Lana Turner's experience, even her sincerely overworked imagination. But it ought to gross its weight in
uranium." They would never make another film together although Lana wanted to, according to the press releases.

In contrast, the forgettable *Nobody Lives Forever,* a midsummer release in 1946, could neither enhance nor disfigure
the shape of Julie's career. He welcomed the opportunity to
play opposite Geraldine Fitzgerald, an actress whose work
he had often admired at times when Warners used her in-
discriminately. She played a rich girl, Julie was out to swindle
her, then they fell earnestly in love. The picture completed
her own Warner contract, and Julie figured she was as happy
to be making the break as he was.

Jean Negulesco, who directed *Nobody Lives Forever,* also
was put on *Humoresque,* which began as something less than
a superproduction but became one in the hands of its portly
producer, Jerry Wald. In the Odets version, *Humoresque*
became so obvious a *Golden Boy* paraphrase that John Garfield said, "You find out what would have happened to Joe
Bonaparte if he had bumped into Helen Wright instead of
Lorna Moon."

The character of rude, virile young violin prodigy Paul
Boray was conceived in Odets's private assessment of John
Garfield's personality and theatrical strength. The role of
Helen Wright—a sophisticated patroness of the arts, adrift in
wealth and alcohol, and starving for sex—was not initially

rated a starring assignment; but Odets did so well in characterizing her that an actress of distinct star quality became a necessity. There was some talk of Tallulah Bankhead or Miriam Hopkins, then Barbara Stanwyck became the preference. Bette Davis had not been ruled out as a possibility. Then Joan Crawford, who had silenced her critics by taking the 1945 Oscar for *Mildred Pierce,* established her own interest in the role . . . and that was that. Helen Wright bore fidelity to the new Crawford image of hardboiled, mature glamour, and she didn't mind that the part was small, if it was strong enough and the billing was large.

Crawford and Garfield may have seemed an improbable combination to people who failed to make the remote connection of Miss Crawford and the Group Theatre. But during her years of marriage to Franchot Tone, Miss Crawford was a charming hostess to the uninhibited New Yorkers who often were summertime freeloaders in their home. Miss Crawford would later say in her autobiography that her marriage to Tone was strongest when his friends from the Group were around to stimulate him. This was why she had given serious thought to studying with the Group. And she had always been a believer in the talent of Odets, who imparted some of his best writing to the Helen Wright characterization.

Garfield remained the protagonist and dominated the footage, but *Humoresque* almost became a Joan Crawford picture in the usual sense. She was the cinematic emphasis. The final print suggested Helen Wright's point of view, and the achievement was the Warner notion of high tragedy: the woman walking suicidally into the sea, as the radiobroadcast of Paul Boray in concert rises in volume—the indefatigable Max Steiner conducting one of his most blaring movie scores.

It was Isaac Stern's violin the moviegoers heard, but Julie properly mastered the fingering for the cameras, simply by learning to play the violin. He took lessons from violinist Harry Zogan, learning to play such elementary tunes as "Yankee Doodle." But his fingering was so realistic that trick photography was not necessary for the closeups—those were the Garfield hands. It was a point of special pride with Julie.

That was only one aspect of a thoroughly researched role. Not surprisingly, some of his best scenes were with Ruth Nelson, the fine actress who stayed with the Group Theatre throughout its official life. She played his mother. And Oscar Levant, long one of Julie's closest friends, had an important role as Julie's sardonic boon companion, dispensing Odets's most inspired character dialogue.

Humoresque would merit study as a textbook for the high-gloss melodrama that became the Warner *chef d'oeuvre* of the forties. It was machine-tooled stuff, but it had a trenchant Garfield performance at its core. And *Newsweek,* endorsing a certain tearjerker for the matinée trade, said Joan Crawford "added swank." The anticipated clash of stars never occurred. Crawford and Garfield maintained a good rapport throughout the project, although there was some uncertainty as to its depth. (A magazine article quoted Robbie Garfield as saying the one actress that worried her was Joan Crawford.) But despite its intimations of prestige, *Humoresque* did not entice Julie into a new Warner pact. He left the studio on schedule, with some tugging of emotions, and on the best of terms with just about everyone there.

Emotional, too, was his reunion with a quorum of Group mainstays, also in 1946, on the stage of Hollywood's Las Palmas Theatre. Joe Bromberg's happy idea was an Actors Lab revival of *Awake and Sing,* since many of the original cast now were anchored in Hollywood. Bromberg directed and repeated his stint as Uncle Morty. The Carnovskys, Art Smith, and Luther Adler reclaimed their old parts; and Julia Adler —Luther and Stella's sister—took over Stella's important role of Bessie Berger. With physical change hardly discernible in him at age thirty-three, Julie still projected the idealism and despair of youth from a stage, and his performance of Ralph Berger was no less secure. The production lacked the crisp discipline of the original. It was mainly a sentimental occasion, and the actors may have been guilty of having too good a time. But weighed against the going Hollywood standard for legitimate fare, it resembled a masterpiece. Selling tickets was no problem, and the run was curtailed only because other commitments intervened—including Julie's to *Body and Soul*. But old wounds were healed without visible scars. Julie was restored to the bosom of his spiritual brethren.

Although 1946 was a year of record prosperity for the film companies, their return to "normalcy" in peacetime was aggravated by labor difficulties that promised industrial turmoil. Even after a blanket twenty-five percent wage increase was given to studio employees in order to end a continuous flurry of strikes, two rival union collectives remained at war with one another. The opponents were the A. F. of L.'s International Alliance of Theatrical and Stage Employees, with a long-established motion picture arm; and the Conference of Studio Unions, organized in 1942 as an umbrella for many tiny craft unions involved in movie production.

The schism had an effect of dividing the previously harmonious Screen Actors Guild into rival factions, revealing a basically conservative posture in those who supported the IATSE. Julie's sympathy was with the CSU, many of whose leaders were his longtime friends and were warriors of the Old Left. The John Garfield signature was affixed to a telegram sent to the IATSE protesting civil rights violations against CSU pickets. Specifically, he was supporting a CSU strike effort to obtain jobs formerly given only to IATSE members. Julie said both unions should have equal rights to work. But the IATSE resisted compromise, saying that the CSU was dominated by Communists.

When the Guild decided, in a showdown vote, to recommend settlement of the dispute through arbitration (essentially siding with the IATSE), Julie went against the CSU and voted with SAG. He said, "All kinds of people are mixed up in this—the kind of people I love. There are guys on the picket line that I've worked with, and they've got wives and kids. But that's why in the end I had to support my Guild, because it has taken the most constructive action to keep these things from happening in America."

As a member of its executive board, Julie liked to inflate his importance to the Guild, but in this controversy he believed he could make an important contribution as peacemaker. But he was bitterly disappointed not to be included on a Guild committee selected to mediate the dispute at an A. F. of L. convention in Chicago. Perhaps significantly, the committee's primary spokesmen would graduate to the national political scene in later years, all as classic Republican conservatives— Robert Montgomery, George Murphy, and Ronald Reagan. (Although still a registered Democrat, Reagan had shed the garments of liberalism. Twenty years later he would become Republican governor of California.)

The Guild accomplished its mission. The strikes were settled through arbitration, and the likelihood of violence was averted. Ronald Reagan said: "It seemed to us that a vital principle morally essential to us all was involved, the principle of arbitration itself . . . arbitration to end and to prevent war, whether between nations or between labor and industry under the American system of private enterprise."

After the smoke cleared, life and moviemaking did appear to return to normalcy in the Hollywood community. But the labor crisis had opened a can of worms. Members of the House Un-American Activities Committee were alerted to the possibility that fabled, fantastic Hollywood was a hotbed of communism, and that the motion picture medium was being used for subversive propaganda.

"I could sign another long-term contract and be a rich, successful guy," Julie told the interviewing Mary Morris, "but I gotta look at myself in the mirror every morning. So I stare at my rich, contented puss and my conscience says, 'Okay, kid, what have you been doing lately?' "

He told everyone he was not becoming his own producer, exactly. The name of the company was Roberts Productions and Bob Roberts was the boss; Julie was merely an employee. But besides being the company's principal financier, John Garfield was also its sole asset.

He said he didn't want to turn movies into a lecture platform, but "there's fear in Hollywood about tackling dangerous subjects, difficult subjects . . . I owe it to myself to be available when some enterprising people want to try something tough."

Oh, he would still do commercial stuff to retain his commodity value at the box office. But he mainly wanted the kind of picture that would be harder to do but might turn out more interesting. He said he wanted to do "zing, spit, fire" pictures.

Julie's friends expected him to take a pratfall. Some thought he would be undone by his faith in Bob Roberts, whom they saw as a parasite—a hanger-on and one-man Garfield entourage. They snickered when Julie said his first effort might be Edgar Allan Poe's *The Tell-Tale Heart*. But they couldn't scoff at the advantageous deal Roberts had negotiated with Enterprise Pictures, the brainchild of such industrial princes as David Loew and David Lewis. Under the Enterprise wing, Roberts and Garfield were without financial obligation; and while they were protected against losses, they would share in the profits.

Julie abandoned the idea of *The Tell-Tale Heart* and entertained other notions, including a life story of Angelo Patri in a kind of *Boys Town* format. Then he read an original script by a young writer and political activist named Abraham Polonsky, whose only credit was the script for a gypsy opera called *Golden Earrings,* with Marlene Dietrich and Ray Milland. And that picture was rumored to be so bad that Paramount was afraid to release it. But Julie trusted his instinct. He decided to take a chance on Polonsky's drama of the fight game, eventually to be called *Body and Soul.*

Even those who were given to belittling Julie's intelligence would often acknowledge his instinctive scent for talent in others. Robbie Garfield was to say: "He had a thing about new people, about giving them a chance in the films he made. He gambled on them and no matter what anyone said about them, he would try again. He said 'They could *direct,*' he said 'They could *write,*' he said 'They could *act*' . . . and most of them succeeded partly because he believed they could."

His director would be Robert Rossen, the favorite screenwriter of his early Warner period, who had tried directing (*Johnny O'Clock*—his own script) and wanted to keep at it.

From the beginning, Abe Polonsky would have a fight on his hands to keep Bob Rossen from rewriting the script.

Julie also hired his favorite cameraman, James Wong Howe. In the cast Julie assembled, only Art Smith represented the Group, in a minor role. But others were veterans who had marched on the Left side of every topical issue: Anne Revere as the boxer's mother; Lloyd Gough, the primary villain; Joseph Pevney as the ill-fated sidekick; and the fine Negro actor Canada Lee as a battered old fighter-turned-trainer.

He settled on Lilli Palmer as the fighter's estranged wife because two of his writer pals—Albert Maltz and Ring Lardner, Jr.—had scripted her first American film (*Cloak and Dagger*) and rated her a capital talent. The Austrian-born Lilli Palmer had become a star in British films and had married Rex Harrison. She accompanied Harrison to Hollywood when he was engaged for *Anna and the King of Siam,* and when she worked into American pictures it was apparent that her English was both excellent and not oppressively British. She agreed to Julie's terms and he gave her costar billing.

The antihero protagonist was cut to the measure of John Garfield. He was a kid from the Bronx who scrapped to the top—champion in a prizefight milieu depicted as an inferno of corruption. Prior to *Humoresque,* any hint of Jewishness in a Garfield characterization was something the studio would purge, but in *Body and Soul* he was again specifically Jewish. Some Garfield intimates—notably Clifford Odets—would interpret the picture as an allegorical commentary on Julie's own life. In that light, the "body" was newcomer Hazel Brooks, representing a composite of all the girls who had tempted Julie to stray from Robbie; and the "soul" was Lilli Palmer. The prizefight business could stand for Hollywood, or for Warner Brothers.

People who bought movie tickets needed no instruction to connect the title with the endearing Garfield characteristics. There was magnetism in the stocky, hard body; and Julie's brand of actor-to-audience communication spelled pure soul. Women responded to the first quality, but the second one was addressed more to the men. Garfield was an actor for both sexes to cherish. They related to him, and his celluloid conflicts often were very similar to their own . . . and never more vividly than in *Body and Soul*.

The fighter has been thoroughly corrupted. He has renounced the wife who loves him but who cannot accept his fall from grace. He has been disowned by his mother. He has obeyed "the system" to the point of tolerating the apparent gang murder of his best friend. And agreeing to take a dive in a championship bout, he has wagered his own bankroll—betting on himself to lose. But a demon stirs within him, summoning his true grit: he wins the fight. He also has won dignity, self-respect, and the wife who had learned of the bribe. Clutching Lilli Palmer at ringside, John Garfield becomes aware of the steely-cold rage of Lloyd Gough and the other mobsters he has betrayed. "What can you do, kill me? Everybody dies."

Body and Soul was filmed in the spring of 1947. Julie took sparring lessons from Mushy Callahan and vowed to do all of his own fight scenes without the use of a double. He enjoyed a wide press coverage mainly for that aspect, and he began to believe some of the news blurbs about his boxing skill. Nor was his confidence shaken by two incidents that occurred during the shooting schedule. While filming a boxing scene in the ring with former welterweight pro Art Darrell, Julie absorbed one of Darrell's hard rights and staggered backward, hitting his head on a camera boom. He was briefly unconscious, and Dr. Forrest Domewood closed Julie's scalp wound with six stitches. Shooting was halted, but Julie was back the next day. Still, the other incident was even more humiliating. At a party he got to boasting about having fought in the Golden Gloves, and he was challenged to a living-room bout by a former Penn State boxing champion. They donned boxing gloves and Julie was decked by two quick, hard punches. Julie was as surprised as Robbie was furious, and he stopped boasting about his boxing prowess. But he continued to show off athletically during the daily shooting, not even relaxing his pace after sustaining his second mild heart attack—attributed to some strenuous rope-skipping Julie did in a series of repeated takes as Hazel Brooks kept blowing her lines during a training camp scene. He was always under doctors' orders to slow down, take things easier; and he was always ignoring the advice.

Body and Soul happened to be as timely as it was good. When it opened in New York in the fall of 1947 to general acclaim as one of the year's best movies, the corruptive influence of big-time gambling on professional and amateur sports—particularly in Manhattan, and especially boxing—was under investigation and getting the headline play in the sport sections. That gave Julie a lot to talk about when he went on a personal promotion tour that was part of his agreement with United Artists. Still obviously an authentic product of New York, he was a sure draw in his own city. But he participated in radio telethons and other special events throughout the country.

Before shooting had been completed on his first independent venture, Julie agreed to play a secondary role in the *Gentleman's Agreement* film that Elia Kazan would direct. Laura Hobson's best-selling novel on the theme of anti-Semitism would be 20th Century-Fox's most ambitious document and 1947 Christmas release, personally produced by Darryl Zanuck.

Gregory Peck was cast as a journalist pretending to be Jewish in order to gain meaningful insight on American anti-Semitism for a magazine article. The part of Dave, the writer's friend—a Jewish lieutenant in the Army—required only half a dozen scenes that added up to little more than twenty minutes on the screen. But the role had an important function to the drama, and Kazan wanted it played by a strong and attractive personality. Not hesitating, Julie said, "I'm doing it for Gadge (Kazan) because the picture says something I believe, and it needs to be said." Julie said *Gentleman's Agreement* would help his career, not hurt it. At the Enterprise Studios he asked David Niven's advice about taking a supporting part, and Niven said when in doubt, be in a hit.

Gentleman's Agreement was a hit, and probably overpraised as pictures that say the right things usually are. Certainly it advanced Garfield's prestige. He received star billing, grouped with Gregory Peck and Dorothy McGuire. *Gentleman's Agreement* pulled in a large supply of Oscar nominations and was the Academy's obligatory choice as best picture. Kazan won, as did Celeste Holm as a supporting actress. And Garfield (whose performance would seem the best thing in the picture when viewed a generation later) could afford to be ignored, for the Academy nominated him as best actor for *Body and Soul*.

There had been stars since the infancy of the movies, but now there was a new class of "superstars"—a term reserved for a select handful of durable screen veterans. Clearly, Julie was moving into that class. He was beginning to feel his powers. There were new propositions for term contracts, there were lavish single-picture offers, and bids to subsidize future Roberts-Garfield productions. Julie savored the attention, but was increasingly distracted by the shadows caused by Hollywood's darkening political situation.

Julie and Robbie again "got involved." In 1947 they attended a Henry Wallace rally at Gilmore Stadium in West Hollywood. A Wallace tour was sponsored by a group called Progressive Citizens of America, then advocating Wallace's presidential candidacy on the Democratic ticket in 1948. The Garfields gave a hundred dollars to the Wallace fund-raising campaign, in effect contributing to the PCA, which would later be identified as a "subversive" group.

Then, in October when *Body and Soul* was playing its first-run Washington engagement, Julie was in a contingent of filmland personalities journeying to the nation's capital to attend hearings of the House Un-American Activities Committee. California State Senator Jack Tenney had named John Garfield as one of the movie actors known as a Communist sympathizer or belonging to Communist-front organizations. (Others identified included Charles Chaplin, Fredric March, and Frank Sinatra.) Tenney resurrected an event of almost two years earlier when Julie and Robbie accepted an invitation to dine aboard a Russian freighter in the Los Angeles Harbor—an occasion honoring Konstantine Simonov, a Soviet journalist visiting the United States at the invitation of the

State Department. Simonov had wanted to meet some movie stars, and the Charles Chaplins also accepted the dinner invitation, as did the Lewis Milestones. Julie had been surprised by the criticism of his action that followed in the press. He said, "I didn't know it was a crime to be hospitable to a guest of the State Department until I read about in the papers the next day." (Julie got it from both directions. Simonov, not impressed by the movie people, criticized them in the Soviet press.)

When asked about Tenney's statements, Julie said: "I voted for Roosevelt and I've always been for Roosevelt, and I guess Senator Tenney doesn't like that. I'm a registered Democrat and I vote the Democratic ticket all the time." (Indeed, he supported the Truman candidacy in 1948 after Wallace failed to mount a drive for the Democratic nomination and became a third-party candidate. Julie had also supported Truman's decision to use the atomic bomb to end the war with Japan.)

The parade of congenial witnesses before HUAC in late 1947 included magnates Jack Warner and L. B. Mayer, director Sam Wood, actors Robert Taylor, Robert Montgomery, Gary Cooper, Ronald Reagan, Adolphe Menjou, and George Murphy, as well as an ominously alarmed Lela Rogers (mother of Ginger). The witnesses were asked if Hollywood was aswarm with Communists, and while all denied that it was, they agreed that a faction of about one percent was extremely well-organized and extremely troublesome. Columnist Howard Rushmore, who once had been fired from the *Daily Worker* for having reviewed *Gone With the Wind* favorably, said, "The Communists didn't bother much with the actors. They were considered ninety-nine percent morons and regarded only with contempt." Sure enough, writers and not actors were the primary victims of the first purge initiated in 1947. And Humphrey Bogart, for one, did not dispute the low rating ascribed to actors. He said, "As politicians, we stink"; and he circulated a petition protesting the hearings, to be forwarded to Congress. Julie failed to sign only because he was giving autographs to WACS and other movie fans that surrounded him while Bogart was circuiting the Capitol corridors with his petition. Although Julie was not in Washington to give official testimony, he spoke out for reporters to hear and record.

"Why should I keep quiet? I pay taxes. Exercising the rights of citizenship is an American principle. If I don't express my convictions, why have them?"

Opposing convictions were getting expressed and were dividing the community of film actors along ideological lines. Adolphe Menjou was the most militant spokesman on the Right, saying: "I'm a witch-hunter and a Red-baiter, and I've read about a hundred and fifty books on communism. I believe America should arm to the teeth, and that every young man should have military training for his discipline, his manhood, his courage, and for the love of his country."

Menjou became the first witness to enumerate specific names the way the committee wanted to hear them. He made pointed reference to the recent dispute between the movie labor collectives, and Menjou's failure to mention John Garfield in his testimony was probably due to Julie's having not backed the CSU in that dispute—as had Edward G. Robinson, whom Menjou cited by name. Yet Menjou failed to mention SAG's function as mediator, or that the differences between the CSU and the IATSE had been resolved through arbitration.

Broadway columnist Earl Wilson offered his own happy solution to "the commie question": take off your clothes, go to bed, go to sleep, and forget it. He said the committee was getting most of its information from dubious sources, citing *Esquire* movie critic John Charles Moffitt's claim that "Broadway was predominately Communist." Wilson said Moffitt's belief was based on "a four-month job he held as a rewrite man on the New York *Sun* twenty years ago."

Many actors mentioned and trained on Broadway talked wishfully of chucking the movie business and returning to their New York roots. Not all of them meant it, and fewer still could overcome the inertia peculiar to southern California living and make it back, even briefly. Among his Hollywood friends,

Julie most admired Fredric March for having achieved a workable formula that permitted both stage and screen work through the years. Yet Julie never doubted that he, too, would get back to the stage as soon as his indenture to Warner Brothers had been completed. He could afford to work below his movieland salary standard, for he had money in the bank. Both Robbie and Julie were generous but penny-wise, a carry-over from the frugality of their have-not times.

Now that investigators were looking for Communists under every Hollywood rock, the Garfields were of a mood to get out of the film colony for awhile. They decided to maintain two residences, one on each coast. Julie thought it would be ideal to spend six months in Hollywood and the other six in New York. He said, "I want to be an actor when I grow up, and you get that in New York." So in December, 1947, the Garfield family packed their clothes and returned to Manhattan, subleasing an elegant triplex on lower Fifth Avenue from Donald Ogden Stewart, the wittiest of Julie's screenwriter friends. It was a significant time for the American theatre, and opportune for Julie to resume active ties with his soulmates.

Although officially disbanded for half a dozen years, the Group Theatre was a more potent influence than ever, shaping the form of the new postwar theatre. The Stanislavsky method had become the major controversy of contemporary acting, not just one of its minor eccentricities. It was in 1947 that Elia Kazan, Cheryl Crawford, and Bob Lewis organized the Actors' Studio, which soon would enlist Lee Strasberg as artistic director; and Sanford Meisner was now the man in charge at the vitally influential Neighborhood Playhouse.

In New York, Julie was reading a lot of scripts. Maxwell Anderson wanted him for *Truckline Café*. It was an old-fashioned "proletarian drama" with a topical concern for the readjustment of returning veterans. A few years earlier, Julie would have accepted any new Anderson play, sight unseen. But the veteran dramatist had not had a major success for several seasons, and Julie thought *Truckline Café* had a lot of good talk but was finally *too* talky.

Anderson read the play aloud to him in a New York dentist's office while Julie endured another reconstruction job on his teeth, again requiring several hours. While the playwright acted out all the parts, Julie made occasional gurgling sounds of response. "My play?" Anderson asked. No; Julie indicated his own teeth. Maxwell Anderson read on, but paused when Garfield nearly screamed. "Your teeth?" Julie managed to say, "No, your play."

He decided against *Truckline Café* but told Anderson of a young actor who had excited Kazan, Stella Adler, and other keen observers of thespian talent. The chap's name was Marlon Brando, and he was cast in the *Truckline Café* lead and ultimately awarded with notices in extravagant contrast to the general panning of the play. This was the occasion that prompted Maxwell Anderson to label the drama critics "the Jukes family of journalism."

Then Elia Kazan showed Julie one of those rare scripts that practically explode with dramatic power—*A Streetcar Named Desire*—by the young Tennessee Williams (who had scored two years earlier with his first Broadway play, the poetically evocative *Glass Menagerie*). Kazan was set to direct the play for producer Irene Selznick, and he wanted Garfield in the part of Stanley Kowalski, the brutish manchild antagonizing the tormented, fragile Blanche Du Bois. Julie admired the play and saw strong possibilities in the Kowalski role, but suspected that Blanche Du Bois would dominate the proceedings. He sought the advice of everyone whose opinion he respected, and in every case he was urged to seize the opportunity. Yet he turned it down. Rejecting intimations of being just plain scared, Julie said: "About *Streetcar,* the reason I didn't do it was just money. I think it's a great play. I just wanted what I thought I was entitled to get. It was a commercial venture being put on for profit, and I wanted the same consideration as an Ingrid Bergman or a Spencer Tracy . . . I deserve that, I guess."

Kazan was disappointed, but not for long. Examining the roster of the newly launched Actors' Studio, he picked Marlon

Brando. The Brando Kowalski was so definitive as to discourage speculation on what Garfield might have made of the role. History doubtless would be grateful to Julie for rejecting *Streetcar*, but he realized he had made a grave mistake. When he saw Anthony Quinn play Kowalski in the national company, he said it proved that an actor of strong individual personality didn't have to imitate the actor who created the role. Both the Brando and Quinn interpretations were valid, he thought, although very different; and he believed there was a boyishness about Kowalski that might have surfaced even better in a Garfield reading.

So when Cheryl Crawford asked Julie to consider *Skipper Next to God*, he said yes rather quickly. The drama by the eminent Dutch refugee from the Nazis, Jan de Hartog, dealt with a sea captain whose cargo was refugee Jews seeking safety in America. Confronted by an order to return the Jews to their homeland where they will almost certainly be annihilated, the captain scuttles his own ship and goes down with it—but only after depositing his passengers safely in lifeboats, near the scene of a scheduled regatta.

An actor playing the *Skipper Next to God* needed almost Christ-like charisma and could not be intimidated by the stilted nature of translated dialogue. Cheryl Crawford rightly sensed that Julie's irreverent approach to dialogue would render it believable, especially since he would have the benefit of Lee Strasberg as director. At that time Julie may have felt safer in Strasberg's care than in Kazan's, although it was also true that *Skipper Next to God* appealed to him because it didn't figure to tie up much of his time. Bob Roberts was getting *Force of Evil* ready for a spring shooting start as their company's second independent film, which caused Julie to reject other scripts which, like *Streetcar*, would involve long-term commitments.

Skipper was supposed to run only four weeks. Julie said it would give him the feel of being on stage again, without the pressure of an expensively mounted, commercially speculative venture. *Skipper* was "experimental theatre" and Julie said it was no big deal. It was one of the American National Theatre Association's noncommercial ventures—the showcasing of a play with literary merit but uncertain popular potential.

Much was made of the fact that John Garfield was accepting the union minimum of eighty dollars a week for the *Skipper* engagement. Julie figured he could afford it, because his salary-plus-profit-percentage arrangement for *Body and Soul* promised to net him almost half a million dollars, and because he had also collected $150,000 for his relatively small role in *Gentleman's Agreement*. By fortuitous coincidence, the Kazan film opened in New York almost to the day of Julie's return to the stage after almost seven years. Julie's excellent notices for *Gentleman's Agreement* seemed to intensify the loud cheers he received for *Skipper Next to God*. Soon it was apparent that the play was capable of selling out for months to come. And Julie said the role of Captain Joris Kuiper was the hardest but most rewarding thing he had accomplished as an actor, in any medium. At the end of January, wealthy producer Blevins Davis took over *Skipper* and transferred it to the Maxine Elliott Theater on Thirty-ninth Street for a commercial run of indefinite duration. Business remained excellent, and the play closed after ten weeks only because Julie had to get to work as principal actor in his *Force of Evil* film.

During *Skipper's* commercial phase, Julie's salary was fixed at $300 weekly, although legend persisted that he was still working for eighty. Julie could have demanded more, but did not want to play the big star against the best interests of the American National Theatre Association, whose Experimental Foundation was to receive half of *Skipper's* profits—that being Blevins Davis's arrangement with Cheryl Crawford. Despite the abbreviated engagement, *Skipper* returned a profit for Davis and enabled him to enrich the Experimental Foundation.

During the *Skipper* run, Julie received an Academy Award nomination as best actor for *Body and Soul*. He was still in New York in March of 1948 when he received a special "Tony"—the Antoinette Perry award given by the American Theatre Wing—for his contribution to New York experimental theatre with *Skipper,* which had just closed. Then the Garfields returned to Hollywood for the Academy Award ceremony, only for Julie to lose out to the veteran Ronald Colman.

The Garfields had experienced a happy season in New York and were reluctant to resume a less exhilarating life in a Hollywood in its winter of discontent. Julie said, "I'm a New Yorker and my wife is a New Yorker and we love New York. My wife thinks I shouldn't be in movies at all. She'd like to stay in New York the year round and I can understand why. They're soft in Hollywood, so busy playing golf and gin rummy that they don't realize they're in the world's most attractive rut."

During their New York stay the Garfields had the Angelo Patris to dinner on Fifth Avenue. The aging, beaming Patri told Julie that "Now you should try your hand at Shakespeare." Some of the friendly Garfield critics from the Group and its offshoots would have scoffed, but Julie was giving some serious thought to The Bard. He said, "Some day I hope to play Romeo, but Romeo with guts, not soft. Romeo was an Italian, and I grew up in Italian neighborhoods. I think I could do it." (Thus he anticipated Franco Zeffirelli's successful film of *Romeo and Juliet* more than two decades later.)

And on a night when the Garfields were attending the fiftieth wedding anniversary celebration of Julie's aunt and uncle in the Bronx, a heavy snow knocked out the taxi service and the Garfields went home on the subway for the first time in years. Normally all subway passengers occupy their seats in stony silence, but Julie and Robbie sensed and enjoyed the stir his presence was causing. They were approached by an elderly couple that had stared pointedly at Julie, and the woman said, "Say, aren't you Julius Garfinkle of Livonia Avenue?" Julie answered that he was, and she said, "Hmmm, I thought so." And then, after a pause: "So what's new with you?"

What was new with John Garfield was *Force of Evil* which, in any event, smacked of traditional Hollywood in no way. Julie boasted that his own company had discovered the director-writer of the age in Abraham Polonsky. During *Body and Soul* there had been some friction between writer-turned-director Bob Rossen and Polonsky over the latter's script, and Abe wanted to be in control of his medium. Julie gave him the opportunity. Working with Ira Wolfert to produce a filmscript from Wolfert's novel, *Tucker's People,* Polonsky got a strong text; and as director he created a powerful, distinctly American film, although not a pretty one by any means. There were superb performances by Garfield, Thomas Gomez, and Beatrice Pearson. Indeed, the movie might arguably be a great one.

But that would be something of an artistic secret, owing to the collapse of the ambitious Enterprise Pictures amalgamation. Clobbered by the expensive debacle of Lewis Milestone's *Arch of Triumph*—the Bergman-Boyer picture that was as disastrous financially as it was critically—the Enterprise ship sank while *Force of Evil* was in the midpassage of production. Metro-Goldwyn-Mayer guaranteed the financing necessary to complete the project, and replaced United Artists as distributor. That M-G-M was not enamored of the finished picture was evident in its subsequent shabby promotion. *Force of Evil* would be the last "major" production released during the calendar year 1948, but the campaign more nearly resembled one for a "B" picture.

Its box office response would be sluggish, and little note would be made of a dramatic "process shot" of John Garfield and Beatrice Pearson in the rear seat of a taxicab: six years earlier but no less brilliant than a famous, similar scene between Marlon Brando and Rod Steiger in *On the Waterfront.*

Nor did anyone suspect that the climactic scene in *Force of Evil,* showing Garfield walking into a cellar of corruption (Orpheus descending into hell) also illuminated Julie as the prophet of his own doom, and the doom for so many of his generation.

By the time *Force of Evil* was a candidate for any kind of artistic claim, all the people involved with its production were in deep trouble.

X

Witches and Phantoms

The United States House of Representatives authorized a Committee on Un-American Activities in 1938. Congressman Martin Dies of Texas, the committee's first chairman and its philosophical catalyst, seemed to feel that communism not only was the most important un-American activity, it was the *only* one. Occasionally the committee would enumerate suspected Communist sympathizers, and one list even included a little girl named Shirley Temple. For the most part, the committee was about as menacing as a small swarm of gnats.

But in 1947 the committee began investigating an amiable composer named Hanns Eisler in an effort to locate and apprehend his brother Gerhart, who they believed was an important Communist agent in the United States. The significance of the Eisler investigation was that it gave the committee a whiff of a lively, party-directed Communist movement within the performing arts. Hanns Eisler had been active in America as a composer for both stage and screen. He had professional ties with the Group Theatre, and a speaking acquaintance with John Garfield.

In his "friendly" 1947 testimony, Jack L. Warner identified writers who had attempted to inject un-American ideas into Warner Brothers film scripts. He implicated several who had written dialogue for John Garfield vehicles, including Albert Maltz, Robert Rossen, and Irwin Shaw. Pressing on, the committee established as its "Unfriendly Ten" a group of Hollywood writers who, as subpoenaed witnesses, refused to cooperate with the committee and were held in contempt. They were the first victims of the Hollywood blacklist and most did some time in prison. Again the roster listed several of John Garfield's intimates: Maltz, Dalton Trumbo, John Howard Lawson, Ring Lardner, Jr., and Herbert Biberman. Although most of the early attention was given to the writers, the blacklist embraced many actors who were less than stars. Joe Bromberg was an early victim. Thoroughly discredited by the committee was Julie's protégé Abe Polonsky—a name so unfamiliar that few knew of his existence, or the fact of his having been blacklisted.

The film colony's liberal element was not passive toward the changing events although it was ineffectual. The petition that Bogart had initiated in Washington finally caught up with Julie at the Beverly Hills Tennis Club, in the form of an "amicus curiae" brief on behalf of the Unfriendly Ten. The brief was circulated primarily by William Wyler on behalf of "The Committee for the First Amendment." Bogart, it seems, had a change of heart and said so in a press conference, for which he was criticized. (The Washington *Post* said, "Bogart's about-face was doubtless due to fear of losing his livelihood as a result of being branded a Communist . . . We are rather sorry for Mr. Bogart, who had nothing at all to be ashamed of until he began to be ashamed.") The petition still contained Bogart's signature as well as those of many other movie notables, among them Lauren Bacall, John Huston, June Havoc, and Richard Conte. It stated in part that "We, the undersigned as American citizens who believe in Constitutional democratic government, are disgusted and outraged by the continuing attempts of the House Un-American Activities Committee to smear the motion picture industry." It went on to say that the hearings were "morally wrong" and curbed the right to "freedom of expression." Julie signed the brief after it was delivered to him at the tennis club by George Wilner, who would later be described as a functionary for Communist party activities in Hollywood.

After the first movement of its witch-hunting symphony, HUAC closed its show for a three-year intermission of fact-finding. Julie was one of many solvent screen stars who, under advice of counsel, furnished the committee (now chaired by Rep. J. Parnell Thomas of New Jersey) with a statement of loyalty to the United States government and a denial of association with Communists—thus hoping to hold the investigators at arm's length.

Hollywood's year of the Great Panic was 1948—not only for its political distress, but because the audience was deserting the moviehouse for television at home, while the Supreme Court was delivering the *coup de grace* by ruling that the major studios had violated the country's anti-trust laws and would have to unload their theatrical holdings. No longer would the big studios dangle fat contract offers to their stars. Even less rosy was the outlook for independent producers.

The Roberts Company did not disband; but with the bottom falling out of the box office, continued independent effort was too risky. There was a business-as-usual show of office activity, but the company's activity narrowed down to its being able to lease a single valuable asset—Garfield himself. And that was an asset of possibly diminishing value, because the House Un-American Activities Committee was defaming some of his past and even present associates, and their shadow tainted him.

There was only one solid offer, but it looked like a humdinger: John Huston wanted Julie to play opposite Jennifer Jones in *Rough Sketch*. In the wake of *The Treasure of Sierra Madre* and *Key Largo,* Huston had a rising reputation, and it figured that *Rough Sketch* had to be a great picture. Julie said it was a political allegory addressed to the House Un-American Activities Committee; but the picture about revolutionary South America contained ambiguities that few moviegoers would try to understand. It would go out to the theaters as *We Were Strangers,* but only briefly. Ticket sales were so skimpy that Columbia, the distributor, simply took it out of circulation shortly after its release, which was deferred until mid-1949. *We Were Strangers* had impressive parts but an undiscernible whole, and the Garfield performance had more authority than definition.

Julie went from the picture assignment to another play

without breaking stride. Clifford Odets emerged from his latest emotional coma to complete a full-length play specifically for John Garfield. *The Big Knife* was about Hollywood, the movie business, and a confused star who was in several untenable positions simultaneously—at home with his wife; at his studio; and in his own conscience. Odets found it impossible to write a play *for* Julie without writing one *about* him.

The Garfields were ready for a permanent move to the East Coast anyway. They had wanted out of Hollywood, so they decided simply to get out. Although Beverly Hills would remain the "official" family residence, the move back to New York in late 1948 was for good. Robbie found a nice apartment on Central Park West, and the Ethical Culture School for David's kindergarten. The Garfields agreed that they wanted their children to grow up and be educated in the East.

Odets now was living at Beekman Place and Fifty-first Street with his wife Betty and their two children. Julie became a daily visitor there, and on many nights he and Odets worked around the clock, talking out all the implications of *The Big Knife* while getting the script into a high polish.

The advance sale for the Broadway engagement was huge and a tour of the principal tryout towns gave assurance of a top-ticket attraction. But when *The Big Knife* opened in February, 1949, it was that sometime thing, the hit that is not a success. It was a drama of political blackmail and spiritual bankruptcy. As a titan of movie industry, Joe Bromberg rather obviously parodied Louis B. Mayer. And many people thought they recognized the play's protagonist—movie star Charlie Castle—as a parody of the actor who was playing him on the stage. It also followed that the role of the unhappy wife (played by Nancy Kelly) could be taken to resemble Robbie Garfield. Julie may not have seen himself in Charlie Castle, an actor who sells himself down the river for movie stardom but would like to get out. Odets resolved Charlie's predicament with a cliché: in the end, the actor kills himself.

The Big Knife ran three months and could have played longer if Julie had so dictated. It hardly mattered what the critics thought of the play's merits; its attraction was a potent movie star in the flesh. Julie was bitterly disappointed that *The Big Knife* was so easily dismissed by the theatre's serious chroniclers.

But Julie's custom was to rebound from disappointment. He said he was a new man, living in the area he knew best. And the play's audiences were filled with adoring women and teen-aged girls. Julie didn't mind that they mobbed him wherever he went.

He and Bromberg were leaving Odets's apartment one afternoon and were accosted by a throng of young girls. They had seen their idol enter the Odets apartment and waited for him to come out. Word got around about who they were waiting for. The crowd grew, and before Julie could make his exit, the street was blocked by the girls. Julie and Joe began walking toward a cab but the girls crushed him against the apartment building's iron fence. Wiggling through to the cab and getting into it were trouble enough, but then the cab was unable to move. When it did, the girls ran alongside, dodging in and out of the traffic, banging on the car's windows. Julie said to Joe Bromberg, "Oh, well, this is my home town." He was very pleased.

Had the critics been more generous in their praise of Odets, Julie might not have quit the play—which, of course, had the effect of closing it. It was explained that the closing was necessitated by another Garfield film commitment, and it was true that Julie had agreed to make *Under My Skin* for 20th Century-Fox. (He signed for $135,000, and did not expect to receive many more one-picture offers at that level.) But he did not report immediately for the filming. When *The Big Knife* closed, Julie sailed for Europe. Ostensibly he was making arrangements for future filming of *The Italian Story* as his own project. It was an earnest venture, and Julie had Fred Zinnemann penciled in as director. *The Italian Story* was about Guido Cantelli, the composer-conductor protégé of Arturo Toscanini. Julie was captivated by Cantelli and looked forward to playing him on the screen, hopefully as soon as *Under My Skin* was completed. But according to the whispers, the real reason he went to France was his infatuation with Micheline Presle.

She was the star of an acclaimed French film of the early postwar issue, *Le Diable au Corps* (*The Devil in the Flesh*). Julie had met her during the filming of *Gentleman's Agreement,* while she paid a visit that culminated in a 20th Century-Fox contract. Her knowledge of art, poetry, and classical music impressed Julie, and it was rumored that he was equally impressed with other aspects of Mlle. Presle. He may have been instrumental in her selection as his leading lady in *Under My Skin.* Whatever Julie's design on the young actress, he did not fare well in France since most of her time was given to Bill Marshall, a Paris-based Hollywood producer. Yet Julie enjoyed visiting the cellars and dance halls on the Left Bank, mingling with the young existentialists he called his "fellow rebels." They clustered around him and he loved it. Here, he was very happy and had a lot of fun. As one observer put it, "They were all rebels together, and not doing too much thinking."

He returned to New York just long enough for a "hello-goodbye" with his family, and to receive—ironically enough—recognition as a "Father of the Year" at a National Father's Day Luncheon at the Waldorf-Astoria (Ralph Bunche was similarly honored). Then Julie went off to Arizona to confer with Dalton Trumbo at Trumbo's ranch. His concern was the script for *The Italian Story;* and if Trumbo was blacklisted, Julie said he could work under a pseudonym. He wanted Trumbo to write the screenplay in any event, although Trumbo's doubt that *The Italian Story* would ever amount to anything commercially may have dissuaded Julie, who soon dropped the idea completely.

But he threw himself into *Under My Skin* with an enthusiasm that was not limited to Micheline Presle. He liked the source material: *My Old Man,* from Ernest Hemingway's collection of Nick Adams stories. But he overrated the script and his leading lady about equally. To a *Collier's* writer,

Julie said: "What an actress! In one scene I'm drunk and I've just beat up my kid. I come roaring into her café while she's singing a song for the customers. She doesn't stop singing and she just looks at me and makes motions with her hands. But what looks, and what motions! This dame knows how to play a love scene from twenty feet away."

Under My Skin was also *Body and Soul* in a different guise. This time the prizefight figure would be in jockey silks, but the crisis was the same. Would the discredited old jockey throw the race, as the gamblers said he must? Or would he remain true to the young son who believes in him? Of course he'll win the race . . . only this time the gangsters really kill him. Julie thought it powerful stuff, and was gratified to be working with Jean Negulesco, the *Humoresque* director who left Warners to become a Fox mainstay.

The audience wasn't so easily convinced, and the audience dwindled. Neither a success nor a failure, *Under My Skin* merely came and went when issued in the spring of 1950. The critical reaction was indifferent, the commercial return only normally disappointing during so troublesome a time for the movie box office. Julie said, "I'm playing Wallace Beery for the first time." But young Orley Lindgren did not become the new Jackie Cooper or Mickey Rooney. And Micheline Presle, making no discernible impression on Middle America, would soon return to France.

Midway during the shooting schedule, there was a month-long shutdown for *Under My Skin* because Julie's hard-driving style was playing havoc with his heart. During a court match at the Beverly Hills Tennis Club he complained of feeling suddenly dizzy. While trying to walk toward a bench, he collapsed. An ambulance sped him to Cedars of Lebanon Hospital where Dr. Lee Siegel diagnosed a myocardial condition—heart muscle strain. Julie was thirty-six, and here was Dr. Siegel telling him he must avoid exertion of any kind for the rest of his life. The advice would go largely ignored, but Julie followed Clifford Odets's advice by giving more serious attention to painting as a pastime. A cruel joke around Hollywood was that Micheline Presle probably caused Julie's heart attack by driving up to Santa Barbara to marry Bill Marshall. No leading lady had ever done that to him while working with him in a movie!

Julie was back on the tennis court before long, and while *Under My Skin* was still before the camera, he accepted another movie starring assignment. Bob Roberts had not been able to raise financing for *The Italian Story* and Julie was not about to pay its production cost from his own pocket. He hoped there was nothing prophetic about the title of his next picture: *The Breaking Point*.

No one in 1950 suggested that *Under My Skin* was a great picture, but *The Breaking Point* would invite that consideration. It was one of only a handful of studio-mill projects to emerge with honor in that lackluster year. Still, it would die at the box office, lost in the chaos of the crumbling studio system. In 1950, not even great pictures could be marketed in the routine way that had worked throughout two decades of talking pictures. Unfortunately, the studios hadn't come up with alternative techniques that were any better.

The Breaking Point was also a Hemingway yarn. It was really *To Have and Have Not*—perhaps the weakest of the Hemingway novels—but it couldn't be called that on the screen because a few years earlier Warners had used the title, but almost none of the story, for the famous Bogart vehicle that introduced Lauren Bacall. ("If you want anything, just whistle.") This time the studio would do a literal version of the book, retaining Hemingway's tragic ending. Instead of getting killed, Bogart had gotten the girl. But Bogart was a winner; and Hemingway's Harry Morgan was a loser.

So Warners summoned John Garfield.

Jack Warner's personal invitation said, in effect, come home for old time's sake, Julie. He generously matched Zanuck's stipend and Julie was hooked. It was a sentimental occasion, reuniting Garfield with his first screen director (Curtiz) and his last Warner producer (Jerry Wald, who had supervised *Humoresque*). What remained at the studio in the way of a contract list did not suggest the Warner legends, but Julie's kibitzing chums—the carpenters, electricians, grips, script girls—were mostly the same faces as before. The fifties did not offer much in the way of security for a screen actor, and Julie decided that if Warners still wanted to talk about a term contract or any kind of multipicture deal, he would listen.

Even Mike Curtiz, with whom Julie had never been chummy or even cordial, welcomed him as a prodigal son and sought his ideas. He did not want to settle for an ordinary picture. He invited Julie and writer Ranald MacDougall to his ranch for congenial preproduction conferences that lasted a week.

"I acted all the parts. If Mike frowned, we'd do some talking, and maybe Randy would do some rewriting. Curtiz wanted to know my secret of being sexy. He decided it was time to get some honest sex into his pictures. I told him I learned everything from Luther Adler, who was a master at making sure all the lights were turned out. I told Mike he should make Luther a technical adviser for all his pictures."

In *The Breaking Point,* honest sex underscored the personal relationship between Harry Morgan and his wife, played by Phyllis Thaxter; and it defined a different relationship with Morgan's sometime lady friend on the side, the nominal costar, Patricia Neal. The story was tragic—about the "little guy" struggling to make a marginal living for his family. Morgan, operating a fishing boat off the Florida keys, smuggles Chinese immigrants and bootleg whiskey in an effort to build up a nest egg, but is ultimately defeated, slain by bandits. His dying statement expressed Hemingway's theme: "One man alone ain't got no chance."

Hemingway himself thought *The Breaking Point* was the best screen adaptation of any of his novels. He said that Harry Morgan as written had never become anything beyond an idea, but that John Garfield made Harry a *person*. It was an Oscar-worthy performance but quickly forgotten, because the picture failed to catch on.

Before filming actually began on *The Breaking Point* (but fortunately for Julie, *after* he had signed with Warners), an article quite damaging to Julie made the papers. John J. Huber, a former FBI undercover man, had told a closed hearing that ten top Hollywood personalities had been used as "drawing cards" by Communist organizations seeking to increase their membership. John Garfield was one of the ten.

Furious and a little frightened, Julie gave the press a statement of his own. "I made several trips during the war to entertain our armed forces, at which time I was thoroughly investigated by the FBI on all counts. The results of those investigations surely should be available now and I stand on them. If they want to string up a man for being liberal, let them bring on their ropes." (Edward G. Robinson, also among those named, gave the press this statement: "Perhaps it would be a good idea to have an investigation of the persons who make such charges. They seem to be as un-American as anything I know.")

There was no more talk of a new contract offer from Warners; and ominously and suddenly, there were no offers at all. The telephone stopped ringing. Scripts stopped coming his way. And Julie got the word from Jerry Wald.

For years Jerry Wald had been advocating a screen biography of Sime Silverman, founder of the show business paper *Variety,* and had been after Julie to take the role. Julie was always occupied. Now he needed a job and Wald was no longer interested, although he planned a spate of new pictures during his new producing partnership with Norman Krasna. Wald said he might be interested later if Julie got "in the clear." Julie was not on the blacklist, but Wald apparently suspected he might be put there at any time. Julie said the film community started treating him "like I was a member of your baseball team but you knew I was going to get traded." The movie people feared that Julie would eventually get the worst of it from HUAC.

When the House committee resumed its center-ring attraction, the oracles said Julie's three-year-old loyalty statement wouldn't keep the sharks at bay; he would almost certainly be called to testify. But he prepared for the worst, and hired the esteemed Louis Nizer as his counsel.

From the time he left Warner Brothers as a free agent and spent his "idle" time in New York, Julie worked with growing intensity toward developing his craft. Despite his measure of artistic accomplishment and more easily measurable popularity, Julie's chronic inferiority complex became more pronounced over the years, not less so. He told Robert Whitehead he had never understood any of the things the Group was talking about—that he'd be left at the post when they started arguing about the fine points of the Method.

He told people he read a lot more than he really did, although he gave a great deal of time to reading—not because he wanted to, but because he felt he had to. He said if he'd been born rich, it wouldn't have mattered that he wasn't educated. But he had known various forms of hunger as a child, and hunger for knowledge dominated "my years of adultery." He tried to close the gap with a late start on education, but then he'd meet a Montgomery Clift who was years younger, but already years ahead of him in learning, just naturally smart as hell.

Julie wondered: could he reach the summit of his profession without true intellect? He said the classics would hold the answer. He wanted to try Chekhov, Strindberg, Ibsen . . .

Sometimes he worked out at the Actors' Studio like an athlete given to sudden bursts of training. He took private instruction and also audited classes given by Stella Adler, Herbert Berghof, and others he regarded as the best coaches. He learned to communicate with Lee Strasberg because, Julie said, Strasberg found a way of coming down to Garfield's own level.

He sought theatrical growth in every form, taking fencing lessons and then ballet training for the bodily discipline they could give him. And he worked again at purging his speech of the Bronx accent. He said that as soon as he could learn to talk he'd like to have a go at playing François Villon.

The growing uncertainty of independent film production also forced Julie to think about being his own producer for the stage. He read Nelson Algren's novel, *The Man With the Golden Arm*, about a poor sucker on junk; and he purchased both the theatre and movie rights, even before he learned that the specter of John Garfield had hovered over Algren throughout the writing of the novel. Algren said if anyone was going to play Frankie Machine, it would have to be John Garfield.

But Hollywood movies still adhered to a rigid production code, and narcotics addiction was not allowed to be depicted on the screen. It could not attain a production code seal, and to release a film without the seal was commercially hazardous, a gamble. Julie said he'd be willing to gamble if the odds improved, and decided to hold on to *The Man With the Golden Arm* until the odds shifted in his favor.

The advent of the Korean War in the summer of 1950 intensified anti-Communist sentiment in the United States and gave HUAC impetus for resuming its hearings in the spotlight's glare. Julie was sad, troubled, worried; and his children were his best therapy.

The Garfield family often got away to Fire Island for delightful weekends and extended vacations. Many years later the grown daughter Julie was to recall that her father "was always so quick to give of his energy. I was so young, but I remember I was always wanting him to carry me piggy-back into the ocean. I only learned later that those were sad days for him, because Hollywood wasn't giving him a chance to work."

His children enjoyed having their father around the house, whether on Fire Island or in the apartment on Central Park West. David, grown professionally into John Garfield, Jr., would say, "I was very young when he was alive, and the few moments between us that I can remember I keep to myself because they were so few, but they all count."

While Bob Roberts tried to work out another picture deal, Julie would take his children to the St. George Playhouse in Brooklyn, or perhaps to a circus that represented a special Easter party for the Police Athletic League.

He could still summon honest laughter when he was "roasted" by the Friars, with old friend Milton Berle as master of ceremonies. But inactivity was grinding him down, and painting wasn't enough for keeping him occupied, although Julie's work improved. (He was proud that Lee Strasberg

would hang "an original Garfield" in his New York apartment.) Julie said: "A lot of actors have hobbies like boats
and horses, but not me. And now that I can't play tennis as
often as I'd like, I'd have to say the stage is my hobby. I much
prefer it to owning a ranch."

But for money's sake, making another film seemed to be
the most sensible idea. Bob Roberts reported that, in any event,
they could not get backers—not even if Julie decided to do
a musical version of *It Happened One Night,* in the nude and
in blackface, to pacify every taste. But they could have an
arrangement with United Artists—a risky one that would have
them shouldering their own financial burden. Julie said he'd
use his own money to underwrite a picture, if necessary, but
the thinking would have to be strictly along commercial lines.

So what kind of story offered the best odds? Julie reasoned
that the tried-and-true package was the way to sell John Garfield to the public. So he chose *He Ran All the Way,* which
would anthologize every cliché of the Garfield formula-picture
—elements that previously had forced Julie to swallow salary
suspension.

The safest thing was John Garfield on the lam, a fugitive
from justice, taken in by a girl who's afraid of him but will
fall in love anyway. Dangerously he lives, because nobody lives
forever. Back there east of the river, they made him a criminal,
those forces of evil . . . so dust be his destiny. John Garfield
living, loving, and losing. The question was whether there
was still an audience willing to see all of it just once more.
He Ran All the Way was shot on both coasts and went into
production in the fall of 1950. It was completed in just six
weeks. Expenses were held to a minimum at every turn. They
couldn't afford sets, so few were built. The inexperienced Jack
Berry was taken on as director, partly because he impressed
Julie but also because he was cheap. Inevitably, it would have
the look of a *little* picture, but Julie said it didn't have to have
the *feel* of one. If he could get the best possible actor for every
role, the rest would take care of itself.

So he played the luckless poor boy who never had a chance.
In a moment of terror and weakness, he kills a cop . . . and

starts running. When they start to close in on him, he takes refuge in the tenement apartment of a simple, sensible family of four. Wallace Ford and Selena Royle were the parents, and Bobby Hyatt their small son. The grown daughter—sad-eyed, hesitant, unsure of herself, dowdy but also rather pretty— would be Shelley Winters.

Suggesting the later *Desperate Hours,* Garfield would hold the girl and her little brother as hostages in the family flat while he plotted an escape. The girl has promised to help him, but is she on the level? He needs a car, and she keeps telling him one is going to come; she's taken care of it and she'll be going with him. But the car doesn't come . . . and they're closing in on him. Believing that the girl has duped him, he makes a run for it. Shot and mortally wounded, he falls into an appropriate gutter along the curb where, slowly, the yellow Ford is just pulling in. And there's the tormented Shelley, faithful after all, weeping in the street as John Garfield's screen career draws unknowingly but typically to its conclusion.

In a luncheon break during the filming of *He Ran All the Way,* Selena Royle got to reminiscing about the last American production of Ibsen's *Peer Gynt* almost thirty years earlier. She had played Solveig to Joseph Schildkraut's Peer. With pretense and pretentiousness, Julie said he'd always wanted to play Peer Gynt. And Selena Royle, regarding him earnestly, said, "It's a good part for you." Julie reminded her of the young Schildkraut.

Julie reread the Ibsen version and said, "Hey, this bird is *me!*" Peer was an engaging liar who could charm women. He was loved by the winsome Solveig, but could not remain true to her, and he was easy prey for a lecherous dancing girl. Peer loved his mother, but could break old Aase's heart by his negligence, then cheer the old woman on her deathbed with fantastic tales that only an adored son could get away with. Peer, the self-deluding braggart, disillusioned at the end, was reunited with the faithful Solveig and sought only to live as a simple, truthful man.

By coincidence, a new version of *Peer Gynt* had been adapted by Paul Green, whose *House of Connelly* had set the Group winging, and whose *Johnny Johnson* had become a legend since the failure of the Group's 1936 production. John Garfield's interest made a Broadway production feasible, although Green's *Peer Gynt* was virtually unstageable, having been fashioned as an outdoor entertainment. But Donald Oenslager came up with some brilliant stage designs and the production was born.

Even the people who most admired Julie's talent thought he was out of his element, although Lee Strasberg showed no hesitation in agreeing to direct *Peer Gynt*. Its theatricality interested him. Julie said, "With me doing Peer, Lee has a good opportunity to find out if he really *is* a genius."

Peer Gynt opened at the ANTA Playhouse on January 28, 1951, for a limited engagement. If business proved exceptional, another theater would house a commercial engagement after its four weeks as part of a special ANTA subscription series.

The reviews were ambiguously favorable—polite but with a hint of condescension. Paul Green's adaptation failed to earn applause. Julie was privately disappointed that his own performance was less than a sensation; he thought himself damned by faint praise. His colorful account of Peer had physical authority in the early passages, but he lacked conviction in the final scenes when he made the full progression from youth to old age. Those he most wanted to please—Clurman, Kazan, and his early mentor James Light—expressed their disappointment either frankly or by their silence. Julie knew his performance had missed the mark, but he was glad to have done it.

His ego was also soothed by *Peer Gynt's* magnetism for the matinée trade. The girls simply wouldn't leave him alone, and Julie liked that. He was an easy touch for an autograph at the stage door exit, and generally accommodating toward the patrons (mostly women) who sought to visit with him backstage. Julie could not always cover his pride when other entertainers sought an audience with him. He was perhaps never more flattered than by a visit from Edith Piaf, the great

French chanteuse who was taking New York by storm in her
club engagement at the Waldorf-Astoria, beginning a national
tour.

Piaf saw a performance of *Peer Gynt* and forgot all about
the play, being so sexually aroused by its star. The indomitable
"Little Sparrow" was a pathetic nymphomaniac, which in itself had an effect of magnifying her artistry to tragic dimension. Hungry for a new lover, Piaf went to the Garfield dressing
room, where Marlene Dietrich introduced her to Julie. She
endured the small talk until the crowd dispersed; then, alone
with Julie, she said forthrightly, "I have to have you." Could
he come to her hotel? Easily seduced by a foreign accent and
certainly flattered by Piaf's reputation as an artist, Julie said
"When?" She answered, "Tonight."

The tryst was arranged, and Julie was punctual. Receiving
him in her suite, Piaf was carefully groomed and beautifully
dressed, indicating that it was no ordinary occasion. A small,
elegant meal was served in the suite. Piaf sought to entertain
Julie with conversation about life and art, apparently intent
on orchestrating a complete night of romance. Julie now was
the impatient one. After the meal he guided Piaf into the
bedroom, where they proceeded to make love. Almost immediately afterward, Julie began preparing himself to leave. The
startled Piaf protested that she had expected he would stay
the night. Julie said he really had to go; anyway, he'd given
her what she wanted, hadn't he?

After Julie left, Piaf burst into furious tears. She would
tell Simone Berteaut (her half-sister and later Piaf's biographer
as well) that she had never been so humiliated: John Garfield
had made her feel like a prostitute. Later when Julie attempted
to visit her again, Piaf refused him hospitality.

There were other episodes, perhaps many. But while Julie
had turned to sex as a mental sleeping pill when despair
threatened to consume him, he was relying less on the old
antidote. Or was he merely burned out, as his poker-playing
pals suggested? They had heard Julie's claim that his relationship with Robbie had strengthened after their return to New
York. And Julie had found that extramarital sex was a thing

that could be given up, like smoking, and as easily resumed.

Rumor persisted that the Garfield marriage was on a crash course. Julie often used Earl Wilson's gossip column as a means for denying reports that he and Robbie were living apart or about to separate, but even the denials fanned the flames of rumor rather than extinguished them. Clifford Odets believed that the Garfields had stabilized their marriage, with prospects of a happy life fortified by their mutual devotion to their children. A dissenting friend of the Garfields said Robbie had adjusted to Julie's indiscretions without forgiving them, and had a real need to get back at him. "Robbie used to enjoy Julie's gullibility. She didn't like the way other people were always putting him on, but she could laugh at him in a way no one else could. But while most people liked Julie just the way he was, she wanted to change him, to improve him. And when that didn't work, she took to ridiculing him. All that cheating he did was really the main problem. Any way she could, she had to cut his balls off."

The Garfields' social life deteriorated when people began to feel taxed by the effort to enjoy Julie and Robbie together. In public they were becoming dueling antagonists—no longer the lovestruck kids from the Bronx who had brought a sweet aroma of ingenuousness into the Group Theatre's worldly-wise atmosphere. Elia Kazan summoned an image that remained fixed in his memory, of Julie resting on a hillside at the Pine Brook summer camp, with Robbie's head in his lap. Julie had stroked his beautiful wife's hair slowly and lovingly as he studied his lines. Kazan contrasted that picture with a visit to the Garfields' nicely appointed apartment on Central Park West, in which sparks of hostility shot around the room as soon as one entered it.

There were accounts of the Garfields working into a quarrel at a party and shouting one another down; of Julie meeting a movie magnate socially, hoping to land a picture offer, but being taunted publicly by Robbie in a way that discouraged the tycoon's interest; and of Julie finding sympathy at home from his children, but not from a wife who did not rate him a novelty attraction. Yet most observers, Kazan included, believed that the Garfield marriage was imperiled not so much by infidelity as by the mounting political pressures.

Clifford Odets, for one, believed that the broadening shadow of the House Un-American Activities Committee was the cause of many broken marriages, eventually including his own to Bette Grayson. The witch-hunt was as devastating a blow to Robbie's morale as to Julie's. Their entire society was involved, and they shared a sense of rage. But the inquisition created a tension that did not encourage patience in human relations. Julie said he and Robbie took out all their grievances on one another, even if they did not concern themselves, because it was the easiest way. Their conflict became more evident when the witch-hunters aroused all of Robbie's wrath. Julie was angry, too, but more obviously he was frightened, and anxious above anything else to protect his professional standing. He would resort to desperate measures, although he knew his wife would never endorse his kowtowing to bloodthirsty Congressional committeemen.

Late in the *Peer Gynt* engagement, he attended a small party with some other cast members, including Karl Malden, Nehemiah Persoff, and Mildred Dunnock (who etched a memorable Aase). Julie learned that HUAC was sending out its first subpoenas of the season, and going for big game. Their main concentration would be on movie actors, and while Julie wasn't in the first wave, someone had inside information that he would be called *soon*.

That was when Julie told Robert Whitehead, "You know, I *wanted* to join the Communist Party. I really did . . . I tried. Hell, I'm a *joiner*. But they wouldn't let me in. Can you imagine that? They thought I was too dumb. They said I couldn't be trusted."

Three and a half years had passed since the House Un-American Activities Committee's first round in its massive investigation of Communist infiltration in Hollywood. Most of the Unfriendly Ten were still serving prison terms. Herbert Biberman, according to his wife Gale Sondergaard, was in jail for having *protected* the First Amendment.

Careers had been stymied if not ruined for good. Persons who might have been Unfriendly in 1947, were prepared to be reluctantly Friendly in 1951 to protect themselves against a professional blacklisting that would deny their right to work at their chosen craft. Robert Rossen, originally an Unfriendly witness, became cooperative when right-wing elements threatened to boycott his upcoming *Brave Bulls* film and force its withdrawal, should he refuse to testify.

Few actors other than exceptionally congenial ones had appeared before the committee during the 1947 sessions. Larry Parks, marked Unfriendly, had been among the scheduled witnesses whose testimony was deferred. When he was summoned by HUAC on March 21, 1951, he was working at M-G-M in a picture called *Love Is Better Than Ever,* for which he had guaranteed billing above the beautiful young Elizabeth Taylor. Obviously his career was worth protecting, and he became a friendly witness.

The grilling of Larry Parks gave other scheduled witnesses a clear idea of what to expect. He got The Works. The session began in the morning, recessed for lunch, and continued in the afternoon for several hours, and the committee achieved its breakthrough: the actor cracked and started to name names, something he surely had not intended to do. The more he told the committee, the more apparent it became that the committee already knew everything he could tell them—about Larry Parks or anybody—and probably knew more. They had done their dirty homework. Nothing really could be gained by forcing testimony from one actor after another except, of course, the public punishment of the individual and the public display of superpatriotism during McCarthyism's finest hour.

They accomplished their mission. Larry Parks's confessional was large-type headline news around the country; so was Sterling Hayden's testimony two weeks later. The irony would soon be apparent. Neither Parks nor Hayden was officially blacklisted. They were simply ruined—Parks more pathetically, for he had been a bigger star at the time. (Hayden eventually regained his professional footing and became a better actor than his early rating; and his autobiography in 1963 renounced

his testimony and expressed his feeling of guilt for having
met with his inquisitors in the first place.) Hayden's inventory
of names given to the committee included Morris Carnovsky.
When specifically asked, Larry Parks said no, he did not recall
having ever seen John Garfield at a Communist cell meeting.

As the plot thickened, it became apparent that every witness confronted the dilemma of damned if they did, and
damned if they didn't. The damnation came not only from
the investigating committee and from public opinion, but
from the peer group—other actors. Some were also involved
in the witch hunt as likely victims but others were "clean"
and mere spectators.

John Garfield accepted his subpoena on March 6—two
weeks before the Larry Parks testimony. On advice of counsel,
he informed the committee of his willingness to give testimony. He was scheduled for April 23, along with actor José
Ferrer and librettist Abe Burrows. Julie started catching hell
from the *Daily Worker,* which had said nice things about
him in the past, but he continued to take thrashing from the
right wing of the national press. Louella Parsons forgave his
recent trespasses now that he was going to be a good boy for
the committee; but Hedda Hopper, an early Garfield fan until
the Communist issue began to possess her, held to her more
recent conviction that Garfield was one of the bad guys.

Old friends pointed the finger at Julie, saying he was selling out. Odets, Kazan, and Lee Cobb pleaded with Julie not
to take the stand; yet eventually all three would be friendly
witnesses, submitting to the wearying ritual of naming the
names. Morris Carnovsky, most admired by Julie as man and
actor, was furious at him.

"Why can't you people understand?" Julie pleaded. "I have
this picture scheduled for release and my own money is
riding on it. If I queer myself with this committee, we're
wiped out . . . Robbie and the kids. I have to do it this
way, and besides, I'm *clean.*"

He had never been a member of the Communist Party but
was he really clean? He had been the zealous joiner, a champion petition signer, giving his name in support of many or-

ganizations and crusades that the committee had decided were organs of subversiveness—perhaps as many as three dozen of them, groups as innocent in sound as the Theatre Arts Committee and the Hollywood Democratic Committee.

Bygone incidents of apparent harmlessness were recalled by the committee to haunt him: during a wartime entertainment junket he had been decorated by Tito's guards and had signed on as a sponsor for the American Committee for Yugoslav Relief; there was the occasion when he, with Charles Chaplin and Lewis Milestone, had been entertained on a Soviet ship anchored off the California coast at an official function honoring the Russian novelist Konstantin Simonov; and there was the National Council of Arts, Sciences and Professions, now being called a Communist front despite its humane charter and mission. Robbie had been with him in many of the seemingly harmless involvements; but then, the committee didn't care about Robbie, for John Garfield was the *name*.

But with his wife, too, Julie was in an untenable position. In a later poker session he told Oscar Levant that the witch-hunt had ruined his marriage just when he and Robbie were getting squared away, and that it was unsalvageable. As he prepared to go on the witness stand, he said it didn't matter which way he turned; there would be something for which he could not be forgiven.

Accompanied by Louis Nizer and Sidney Davis as counsel, Julie arrived in Washington for his turn in the committee spotlight. Having fretted for days about what was coming, he experienced something like opening-night excitement.

"They're out to fuck me," he muttered just before taking the stand, "but I'm not going to let them." He had joked that he would be playing this act just for the critics, and that he was going to have to be a better actor than he'd ever been before.

FRANK TAVENNER, JR. (counsel for the committee): Will you state your full name, please?
GARFIELD: John Jules Garfield.
TAVENNER: Mr. Garfield, when and where were you born?

GARFIELD: I was born in New York City, on the East Side, March 4, 1913.

TAVENNER: What is your present address?

GARFIELD: I pay taxes in California. I guess I would say 1052 North Carroll Drive, Los Angeles, is my business and present address, although my children go to school in New York City.

TAVENNER: Where are you now living, in New York or California?

GARFIELD: I live in both California and New York. I consider myself legally a resident of California.

TAVENNER: What is your profession?

GARFIELD: Actor.

TAVENNER: Will you give the committee a brief statement of your educational training for your profession.

(The brief statement covers his public schooling, the Angelo Patri influence, the Eva LeGallienne apprenticeship, the early plays and then the Group Theatre, to the time of his departure for film work.)

TAVENNER: Trace briefly your experience in Hollywood in your profession.

GARFIELD: I came to Hollywood in 1938. I think I made approximately thirty-one pictures. The first picture was called *Four Daughters.* It was produced by Warner Brothers. I was under contract to Warner Brothers seven and a half years and we made many outstanding, fine pictures at Warner Brothers. One or two or three come to my mind such as *Destination Tokyo; Air Force,* the story of the Air Corps during the bombing of Pearl Harbor; and one I am particularly proud of, *Pride of the Marines,* the story of Al Schmid of Guadalcanal.

TAVENNER: Your experience with Warner Brothers for seven and a half years brings us up to the middle of 1945, I assume.

GARFIELD: Or 1946. Then I went into business for myself. I produced, or helped produce, *Body and Soul,* then played in *Gentleman's Agreement,* which I had nothing to do with except work for 20th Century-Fox. I worked for Columbia in *We Were Strangers* and played in *Force of*

Evil, an exposé of the numbers racket. The last picture I did was *He Ran All the Way,* which I did myself.

TAVENNER: Mr. Garfield, after you were served with a subpoena to appear before this committee as a witness, the New York *Times* carried a statement attributed to you which is as follows: "I have always hated communism. It is a tyranny which threatens our country and the peace of the world. Of course, then, I have never been a member of the Communist Party or a sympathizer with any of its doctrines. I will be pleased to cooperate with the committee." Were you correctly quoted in the news article which I have just read?

GARFIELD: Absolutely.

TAVENNER: Is it a fact that you have always hated communism, as stated in that news release?

GARFIELD: Absolutely, yes.

TAVENNER: Are you of the opinion and belief that communism is a tyranny which threatens our country and the peace of the world?

GARFIELD: I believe so. I think it is a subversive movement and is a tyranny and is a dictatorship and is against democracy.

TAVENNER: Have you ever been a member of the Communist Party?

GARFIELD: I have never been a member of the Communist Party.

TAVENNER: If you are willing to cooperate with this committee . . . it will be necessary to ask you questions relating to your knowledge of Communist activities in that field, and especially about your own conduct in connection with organizations to which you have belonged and as to experiences which you have had. I understand you are willing to cooperate with the committee?

GARFIELD: I will answer any question you put to me.

(After a brief exchange reviewing previous answers, committee counsel produces a document.)

TAVENNER: I have before me the December 10, 1936 edition of the *Daily Worker,* which has a column in it entitled "A YCL Drama Against War" and a subheading entitled "League Plans Gigantic Pageant for Lenin Memorial."

In the course of that article appears the statement that "Jules Garfield of the Group Theatre is lending a hand in the promotion of this program." The program, of course, was a Young Communist League program. Will you examine it and state whether or not you did participate in any way, lending your influence or your help to the organization of that program by the Young Communist League of New York?

GARFIELD: I have no knowledge of lending my name to this organization, particularly an organization called the Young Communist League, because, believe me, if I had heard of such a name I would have run like hell. I have absolutely no knowledge of this. None whatsoever.

(Citing reference to membership in the Group Theatre, committee counsel asks what the Group Theatre is. Julie's description is bland, accurate, and fairly complete in outline.)

TAVENNER: While you were a member of the Group Theatre, did anything occur to you to lead you to believe there was Communist activity within the Group in the form of an effort to influence its action or the way in which it operated?

GARFIELD: It was purely run on an artistic basis. Of course the actors on Broadway used to call us peculiar because we didn't accept employment on the outside, and took much less money than we usually would get, because we wanted to work in a certain way. They thought that was kind of strange.

(Counsel asks about the Group's summer camps, specifically Ellenville, New York, and witness explains the nature of the rehearsal camps.)

TAVENNER: Do you recall any occasions when, at those camps, people were brought in who attacked the principles of our form of government?

GARFIELD: I do not, sir. I do recall that one or two of the directors had just come from Moscow where they had seen the Moscow Art Theatre, and they talked about that. That is my best recollection. It is pretty long ago.

TAVENNER: What were the circumstances which led to your going to Hollywood?

GARFIELD: Well, I had turned down Hollywood for five years. Then I was promised the lead in a play. It is a very personal story but I don't mind telling you. I had a falling out with some of the directors in the Group on the basis of the part I was supposed to get and didn't get, so I was a little angry and signed a contract. Warner Brothers signed me at that time.

TAVENNER: Were you acquainted with Harold Clurman? C-l-u-r-m-a-n?

GARFIELD: He was one of the directors of the Group Theatre.

TAVENNER: What part did he play in your going to Hollywood?

GARFIELD: He was against my going to Hollywood. He wanted me to stay with the Group Theatre.

(Committee counsel, apparently surprised by the answer, switches the subject and asks Julie about such names as Elizabeth Leech, Margaret Potts, and Barbara Myers, which he does not recognize.)

TAVENNER: Did you become acquainted with a person by the name of Eleanor Abowitz, A-b-o-w-i-t-z?

GARFIELD: That is a familiar name but I didn't become acquainted with her. It is a familiar name.

TAVENNER: Do you recall an incident when she made arrangements for you to make a speech on behalf of Charlotte Bass, who was a candidate for city council in Los Angeles?

GARFIELD: I never spoke for Charlotte Bass for city council. I spoke for Helen Gahagan Douglas, but not Charlotte Bass.

TAVENNER: In Hollywood did you become acquainted with a person by the name of Sidney Benson?

GARFIELD: I know that name, too. It is a familiar name.

TAVENNER: I think he also went by the name of Sidney Bernstein. Does that strike a bell with you?

GARFIELD: No. I know a Benson who is a writer, a radio writer. But the Abowitz name strikes a bell with me.

TAVENNER: What do you know about the activities of Eleanor Abowitz.

GARFIELD: I don't know anything about her activities. I remember hearing that name before.

TAVENNER: Were you associated at any time in a business way with Hugo Butler?

GARFIELD: He was a writer.

TAVENNER: Were you associated with him at any time in the production of a picture?

GARFIELD: Yes, yes, yes.

TAVENNER: What picture was that?

GARFIELD: A picture called *He Ran All the Way,* just recently, six or eight months ago.

TAVENNER: When did he write that script?

GARFIELD: This past summer, because we shot the picture in October.

TAVENNER: Do you have any knowledge or information to cause you to believe that he was a member of the Communist Party?

GARFIELD: None whatsoever. The only relationship I had with him was purely on a craft basis, the picture and the writing of the script.

TAVENNER: Are you acquainted with Herbert Biberman?

GARFIELD: I know him casually. I didn't socialize with him.

TAVENNER: Did he at one time endeavor to get you to endorse an advertisement to Open the New Front Now— that program?

GARFIELD: Can you tell me what year that was?

TAVENNER: I should have said Second Front instead of New Front. It was the period along the latter part of 1942.

GARFIELD: In other words, you mean the Russians! In other words, the period we were allies with the Russians?

TAVENNER: Yes.

GARFIELD: I don't specifically remember it, but I certainly felt, as everyone felt, that the Russians were our allies, and therefore we tried to help them as much as possible.

TAVENNER: I am not asking about your views. I am asking about what Biberman did, if you recall.

GARFIELD: I don't know. I couldn't answer that.

TAVENNER: Did you at any time make any contributions to a publication known as the *New Masses?*

GARFIELD: I might have subscribed to it from a dramatic, literary point of view, but I never made any contributions.

TAVENNER: The *New Masses* is known as a Communist publication. There were other publications.

GARFIELD: For instance, I subscribe to the *Christian Science Monitor* and *Time* magazine.

TAVENNER: I am not talking about subscribing. Did you make a contribution to the *People's World,* the *Daily Worker,* and those papers?

GARFIELD: No, sir.

TAVENNER: Were you acquainted with Hanns Eisler?

GARFIELD: I knew him, yes.

TAVENNER: What was the occasion of your knowing him?

GARFIELD: He worked in Hollywood as a musician. I met him at cocktail parties, as I met many other people. That is my acquaintance with him. He never scored any picture I was in.

TAVENNER: Did you have any occasion to believe he was a member of the Communist Party?

GARFIELD: None whatsoever. As a matter of fact, these people—we never discussed politics. They never did trust me. I was a liberal, and I don't think the Communists like liberals, and I was quite outspoken about my liberalism.

(The surprised committee counsel engages in discussion with committee members Bernard Kearney and Morgan Moulder, and with chairman John Wood—successor to J. Parnell Thomas. Most names previously discussed are identified as known Communists. Other names are discussed inconclusively in another series of questions given to the witness. Then committee counsel questions witness about his association with Actors' Laboratory.)

GARFIELD: I was never associated with Actors' Lab. I did a play for the veterans' program, not at the Actors' Lab but at the Las Palmas Theatre. They had a veterans program to give scholarships under the GI Bill of Rights.

TAVENNER: Was your personal secretary at that time a girl named Helen Schlain?

GARFIELD: Sloate, not Schlain; S-l-o-a-t-e. I had a girl who worked for me by that name.

TAVENNER: Did she also go by the name of Helen Schlain?

GARFIELD: Not to my knowledge.

TAVENNER: Did she hold an official position in the Actors' Laboratory as a secretary or something of that nature?

GARFIELD: She hung around there. I don't know what her position was. I had no knowledge of her activities.

(The topic is shifted toward Julie's activities as a member of the Screen Actors Guild executive board.)

GARFIELD: I was on the board for six years and during the period of this strike, we of the Screen Actors Guild tried in every way possible to stop it. As a matter of fact, some of us were accused of being sympathetic to the Conference of Studio Unions, which was the other side, at the beginning. Then we proceeded to get all the information we could, and we discovered the CSU didn't want to settle the strike.

(Minutes of a meeting of the board of directors of the SAG are introduced, read, and discussed.)

TAVENNER: During the period in which the Communist Party was interesting itself in this particular strike movement, was there any time when your views coincided with the Communist Party views and aims in connection with the strike, or were they at all times divergent?

GARFIELD: I would say at most times they were divergent, but I didn't know their point of view. Once I remember a meeting of actors at a private home which I heard about and went to. Ronald Reagan was there and when he saw me he was surprised, and when I saw him I was surprised, and we reported this at a meeting, that there were special meetings being held. The membership of the Screen Actors Guild voted 98.9 percent against supporting this strike, eventually.

(Committee member Harold Velde interrupts a lengthy discussion about the Screen Actors Guild with a question.)

VELDE: I don't think you have answered the question that counsel asked you. He asked if you knew any Communist Party members.

GARFIELD: Officially, do you mean?

TAVENNER: Either from statements they made to you or from what you learned about them?

GARFIELD: No, sir.

(Extended discussion follows concerning the strike vote—
sample exchange given.)

TAVENNER: Was Anne Revere one of those who voted
on that same resolution?

GARFIELD: I am sure she did. She was a member of the
board of the Screen Actors Guild.

TAVENNER: Do you know how Anne Revere voted?

GARFIELD: Well, it is pretty difficult to remember. I
know how I voted.

(Committee counsel returns to direct questioning.)

TAVENNER: It appears that you sponsored a dinner at the
Ambassador Hotel in Los Angeles on February 4, 1945,
under auspices of the Joint Anti-Fascist Refugee Committee,
for the purpose of raising funds.

GARFIELD: I have no knowledge of being a member of
that organization, and I don't have any recollection of spon-
soring that dinner.

TAVENNER: I will check to make certain of the exact date
and circumstances and we will return to the question. Let
me ask you if you recall at such a meeting that you introduced Paul Robeson?

GARFIELD: I don't have any recollection. I possibly could
have gone to it, but I was never a member of it.

TAVENNER: You would recall if you introduced Paul
Robeson, wouldn't you?

GARFIELD: I certainly would.

TAVENNER: Do you recall?

GARFIELD: I don't recall it. If it was during the war, then
it is possible that it might have happened.

(Committee counsel, evidencing some exasperation, introduces the names of other organizations of believed Communist
posture with which witness may have been affiliated.)

GARFIELD: I would like to point out what a difficult and
tough situation a guy like me is in, because I get a million
requests from organizations, some very worthy ones, because I am in this situation where I am in the public eye
and people think, "He is a nice guy, maybe he will do it
for us," and so forth. I have a letter from the National
Citizens' Political Action Committee dated August 7, 1945

. . . I answered "no" but it is just possible that a thing like this would come to me and I would throw it in a wastebasket, and three months from now I would be on this committee . . .

(Donald L. Jackson, a California congressman whose constituency embraces most of the film colony, is the man who replaced Richard Nixon as a committee member upon the latter's election to the United States Senate.)

JACKSON: Mr. Garfield, isn't every other person in the motion picture industry in precisely the same position?

GARFIELD: Pretty much so, yes.

JACKSON: Isn't it true there are literally hundreds of people in the industry whose actions have never made them suspect?

GARFIELD: Possibly, but I have always been an outstanding liberal.

VELDE: You mentioned a while ago that the Communist Party didn't trust you.

GARFIELD: They don't trust liberals.

CHARLES POTTER (member): Many times they use liberals?

GARFIELD: They try; yes, sir.

JACKSON: I would say Alger Hiss was known as a very outstanding liberal. Certainly he gained some level of approval and acceptance by the Communist Party.

(Complicated discussion follows, primarily about the Committee for the First Amendment—on behalf of the Unfriendly Ten, with tangent discussion of witness's contributions to Yugoslav Relief, his support of the Abraham Lincoln Brigade advocating a break with Franco's Spain, and his role in official hospitality toward the Soviet author, Konstantin Simonov.)

TAVENNER: As you look back on your activity in connection with the Committee for the First Amendment, do you now take the same view, or do you feel that this committee should properly investigate communism in the motion picture industry?

GARFIELD: Pretty much, except for one thing. There is a big difference between fighting for a legitimate political party and fighting for a subversive group, which I consider

the Communist Party to be, and there is where I would
differ today.

TAVENNER: You now consider it a subversive group rather
than a political party?

GARFIELD: Exactly. I am a Democrat, and if you were a
Republican I would fight like the devil for your right to
speak up. But I feel that these people are not a legitimate
political party. It creates a lot of confusion. People say,
"This party is on the ballot," and they think it is automatically
a legitimate party. It seems to me if the Communist Party
was outlawed it would help clear up a lot of confusion on
that point.

WOOD: You have indicated some knowledge of the Communist Party and its activities. How could you possibly
know anything about its activities if you didn't know who
its members were?

GARFIELD: I had no knowledge who its members were,
and didn't know all its workings.

(There is digression into Julie's views on the Henry Wallace
1948 Presidential candidacy and Julie says he deserted Wallace because the Communists had "captured him.")

WOOD: Let me ask you categorically, have you any knowledge of the identity of a single individual who was a member
of the Communist Party during the time you were in Hollywood?

GARFIELD: No, sir.

(Counsel introduces names of additional organizations and
individuals with referrals to specific meetings and incidents.
Witness gives testimony consistent in tone and content with
all that has gone before. Counsel has no further questions.
Rep. Moulder compliments the witness on his statements and
says a person should not be condemned for being a liberal;
after all, Jefferson was one and so was Lincoln. Reps. Walter
and Frazier have no additional questions. Rep. Velde does)

VELDE: I want to straighten out the matter of whether
you signed a petition to abolish this committee in 1947 or
1948.

GARFIELD: I say I never did sign.

VELDE: You are quite positive you did not sign such a petition?

GARFIELD: Quite positive; yes, sir.

(After some additional questions—seemingly frivolous and unrelated—Rep. Velde has none left, nor does Rep. Kearney, but Rep. Jackson does.)

JACKSON: I am still not convinced of the entire accuracy you are giving this committee. It is your contention you did not know, during all the time you were in New York affiliated with the Group Theatre, which for all its artistry was pretty well shot through with the philosophy of communism—

GARFIELD: That is not true.

JACKSON: That is a matter of opinion. You contend during all that time in New York you did not know a Communist?

GARFIELD: That is right.

JACKSON: And that during the years you were in Hollywood and in close contact with a situation in which a number of Communist cells were operating, with electricians, actors, and every class represented, that during the entire period of time you were in Hollywood you did not know of your own personal knowledge a single member of the Communist Party?

GARFIELD: That is absolutely correct, because I was not a party member or associated in any shape, way or form.

JACKSON: During that period it might interest you to know attempts were made to recruit me into the Communist Party, and I was making $32.50 a week.

GARFIELD: They certainly stayed away from me, sir.

JACKSON: Perhaps I looked like better material. You were never approached at any time to join the Communist Party?

GARFIELD: That is right, Mr. Jackson. I might say, if at any time that had happened, I would have run like hell.

JACKSON: I must say, Mr. Chairman, in conclusion, that I am still not satisfied.

(Nor is committee counsel, who resumes questioning after another complicated digression.)

TAVENNER: Is Mr. Hugo Butler still associated with you in a business way?

GARFIELD: No, sir; absolutely not. He hasn't been for the last four months.

TAVENNER: You spoke of Jack Berry.

GARFIELD: He was the director.

TAVENNER: Yes, of your picture. Do you know where he is now?

GARFIELD: No. The picture was completed in November. I went to New York to do a play, *Peer Gynt*.

TAVENNER: We have been unsuccessful in locating either Hugo Butler or Jack Berry. We have subpoenas for them.

(With no other questions forthcoming, witness asks permission to read a brief statement and chairman indicates he may proceed.)

GARFIELD (reading): "When I was originally requested to appear before the committee, I said that I would answer all questions fully and without any reservations, and that is what I have done. I have nothing to hide and nothing to be ashamed of. My life is an open book. I am no Red. I am no 'pink.' I am no fellow traveler. I am a Democrat by politics, a liberal by inclination, and a loyal citizen of this country by every act of my life."

Officially excused under subpoena, Julie thanked the chairman and shook his hand. He also exchanged handshakes and small talk with Rep. Velde and Rep. Moulder, from whom there was a visible stirring of adulation for John Garfield. But Jackson and Kearney in particular made no effort to disguise their hostility.

The relieved expressions on the faces of Julie's attorneys assured him that he'd come through the ordeal nicely. He felt briefly exhilarated. He had not failed in his footwork: he'd feinted, back-pedaled, dodged while they jabbed; they had scratched him up a bit but hadn't landed any solid blows or uppercuts. They hadn't broken him. He heard that there hadn't been a testimony quite like it in the annals of HUAC.

Julie's feeling of deliverance wore away within a day or two—as long as it took the newspaper columnists to go to work on him. They discredited his testimony and asked a few questions of their own.

How could Garfield be so naive (stupid?) as to deliver such testimony? How could he expect the committee to believe it? *Did* they believe it?

The *Daily Worker,* lashing out at one of its old pets, branded Garfield a traitor for having disowned the things he had long and ardently professed to believe in. Archer Winsten, a voice characteristic of the liberal New York *Post,* said flatly that no one could have possibly lived in New York during the thirties and not have known a single Communist.

Julie began to sense that he was not yet out of the woods when a major article in the May 23 *Variety* revealed that HUAC was having afterthoughts about the Garfield testimony. At Congressman Jackson's urging, the committee would turn the transcript of Garfield's testimony over to the FBI. A cross-referencing of Garfield's statements against information that might be contained in the FBI records would determine whether a perjury claim might be in order against Garfield.

Nor was Julie consoled by the chilly reception at Club 21 or Toots Shor's or any of his old haunts. He had expected gratitude from his old pals for his effort to keep them in the clear. His sin was in having testified at all. It had made his estrangement from Carnovsky permanent.

First commercial returns on *He Ran All the Way* mired Julie in a deeper gloom. Its first-run dates in July made it evident that it would do well to break even; it was more likely that Julie would not recover all of his investment. The irony was that a picture made to box-office formula got a better press than it courted. Critics saw it as a breakthrough for crime drama, because persons other than the lead fugitive were characterized fully and realistically. Garfield commanded the audience's pity, but the primary sympathy was with the family he threatened. Despite its grainy B-picture look, *He Ran All the Way* was a forceful entertainment. But the box office receipts were disappointing.

Money worries held Julie under siege. He and Robbie were still comfortable but the future was clouded. He felt a need to be working again for peace of mind and for income, and struggled anew with *The Man With the Golden Arm.* Julie hired a writer to try for an approach that would pacify the Johnston Office, but the problem remained unsolved and the writer was let go. Julie contacted the studios, advertising his availability. Following up a report that one company was seeking "a John Garfield type" for a western, Julie had an intermediary suggest that the authentic prototype should be considered. The response was "Yes, we need a Garfield *type* but we can't use Garfield."

It was now common knowledge that he had signed forty-two petitions and had given his name to as many as thirty-two organizations identified with the "Red front"—groups as innocent in sound as the Hollywood Democratic Committee and the American Committee for Yugoslavian Relief. Julie was not officially blacklisted, but he was rat poison anyway. In her autobiography, *The Gift Horse,* the German actress Hildegard Knef (who would befriend Julie shortly after the incident told of a covert poolside discussion at Tyrone Power's house, in which Julie became a dominant topic of sad conversation. When someone said, "Garfield's finished," Marlene Dietrich said, "Yes, because he refused to give names," under her breath, bitterly; then she added loudly, "We're all whispering as though we were living under Hitler!"

In the fall of 1951 the ABC television network planned a dramatic series called *Counsellor-at-Law,* based on Elmer Rice's original play and characters, to be scripted by Rice himself. The idea was that Garfield would take the old Paul Muni role of George Simon. Julie thought it appropriate that the same play that had boosted him on the stage could be his essential start on television. But even when Elmer Rice protested that no other actor would be satisfactory, the ABC people indicated they could not consider hiring John Garfield. Out of loyalty to Julie, Rice resigned his function and the venture fell through. But the incident fired Julie's determination to clear himself with HUAC, even recanting his testimony if necessary.

For comfort, Julie turned more and more to his children. On Father's Day in 1951, the Ethical Culture School had a special celebration and he sat in the audience while eight-year-old David and five-year-old Julie Roberta joined the other children in singing the school song. After the program he obliged audience and students alike with his autograph. When the impatient David wanted to leave, Julie said, "You must remember, your father is a very famous man." But David didn't seem to understand.

Meanwhile, Clifford Odets had started once again to work on a play idea for Julie. When his marriage to Bette Grayson seemed to be foundering, the playwright and Julie again turned to one another for boozy solace. Odets alerted Julie to the playscript of *Fragile Fox* by a new writer, Norman Brooks. The title alluded to a company of combat infantry, and Julie was attracted by the antihero protagonist, a paranoid. He took an option on the play and undertook a search for a producer. If he couldn't find one, he said he'd produce it himself and get Lee Strasberg to direct; then, if it was a hit, he might star in a movie version for his own company, and direct it himself. Julie's burst of self-confidence was short-lived because no producer came forth, nor was he able to raise money on his own. Finding his name so risky as to discourage even minor speculators on Broadway, Julie plunged into an emotional panic.

Odets saw the signs, and now it was his turn to bail Julie out. While Odets's emotional equilibrium still was a yo-yo on a fragile string, he was in one of his "up" periods despite having troubles of his own with HUAC. He had reconciled with his wife, based on his agreement that she could resume her acting career. Then, the *Night Music* play that had failed in 1940 (but remained his favorite) was getting a revival under the ANTA banner by Robert Whitehead, who rated the play a possible lost masterpiece. Whitehead and Odets were discussing the possibility of working Garfield into the *Night Music* cast (in the role that would be played, instead, by the unknown Rod Steiger), when Julie's disappointing *Golden Boy* experience was recalled. Whitehead suggested that it wasn't too late for Julie to play Joe Bonaparte, and that ANTA might revive *Golden Boy*.

XI

The Shore Dimly Seen

Julie was thirty-eight. The first gray hairs were appearing, but only to the up-close observer. He had acquired a slight puffiness around the eyes, but that only betrayed his dissipation and was not symptomatic of onrushing age. There was still a boyishness about him that could be entirely convincing when projected from the stage, as the opening scenes of *Peer Gynt* had proved.

Everything about the *Golden Boy* project seemed right. The play was overripe for revival. Julie liked the idea and was immediately available. Robert Whitehead had no difficulty getting the ANTA board to support a production that would have John Garfield in the star role. Elia Kazan, while much in demand and with energies subdivided by major directorial assignments for both stage and screen, agreed to manipulate his schedule to direct the revival.

Julie was out to prove that Harold Clurman had made a mistake back in 1937 by denying him the title role. He was determined to play the hell out of it, and he hoped that the Lorna Moon role might be played by either of two girls who had recently been leading ladies to him in pictures—Beatrice Pearson or Patricia Neal, neither of whose screen careers was being advanced. But there was a minor complication. Bette Grayson decided she wanted to play Lorna Moon, and Odets became her advocate because he was trying to save their marriage. Her inadequacy was obvious, and it would take something away from the production. But obviously, she'd get the part.

Then Kazan withdrew as director. Under subpoena by HUAC, he agreed to testify and had to prepare his case. Odets took over the direction of *Golden Boy,* thus killing any chance of saving his marriage. Bette Grayson kept the part of Lorna Moon but tangled with her husband when he sought to direct her, however patiently. They made a permanent break and were divorced soon afterward.

Otherwise the production took on aspects of a Group homecoming. Art Smith now played Tom Moody, the fight manager. And Lee J. Cobb, who had acted a neighbor in the original production, came back to do Papa Bonaparte . . . and do it better than he had played it in the William Holden picture. (Cobb, having attained theatrical eminence as Willy Loman in Arthur Miller's *Death of a Salesman,* now rated costar billing with Garfield.) Curt Conway and Tony Kraber had bit parts, and several young actors groomed mainly by Kazan at the Actors Studio took the well-defined supporting roles—Jack Warden, Arthur O'Connell, Jack Klugman; and a dazzling Joseph Wiseman, doing Kazan's old stage role of underworld promoter Eddie Fuselli. The revival's popular subtitle, applied by its playwright, was "Garfield's Revenge."

The out-of-town tryout itinerary began in Hartford. It was snowing when *Golden Boy* opened there, but the people weren't intimidated. The playhouse was filled. The production seemed to go well, and Julie was secure in his performance. His Joe Bonaparte was fierce, colorful, touching. *Golden Boy* was still an "audience play," and the cheering for John Garfield indicated that if he was on the skids as a "name," the Hartford people hadn't been informed. A healthy advance sale was reported in New York, and the revival's unqualified success was never in real doubt.

The Hartford opening was an occasion for a dinner party attended by some people who had come up from New York. Robbie Garfield was conspicuously absent, so Julie went alone to the gala. Stirred into a nervous excitement by the opening, he was in a talkative mood. And he found a good listener.

Iris Whitney was a close friend to Mrs. Robert Whitehead,

who introduced her to Julie. A former actress who had become an interior decorator, Iris Whitney was a career bachelor girl, age thirty-six, coolly pretty and casually elegant. Julie engaged her in conversation most of the evening. She returned to New York but Julie remained curious about her, and told Whitehead that Iris Whitney was "the kind of girl I could really go for." Whitehead didn't know what to make of it. For all his well-known carousings, Julie had never been one to become seriously "interested" in a woman other than his wife; and officially Julie was still living at home.

He passed his thirty-ninth birthday just before *Golden Boy* settled into the ANTA Theatre for its New York engagement. Yet his immersion into Joe Bonaparte seemed to have restored Julie's youth. He briefly forgot all his troubles and recaptured the old charm. The romantic fire reignited within him, and he made no secret of having looked up Iris Whitney.

She was acquainted with people on the more refined and affluent edges of show business, and Julie found her conversation a pleasant departure from the ego-driven discussions of acting and politics. But whatever their topic, eventually they got to talking about John Garfield. Being with Iris Whitney would put Julie in a reflective mood. Now he tended to review his odyssey as one seeking to discover a fatal turning point. Iris Whitney offered the kind of hand-holding assurance Julie required. (One of her own friends described her as a combination of Florence Nightingale and Mata Hari: humane and sympathetic, and possibly predestined for some form of martyrdom.)

Not even the *Golden Boy* success could alter Julie's apparent belief that he had been playing a game that was now over, and he had lost. Talking freely about his sexual peccadillos, he repeatedly asked Iris Whitney, "What was I trying to prove? What in God's name was I trying to prove?"

Golden Boy opened on March 12 for a limited engagement of four weeks. "Garfield's revenge" became his sentimental vindication. The run was extended an additional three weeks to meet the demand for seating. But shortly before the closing, the company's bliss was jarred by Elia Kazan's rendez-vous with the witch-hunters.

In a prepared statement, Kazan named a battery of actors and other show people with whom he had engaged in Communist Party activities during his early, brief tenure as a card-holding member. The enumeration was not given in a spirit of betrayal; Kazan merely was giving a matter-of-fact summary of what the committee would have tried to pound out of him. He sought to break clear of the wolves in a single action, rather than have them still snapping at his heels, as they were at John Garfield's.

Kazan specified that he had been instructed by party officials to gain ideological control of the Group Theatre. This never happened, he said, because the three directors were successful in keeping art, not politics, as the Group's primary concern. But he named several Group actors as party members, including Art Smith and Tony Kraber of Julie's *Golden Boy* revival cast. The company engaged in heated controversy over what Kazan should and should not have revealed. Julie, appreciative of Kazan's dilemma, did not participate in the argument. Nor did Clifford Odets, who confided to Julie that he would obey his lawyer's advice when it was his turn to testify. He would do exactly as Kazan had done: tell the truth.

Julie thought he felt a tightening vise. He heard that Louis Russell, an investigator employed by the relentless committee, was still reviewing Garfield's ten-month-old testimony for possible implications of perjury. From his agents at MCA he learned that he was the preferred choice for a 20th Century-Fox picture planned for fall production, but that the role would not be offered until Julie's status with the investigating committee was finally resolved. The picture was *Taxi*, and it would be shot mostly in New York City. Julie wrote a solicitous letter to Spyros Skouras, the president of 20th Century-Fox, seeking advice on what he should do to earn confirmation for the star role in *Taxi*.

The laconic Art Smith, who became Julie's sounding board during the *Golden Boy* revival and retained that function after the closing, had a track on Julie's panic. He believed that Julie, by seeking advice from everyone he knew, simply was getting too much advice and becoming confused. He also was beginning to talk aloud to himself—in his dressing room, at Toots Shor's and other haunts, and during the long solitary walks that were a new thing for Julie.

In effect, Julie was asking himself one question. When the blows are coming at you in every direction and you're too groggy to land counterpunches, which course do you take? Do you stand there and get killed, or do you just throw in the towel and collect your lesser share of the purse? Julie's attorneys were advising him to stay cool, to keep patience; they believed he was out of danger, that there would be no more harassment from HUAC. But Julie had abandoned his faith in legal counsel, as with every other form of advice. He decided to play the game his own way.

It seemed to Julie that the theatre and film people who resisted the HUAC probings, either on the witness stand or off it, were ruined professionally, possibly for all time. But those who had swallowed their pride and told the committee what it wanted to hear were risking and absorbing the abuse of the liberals, but figured to ride out the storm and emerge with their professional status no less secure.

He heard that the Anti-Defamation League of B'nai B'rith was an effective intermediary between the investigators and the Jewish professionals who sought the League's assistance. Julie was an old acquaintance of the League's general counsel, Arnold Forster, another poor-born Bronx boy who had made good. Forster advised Julie against another confrontation with HUAC, which would be defaming in any event. A more popular form of confession would be the kind given directly to the press, and it could also be lucrative. Forster got the *Look* editors aroused over a possible Garfield tell-all, and agreed to collaborate with Julie on an article of major length that would culminate in John Garfield's appearance on a *Look* cover.

Now Julie's strategy would be to paint himself as a dupe of the Communists, rather than a cheerleader. And since he was still under an insinuating attack by right-wing newsmen, Julie decided to make peace with them even before his about-face was recorded in *Look.* He telephoned Victor Riesel, the virulent anti-Communist labor columnist of the New York *Mirror,* and arranged an appointment.

On Thursday, May 8, Julie met with Riesel at Sardi's for lunch. He told Riesel he was preparing a document that would cover every aspect of his political involvement, in and out of the theatre, over a twenty-year period. He wasn't out to "get" anybody but would reveal names when necessary. Riesel agreed to help circulate the news of John Garfield having been "used" by the Reds.

Julie met again with Forster later that same day. The arrangement with *Look* had been confirmed, and the editors had come up with a title: "I Was a Sucker for a Left Hook." Properly displayed, the *Look* piece figured to build Julie into a tragic hero but a *patriotic* one, and he'd be "hot" again. From the West Coast he learned that 20th Century-Fox already knew that the *Look* exposure was targeted for a fall issue. Not only did this make the *Taxi* film almost a certainty for Julie, it enhanced the possibility of a 20th Century-Fox term contract that would deliver him from financial worry. The studio might even finance the stage production of *Fragile Fox* for Julie. The only thing that remained was his and Forster's bringing the article into shape.

He did not keep his regular Thursday night poker-playing date with Ray Bloch, Irving Mansfield, and other denizens of Manhattan who were his longtime pals. Presumably he spent the night at home, not playing poker or engaging in any frivolity. The next day Julie moved out of the Garfield apartment on Central Park West for the last time. He would not discuss the factors that caused the break, but indicated it was no temporary thing. He told Earl Wilson there would be a divorce, but to hold off announcing it, "just in case." Julie's friends who were privy to his "manifesto" (as he called the document for *Look*) concluded that Robbie Garfield's opposition to his plotted confession triggered their climactic separation. Julie rented a suite at the Warwick Hotel and went into confinement.

His only visitor there would be Forster. They reached accord on the content of the magazine article and determined its shape; then Forster left Julie alone to complete the text. Quoted by Stefan Kanfer in *A Journal of the Plague Years,* Forster found John Garfield "tractable, understanding and terrified . . . He was guilty of two things—of loving people and of being naive. For his naiveté, he paid with his reputation."

On the day he moved into the Warwick, Julie also read the New York *Times* obituary for Canada Lee, the majestic Negro who had a good role in *Body and Soul.* Lee's death at age forty-five was attributed to high blood pressure. In the previous October, Mady Christians (age forty-four) had died of "natural causes" similar to those that claimed J. Edward Bromberg (age forty-eight) on December 6, 1951. It was noted that the Lee, Christians, and Bromberg deaths all occurred shortly after the actors were ground to pieces by HUAC. They were whispered suicides, but Philip Loeb was a confirmed one. Yet the committee kept pounding away, citing every grim statistic as its proof and vindication.

On Sunday, May 18, Julie completed his sixteen-page confession and emerged from his hotel. He wanted to explain what he was doing, in hope of obtaining understanding from the people he feared would come down hard on him as a squealer. He telephoned the Odets apartment and got no answer; then he remembered that the playwright had gone to Washington, there to meet his interrogators the very next day.

Julie visited Iris Whitney, but only briefly; she had other guests. How he spent Sunday evening would remain a mystery, but there would be later reports of people in the Bronx saying they saw John Garfield that night, walking alone near one of his old neighborhoods.

He had been under doctor's advice to forego tennis and had not been on a court for several weeks. But on Monday morning he played several hard sets with Steve Widdoes at Columbia University, and boasted that after having not been to bed the night before, he could still win a match.

Then he went to a baseball game with Howard Lindsay, and they made a date for poker at Lindsay's house later that evening. Russel Crouse, Lindsay's collaborator on many successful plays, was summoned. So was Oscar Levant. Julie drank and lost heavily, but while his friends remarked sympathetically about his obvious exhaustion, they played into the small hours at Julie's own insistence. A discussion topic around the card table was Clifford Odets's testimony before HUAC. It began that day and would carry into Tuesday.

He did not return to the Warwick, but went to the New York Athletic Club on Tuesday morning for a massage. He listened to the concluding segment of Odets's testimony, which was carried by radio. Odets's long, painful account enumerated a sufficiency of names and offered a capsule history of the revolutionary drama—which the committee could not, or would not, distinguish from communism. It saddened Julie, as it did other listeners, that Odets would identify as one of the important party functionaries the same Joe Bromberg whose eulogy he had penned in the New York *Times* only months before. Julie made a telephone call, then left the Athletic Club saying he was going home for a talk and some lunch with his wife.

But Art Smith, who had an early afternoon drink with Julie in the Astor bar, said Julie had skipped both breakfast and lunch and looked the part. Julie was also talking, although dubiously coherent, about having had a change of mind on "spilling the soup" to *Look*.

According to Hildegard Knef, she also saw John Garfield on Tuesday afternoon. Either by accident or design, he turned up at the Plaza Hotel where she was staying, and went with her to a cocktail party for which he was not dressed. He also needed a shave, but not so much as he seemed to need someone to talk to. Julie mumbled, "It's not good to be seen with me," to the German actress, who noted that he was smoking an unbroken chain of cigarettes. When Hildegard Knef said she would be flying back to Germany the next day, Julie said, "You still got a lot of Nazis? I'm a Jew." He wanted to get her off alone for a talk but she explained that she had to get ready for a party at Club 21 that Spyros Skouras was giving in her honor. She suggested that Julie might try her later. He said he would. He returned to his hotel to make himself presentable, and may have considered going to Club 21 where he was still welcome . . . and where he could perhaps ingratiate himself with Spyros Skouras, who now was of primary importance to Julie professionally.

Instead he called on Iris Whitney, later that afternoon in her apartment at 3 Gramercy Park. Now he was spiffy, but still drawn and haggard from having not slept for three days. Yet he was in subdued good spirits, and he said it would be his pleasure to take Miss Whitney to dinner. At Luchow's they dined slowly and enjoyably; and when they walked back to her apartment, Julie wanted to sit in the park.

Gramercy Park is small and lovely, the exclusive domain of the people residing around it. Iris Whitney unlocked the gate with her own key. They sat in the darkness of presummer on a park bench and talked quietly. Then Julie rose from the bench and walked over to regard the only statue in the park, a handsomely sculptured Edwin Booth.

"I wonder how good an actor he thought I was," Julie mused, "or if he knew how good I might have become." In his reflective mood Julie was employing the past tense. He seemed no longer interested in the future, or even in the present. Oscar Levant would say that toward the end, Julie talked as one who doubted his own existence.

In the park he complained of feeling suddenly ill and suspected something he may have eaten. Iris Whitney thought he was merely capitulating to fatigue. He was becoming chilled, so they left the park and returned to her apartment. She offered him tea, but Julie said he should leave, that he was beginning to feel really terrible. Miss Whitney decided to telephone a doctor, but Julie said he didn't need a doctor, he needed rest. He was drowsy and vague, and when Miss Whitney decided to put him to bed, he did not object.

He fell asleep almost immediately in her bedroom. Iris Whitney was concerned, but she noted that Julie seemed to be resting comfortably and breathing regularly and deeply. She stayed up for several hours, checking on Julie periodically. She made some orange juice and placed a glass on the nightstand by the bed, for Julie to have when he awoke. Then she went to sleep on the living room sofa.

When morning came, Iris Whitney looked in on Julie again. The full glass of orange juice was untouched. Unable to stir Julie, she telephoned Dr. Charles Nammack, her own physician. But she already knew that this time the golden boy had taken the full count.

XII

John Garfield Lives

New York had not had a funeral to match it since all those desperate women dismantled Frank Campbell's establishment a generation earlier to get a last look at Rudolph Valentino. John Garfield lay in state in a small funeral home on Seventy-sixth Street, but about 500 persons filed past his bier before the doors were closed to the public, at the request of the Garfield family. A mob gathered outside and tied up traffic, and threatened other mayhem. Police waged a tugging, pushing battle with the spectators, until the family relented and allowed the doors to be reopened. Seven thousand persons viewed the body on Thursday; and in the hours after school was dismissed, bobby-soxers dominated the throng, wailing uninhibitedly. Souvenir hunters tried to pick at Julie's coffin, even his clothing.

Clifford Odets, having just returned from his ordeal of Washington testimony, buried his face in his hands upon seeing Julie in the opened casket, and wept violently. That evening Odets assisted Robbie Garfield in receiving Julie's relatives and friends.

On the following day, ten thousand persons crowded the street outside the Riverside Memorial Chapel, where the afternoon services were conducted by Rabbi Louis Newman of Temple Rodeph Sholom. The rites of the Hebrew Reformed faith were attended by most of the notables of the Broadway theatre, and many from Hollywood. A funeral cortège of ten limousines followed the hearse to Westchester Hills Cemetery in Mount Hope, New York. Robbie Garfield's eyes were shielded by dark glasses throughout the graveside service, and she held her jaw tight and firm while her children wept freely. Rabbi Newman said, "He came like a meteor, and like a meteor he departed."

So New York saluted one of its own not as an outcast for having died under awkward circumstances, but as a folk hero. The kid who was a star throughout his movie career became a superstar in death. But the press scandalized his passing. Newspapers screamed that John Garfield, not officially separated from his wife, had died of a heart attack in the apartment of a woman the general public had not heard of. The news media defamed Iris Whitney by insinuation, and many readers equated her with an easy pick-up. (In Hollywood the sardonic consensus was that the *style* of his death particularly befitted John Garfield.)

Still, the press coverage was less lurid than it might have become. Before Dr. Nammack had arrived at Iris Whitney's apartment to give the death pronouncement, Miss Whitney had telephoned Robert Whitehead and he arrived almost immediately, relieving her of the ordeal of handling the inevitable battery of reporters and police. After Robbie Garfield had been notified, press agent Barry Hyams—an old friend— represented the Garfield family in its dealings with the media, helping to convey a measure of decorum to the tragedy. But selling papers was a business after all; and so, it seemed, was giving legal counsel. Robbie Garfield received a bill from the Nizer firm for "services rendered". . . on the day of Julie's funeral.

For several days afterward, the papers carried postscripts to the John Garfield story with the rhythm of curtain calls. First it was revealed that the actor had left home only ten days before he died. Earl Wilson noted that a memo on his own desk at the time of Julie's death carried a reminder to "check with John Garfield about possible reconciliation with his wife." Victor Riesel wrote of John Garfield's intention to disclose his Red-flavored history, and said the Communists had woven a web around Garfield by playing on his emotional sympathy for underdogs.

Two weeks after Julie's death, his will was filed. The estate of "more than $100,000" was left entirely to the wife who had also been his childhood sweetheart.

The political information took on irony. The House Un-American Activities Committee and the Federal Bureau of Investigation affirmed that they had closed their books on the John Garfield case just before the actor's death. Julie had died in the clear.

Hedda Hopper thought Julie's passing was somehow glorious. She wrote: "John Garfield's friends and fans are happy: before he died, he made a full confession."

• When *Fragile Fox* was finally presented on Broadway in the fall of 1954, the role Julie had coveted was played by his *alter ego,* Dane Clark. The play was not commercially successful, but it was turned into an impressive 1956 film (retitled *Attack*) by Robert Aldrich, who had been assistant director for *Body and Soul.* Otto Preminger obtained movie rights to *The Man With the Golden Arm,* and when he was also unable to reach an agreement with the movie industry's own censors, he decided to make the picture anyway and release it without a production code seal. The risk worked; the picture made money and was deemed an artistic success as well. Frank Sinatra was much admired in the role of Frankie Machine, but Nelson Algren said he had conceived the character in John Garfield's image and that only Garfield should have played it.

The blacklisting was not curtailed although the practice eroded as public opinion shifted. Most of Julie's associates, while permanently scarred, eventually regained their professional footing. (However, Abraham Polonsky and Jack Berry —Julie's hand-picked directors—went fully twenty years without acknowledged screen credits.) Clifford Odets's career flourished again for another decade before his own death, both on stage (*The Flowering Peach*) and screen (most notably, *Sweet Smell of Success,* in which Tony Curtis enacted a role Odets had designed for Garfield many years earlier). But Odets never returned to the writing of *By the*

Sea, the play that would have had Julie starring again on Broadway during the season that followed his death.

In 1955 Robbie Garfield married Sidney Elliott Cohn, a leading New York attorney with whom Julie had been acquainted. But the Garfield children came of age with a strong awareness of their father. Robbie had obtained prints of most of the Garfield films, and they screened them often in their private projection room. Perhaps not surprisingly, both son and daughter were to become actors. As John Garfield, Jr., David has shown promise in several screen roles, despite having had no major opportunity, while Julie Garfield has been an appealing young actress, primarily of the Off-Broadway stage.

In formulating the reality of John Garfield, the researcher must contend with myth and bogus legend. Strange stories abound, and there have been books *about* or seemingly alluding to John Garfield, some in the guise of fiction. Although her memoir has been largely discredited, the late Barbara Payton's *I Am Not Ashamed* may have popularly distorted the nature of Julie's sexuality, at about the same time that *Prince Bart* was a best-selling novel. In 1954 Jay Richard Kennedy, who had been an acquaintance of Julie's but hardly a true friend, wrote *Prince Bart* and modeled his title character too obviously, and therefore unsatisfactorily for fiction. So much about Bart Blaine was unmistakably John Garfield that many readers accepted all of the content as gospel. In the Kennedy novel, film star Bart Blaine is fading in the popularity charts, nursing a vulnerable heart, and is propelled mainly by sexual compulsion. He pursues a death wish out of his obsessive guilt. The novel contained passages of impressive writing but was dismissed by literary critics for the same reason that caused Julie's friends to scorn it: it imparted no warmth to Bart Blaine, nor the sympathy of understanding. Bart lacked beauty of character, and he did not really indicate a great talent; he was merely weak. Still, the novel may have helped fuel the bizarre, apparently eternal rumors of How John Garfield Really Died.

Indeed, he did not die in the well-known saddle, but as Iris Whitney and Robert Whitehead said he did. Julie was too spent physically to have lived up to the apocryphal stories that have lacquered his legend.

After the Garfield name had been in eclipse for awhile, the legend came full-flame in the sixties. Reassessing the Hollywood legacy, the young inquisitive Film Generation rehabilitated him. By lionizing John Garfield as their own new discovery, they incited a revaluation of an actor most of them did not remember, but who is a mirror of their own lives. Even more significantly, the Garfield renaissance is also in keeping with a recent complete turnabout in the mythology of movie stardom.

Gone, now, is the Hero—that paragon who will settle all the issues and emerge the master of his fate, and will also get the girl if he wants her. Today's dominant film image is the antihero, rooted not in romance but in sociology. The new protagonist is a hybrid of plus and minus factors, not one of the Establishment but a rebel against it . . . and not a likely bet to win.

Some chroniclers have assumed that Marlon Brando introduced the line that would include Paul Newman and Steve McQueen, James Dean briefly, and the eventual Dustin Hoffmans and Al Pacinos. Other genealogists have recognized Montgomery Clift as the more influential antecedent of the new style. Yet it began with Garfield, although it remained for a later generation to recognize this.

As the forerunner of Brando, Clift, and Newman, John Garfield is a special image of the movies, and was the prophet of the New Actor on film. But ultimately he must be considered not as an image but as an artist.

He groped to understand the complexities of the Stanislavsky system and to incorporate it into his craft; yet in a way that he did not understand, he remained rather apart from the more illustrious Group Theatre actors, the ones he sought to emulate. He was not able to do what they did: immerse themselves in their roles so thoroughly as to deny their own personalities. In all of his best work, Julie's volatile force was the unmistakable Garfield personality. He compensated for his lack of intellect with a pure, raw talent and an innate sensitivity the Group could not have given him. And personality, after all, is the mechanism of a Star.

He liked to say he was just a dumb kid from the Bronx; but that was what made him special. His approach to a role was instinctive, irreverent, amoral; and nourished by those qualities, each Garfield characterization assumed a life of its own with more dimension than the dramatist had envisioned. There is no doubting that he conveyed a magic from the stage; but present and future generations will measure him, finally, by the unique legacy that is the living screen.

Surely, though, he was a product of his times. He was depression's child, hungry for the promise of democracy, seeking only what Ralph Berger sought in *Awake and Sing:* a chance to get to first base. He did not express the American dream, but the hopeful idealism of the underprivileged.

And while he lived, Julie obeyed the only law of the street: *don't rat on nobody.*

Envoi

A Prose Eulogy to John Garfield by Clifford Odets
(In the "Drama Mailbag" of the New York *Times,*
May 25, 1952)

To the Drama Editor:

The use of your valuable space is asked to say a few words about
the gifted John Garfield, star of the American stage and screen,
and his untimely death last week, so stunning to all of his ad-
mirers and friends.

These past two years he was tired, no doubt. He had had his
share of career troubles—financial projects gone wrong, witch-
hunters searching his closets, attacks in part of the press for
alleged impolitic activities, and sometimes bad health to boot.
But Garfield's abundant and energetic nature did not flag in its
outpouring of plans and work.

He had finished only recently a not unsuccessful ANTA revival
of "Golden Boy," the third play he had done for that high-
minded organization; "Skipper Next to God" and "Peer Gynt"
in an adaptation by Paul Green, being the previous productions
to which Garfield had generously donated his valued services.
His next plans were to join Franchot Tone for a few summer
weeks of stock in Florida and to help produce, later in the year,
a first play by Norman Brooks, a new and talented writer. After
this would have come my play-in-work, "By the Sea."

In these keen and bitter times, highly placed and so open to any
wild attacks, Garfield remained extraordinarily free of malice
and meanness—they were nowhere in his nature. Despite any
and all gossip to the contrary, I, who was in a position to know,

state without equivocation that of all his possessions Garfield was proudest of his American heritage, even rudely so. In all ways he was as pure an American product as can be seen these days, processed by democracy, knowing or caring nothing for any other culture or race.

His climb from bare poverty to stardom illustrated for him one of the most cherished folkways of our people. His feeling never changed that he had been mandated by the American people to go in there and "keep punching" for them. His success, as he felt it, was the common property of millions, not peculiarly his own. This, I submit, was a basic purity of which not even Garfield himself was conscious.

Few actors on our stage throw themselves into their work with the zest displayed by Garfield; only those who had not known him before would be surprised by his rehearsal period humility. Affectionate by nature, charming and often refreshingly candid, he mostly reserved for friends a glimpse of something true and precious—the ardor of a boy for learning and growth.

Many believed, and among them such critics as Brooks Atkinson and Richard Watts, Jr., in their last reviews, that John Garfield at 39 was just beginning to reveal himself as an actor in terms of wider range, new sensitivity and maturity. They were correct, for the sheen of Hollywood fooled him only a little; and one may surmise that in his work he felt himself a beginner, while in his life he had come to know himself as a man seeking his identity.

I ask, finally, to be permitted to forget the present hushed austerities and say, simply, "Julie, dear friend, I will always love you."

CLIFFORD ODETS

New York, N. Y.

The Films of John Garfield

1. FOUR DAUGHTERS (Warner Brothers)

August 1938. Producer, Hal B. Wallis. Associate producer, Henry Blanke. Director, Michael Curtiz. Screenplay, Julius Epstein and Lenore Coffee, from the story "Sister Act" by Fannie Hurst. 91 minutes.

Cast: Claude Rains, Priscilla Lane, Jeffrey Lynn, Gale Page, John Garfield, Rosemary Lane, Lola Lane, Frank McHugh, May Robson, Dick Foran, Vera Lewis, Tom Dugan, Eddie Acuff.

2. THEY MADE ME A CRIMINAL (Warner Brothers)

January 1939. Producer, Hal B. Wallis. Associate producer, Max Siegel. Director, Busby Berkeley. Screenplay, Sig Herzig, adapted from earlier screenplay, *The Life of Jimmy Dolan,* by David Boehm and Erwin Gesler, based on the story by Bertram Millhauser and Beulah Marie Dix. 92 minutes.

Cast: John Garfield, Claude Rains, Gloria Dickson, Billy Halop, Bobby Jordan, Leo Gorcey, Huntz Hall, Gabriel Dell, Bernard Punsley, Ann Sheridan, May Robson.

3. BLACKWELL'S ISLAND (Warner Brothers)

March 1939. Producer, Bryan Foy. Director, William McGann. Original screen story, Crane Wilbur and Lee Katz. Screenplay, Crane Wilbur. 71 minutes.

Cast: John Garfield, Rosemary Lane, Dick Purcell, Victor Jory, Stanley Fields, Morgan Conway, Granville Bates, Anthony Averill, Peggy Shannon, Charley Foy, Norman Willis, Joe Cunningham.

4. JUAREZ (Warner Brothers)

May 1939. Producer, Hal B. Wallis. Director, William Dieterle. Screenplay, John Huston, Aeneas MacKenzie, and Wolfgang Reinhardt, based on the play *Maximilian and Carlota* by Franz Werfel, and the novel *The Phantom Crown* by Bertita Harding. 133 minutes.

Cast: Paul Muni, Bette Davis, Brian Aherne, Claude Rains, John Garfield, Donald Crisp, Gale Sondergaard, Gilbert Roland, Joseph Calleia, Henry O'Neill, Pedro deCordoba, Harry Davenport, Montagu Love, Georgia Caine, Walter Fenner, Alex Leftwich, Louis Calhern, Monte Blue, Walter Kingsford, Vladimir Sokoloff, Grant Mitchell.

5. DAUGHTERS COURAGEOUS (Warner Brothers)

July 1939. Producer, Hal B. Wallis. Associate producer, Henry Blanke. Director, Michael Curtiz. Original screenplay, Julius J. Epstein and Philip G. Epstein, suggested by the play *Fly Away Home* by Dorothy Bennett and Irving White. 108 minutes.

Cast: John Garfield, Priscilla Lane, Claude Rains, Jeffrey Lynn, Fay Bainter, Rosemary Lane, Gale Page, Lola Lane, Donald Crisp, May Robson, Frank McHugh, Dick Foran.

6. DUST BE MY DESTINY (Warner Brothers)

October 1939. Producer, Hal B. Wallis. Associate producer, Louis Edelman. Screenplay, Robert Rossen, from the novel by Jerome Odlum. 89 minutes.

Cast: John Garfield, Priscilla Lane, Alan Hale, Frank McHugh, Billy Halop, Bobby Jordan, Charley Grapewin, Henry Armetta, Stanley Ridges, John Litel, Moroni Olsen, Victor Kilian, Marc Lawrence.

7. THE CASTLE ON THE HUDSON (Warner Brothers)

February 1940. Producer, Hal B. Wallis. Associate producer, Samuel Bischoff. Director, Anatole Litvack. Screenplay, Seton I. Miller and Brown Holmes, adapting Courtney Terrett's earlier screenplay, *20,000 Years in Sing Sing,* based on the book by Lewis E. Lawes. 80 minutes.

Cast: John Garfield, Ann Sheridan, Pat O'Brien, Burgess Meredith, Jerome Cowan, Henry O'Neill, Guinn Williams, John Litel, Margot Stevenson, Willard Robertson, Nedda Harrigan, Edward Pawley, Billy Wayne, Barbara Pepper.

8. SATURDAY'S CHILDREN (Warner Brothers)

May 1940. Producer, Hal B. Wallis. Associate producer, Henry Blanke. Director, Vincent Sherman. Screenplay, Julius J. Epstein and Philip G. Epstein, from the play by Maxwell Anderson. 103 minutes.

Cast: John Garfield, Anne Shirley, Claude Rains, Roscoe Karns, Lee Patrick, Dennie Moore, George Tobias, Elizabeth Risdon, Berton Churchill.

9. FLOWING GOLD (Warner Brothers)

August 1940. Producer, Hal B. Wallis. Associate producer, Harlan Thompson. Director, Alfred E. Green. Screenplay, Kenneth Gamet, based on the novel by Rex Beach. 82 minutes.

Cast: John Garfield, Frances Farmer, Pat O'Brien, Raymond Walburn, Cliff Edwards, Tom Kennedy, Granville Bates, Jody Gilbert, Edward Pawley, Frank Mayo.

10. EAST OF THE RIVER (Warner Brothers)

November 1940. Producer, Hal B. Wallis. Director, Alfred E. Green. Screenplay, Fred Niblo, Jr., from a story by John Forte and Ross B. Wills. 74 minutes.

Cast: John Garfield, Brenda Marshall, Marjorie Rambeau, William Lundigan, George Tobias, Moroni Olsen, Douglas Fowley, Jack LaRue, Paul Guilfoyle.

11. THE SEA WOLF (Warner Brothers)

March 1941. Producer, Hal B. Wallis. Director, Michael Curtiz. Screenplay, Robert Rossen, from the novel by Jack London. 101 minutes.

Cast: Edward G. Robinson, John Garfield, Ida Lupino, Alexander Knox, Gene Lockhart, Barry Fitzgerald, Stanley Ridges, Francis McDonald, Howard daSilva, David Bruce, Frank Lackteen.

12. OUT OF THE FOG (Warner Brothers)

June 1941. Producer, Hal B. Wallis. Associate producer, Jerry Wald. Director, Anatole Litvak. Screenplay, Robert Rossen, Jerry Wald, and Richard Macaulay, from the play *The Gentle People* by Irwin Shaw. 90 minutes.

Cast: John Garfield, Ida Lupino, Thomas Mitchell, Eddie Albert, John Qualen, George Tobias, Aline MacMahon, Leo Gorcey, Odette Myrtil.

13. DANGEROUSLY THEY LIVE (Warner Brothers)

January 1942. Producer, Mark Hellinger. Director, Robert Florey. Original screenplay, Marion Parsonnet. 84 minutes.

Cast: John Garfield, Nancy Coleman, Raymond Massey, Moroni Olsen, Lee Patrick, Christian Rub, Ilka Gruning, Roland Drew, Frank Reicher, Esther Dale, John Harmon, Ben Weldon.

14. TORTILLA FLAT (Metro-Goldwyn-Mayer)

May 1942. Producer, Sam Zimbalist. Director, Victor Fleming. Screenplay, John Lee Mahin and Benjamin Glazer, from the novel by John Steinbeck. 101 minutes.

Cast: Spencer Tracy, Hedy Lamarr, John Garfield, Frank Morgan, Akim Tamiroff, Connie Gilchrist, John Qualen, Sheldon Leonard, Donald Meek, Allen Jenkins, Henry O'Neill.

15. AIR FORCE (Warner Brothers)

February 1943. Producer, Hal B. Wallis. Director, Howard Hawks. Original screenplay, Dudley Nichols. 122 minutes.

Cast: John Garfield, Gig Young, Harry Carey, Arthur Kennedy, George Tobias, John Ridgely, James Brown, Faye Emerson, Charles Drake, Stanley Ridges, Moroni Olsen, Ann Doran, Edward Brophy, Ward Wood, Ray Montgomery, Willard Robertson, Addison Richards, Dorothy Peterson, Tom Neal, Ruth Ford, James Flavin, James Millican.

16. FALLEN SPARROW (RKO Radio)

August 1943. Producer, Robert Fellows. Director, Richard Wallace. Screenplay, Warren Duff, from the novel by Dorothy B. Hughes. 94 minutes.

Cast: John Garfield, Maureen O'Hara, Walter Slezak, Patricia Morison, Martha O'Driscoll, Bruce Edwards, John Banner, John Miljan, Hugh Beaumont, Sam Goldberg.

17. THANK YOUR LUCKY STARS (Warner Brothers)

September 1943. Producer, Mark Hellinger. Director, David Butler. Screenplay, Norman Panama, Melvin Frank, and James V. Kern, from an original story by Everett Freeman and Arthur Schwartz. 128 minutes.

Cast: Dennis Morgan, Joan Leslie, Eddie Cantor, S. Z. Sakall, Edward Everett Horton, Ruth Donnelly, Mike Mazurki, Henry Armetta, Humphrey Bogart, Jack Carson, Bette Davis, Olivia deHavilland, Errol Flynn, John Garfield, Ida Lupino, Ann Sheridan, Dinah Shore, Alexis Smith, Willie Best, Alan Hale, Hattie McDaniel, George Tobias, Spike Jones.

18. DESTINATION TOKYO (Warner Brothers)

December 1943. Producer, Jerry Wald. Director, Delmer Daves. Screenplay, Delmer Daves and Albert Maltz, from a story by Steve Fisher. 134 minutes.

Cast: Cary Grant, John Garfield, Alan Hale, Dane Clark, Warner Anderson, William Prince, Robert Hutton, John Ridgely, John Forsythe, Faye Emerson, Tom Tully, Peter Whitney, William Challee, Whit Bissell.

19. BETWEEN TWO WORLDS (Warner Brothers)

May 1944. Producer, Mark Hellinger. Director, Edward A. Blatt. Screenplay, Daniel Fuchs, from the play *Outward Bound* by Sutton Vane. 111 minutes.

Cast: John Garfield, Paul Henreid, Eleanor Parker, Sydney Greenstreet, Edmund Gwenn, George Tobias, George Coulouris, Faye Emerson, Sara Allgood, Dennis King, Isobel Elsom.

20. HOLLYWOOD CANTEEN (Warner Brothers)

December 1944. Producer, Alex Gottlieb. Director, Delmer Daves. Original screenplay, Delmer Daves. 123 minutes.

Cast: Dane Clark, Janis Paige, Robert Hutton, Bette Davis, Joan Crawford, Barbara Stanwyck, John Garfield, Ida Lupino, Jack Benny, Paul Henreid, Dennis Morgan, Joan Leslie, Alexis Smith, Eddie Cantor, Sydney Greenstreet, Peter Lorre, Jack Carson, Jane Wyman, Zachary Scott, Helmut Dantine, Joe E. Brown, Eleanor Parker, The Andrews Sisters, Roy Rogers, Irene Manning, Dolores Moran, William Prince, Faye Emerson, Alan Hale, Craig Stevens, Kitty Carlisle, John Ridgely, Andrea King, Joan McCracken, Victor Francen, Donald Woods, Joyce Reynolds, Joseph Szigeti, Jimmy Dorsey and his band, Carmen Cavallaro and his orchestra.

21. PRIDE OF THE MARINES (Warner Brothers)

August 1945. Producer, Jerry Wald. Director, Delmer Daves. Screenplay, Albert Maltz, from a book by Roger Butterfield. 119 minutes.

Cast: John Garfield, Eleanor Parker, Dane Clark, John Ridgely, Rosemary DeCamp, Ann Doran, Ann Todd, Warren Douglas, Don McGuire, Tom D'Andrea, Mark Stevens, Rory Mallinson, Anthony Caruso, Moroni Olsen.

22. THE POSTMAN ALWAYS RINGS TWICE (Metro-Goldwyn-Mayer)

February 1946. Producer, Carey Wilson. Director, Tay Garnett. Screenplay, Harry Ruskin and Niven Busch, from the novel by James M. Cain. 113 minutes.

Cast: Lana Turner, John Garfield, Cecil Kellaway, Hume Cronyn, Leon Ames, Audrey Totter, Alan Reed, Jeff York, Charles Williams.

23. NOBODY LIVES FOREVER (Warner Brothers)

September 1946. Producer, Robert Buckner. Director, Jean Negulesco. Original screenplay, W. R. Burnett. 101 minutes.

Cast: John Garfield, Geraldine Fitzgerald, Walter Brennan, Faye Emerson, George Coulouris, George Tobias, Robert Shayne, Richard Gaines, James Flavin, Ralph Peters, Richard Erdman, William Edmunds.

24. HUMORESQUE (Warner Brothers)

December 1946. Producer, Jerry Wald. Director, Jean Negulesco. Screenplay, Clifford Odets and Zachary Gold, from a story by Fannie Hurst. 126 minutes.

Cast: Joan Crawford, John Garfield, Oscar Levant, J. Carroll Naish, Ruth Nelson, Tom D'Andrea, Joan Chandler, Paul Cavanagh, Peggy Knudsen, Craig Stevens, Richard Gaines, John Abbott, Fritz Leiber, Don McGuire, Bobby Blake, Tommy Cook.

25. BODY AND SOUL (Enterprise-United Artists)

September 1947. Producer, Bob Roberts. Director, Robert Rossen. Screenplay, Abraham Polonsky. 104 minutes.

Cast: John Garfield, Lilli Palmer, Hazel Brooks, Anne Revere, William Conrad, Joseph Pevney, Canada Lee, Lloyd Gough, Art Smith, James Burke, Virginia Gregg, Joe Devlin.

26. GENTLEMAN'S AGREEMENT (20th Century-Fox)

December 1947. Producer, Darryl F. Zanuck. Director, Elia Kazan. Screenplay, Moss Hart, from the novel by Laura Z. Hobson. 119 minutes.

Cast: Gregory Peck, Dorothy McGuire, John Garfield, Celeste Holm, Anne Revere, June Havoc, Albert Dekker, Dean Stockwell, Jane Wyatt, Sam Jaffe, Ransom Sherman, Nicholas Joy, Harold Vermilyea, Roy Roberts, Kathleen Lockhart, Curt Conway, John Newland, Robert Warwick, Gene Nelson, Robert Karnes.

27. FORCE OF EVIL (Enterprise-M-G-M)

December 1948. Producer, Bob Roberts. Director, Abraham Polonsky. Screenplay, Abraham Polonsky and Ira Wolfert, from the novel *Tucker's People* by Ira Wolfert. 83 minutes.

Cast: John Garfield, Beatrice Pearson, Thomas Gomez, Roy Roberts, Marie Windsor, Howland Chamberlin, Paul McVey, Jack Overman, Tim Ryan, Stanley Prager, Beau Bridges, Paul Fix, Barbara Woodell, Raymond Largay, Barry Kelley, Allan Mathews, Georgia Backus, Sid Tomack.

28. WE WERE STRANGERS (Horizon-Columbia)

May 1949. Producer, Sam Spiegel. Director, John Huston. Screenplay, Peter Viertel, from an episode in the novel *Rough Sketch* by Robert Sylvester. 107 minutes.

Cast: Jennifer Jones, John Garfield, Pedro Armendariz, Gilbert Roland, Ramon Novarro, Wally Cassell, David Bond, Jose Perez, Morris Ankrum, Tito Rinaldo, Leonard Strong.

29. UNDER MY SKIN (20th Century-Fox)

March 1950. Produced by Casey Robinson. Directed by Jean Negulesco. Screenplay by Casey Robinson, from the story "My Old Man" by Ernest Hemingway. 86 minutes.

Cast: John Garfield, Micheline Presle, Luther Adler, Orley Lindgren, Noel Drayton, A. A. Merola, Ott George, Paul Bryar, Ann Codee, Steve Geray.

30. THE BREAKING POINT (Warner Brothers)

October 1950. Producer, Jerry Wald. Director, Michael Curtiz. Screenplay, Ranald MacDougall, from the novel *To Have and Have Not* by Ernest Hemingway. 98 minutes.

Cast: John Garfield, Patricia Neal, Phyllis Thaxter, Juano Hernandez, Wallace Ford, Edmon Ryan, Ralph Dumke, Guy Thomasan, William Campbell, Sherry Jackson, Victor Sen Yung, James Griffith.

31. HE RAN ALL THE WAY (United Artists)

July 1951. Producer, Bob Roberts. Director, Jack Berry. Screenplay, Hugo Butler and Guy Endore, based on the novel by Sam Ross. 79 minutes.

Cast: John Garfield, Shelley Winters, Wallace Ford, Selena Royle, Gladys George, Norman Lloyd, Bobby Hyatt.

(John Garfield also appeared unbilled in a bit part in *Footlight Parade*, a Warner Brothers 1933 film, and as one of several "surprise cameos" in Franchot Tone's independently made 1949 film, *Jigsaw*.)

Index

280